CAMBRIDGE STUDIES IN AMERICAN LITERATURE AND CULTURE

A House Undivided

Cambridge Studies in American Literature and Culture

Editor
Albert Gelpi, Stanford University

Advisory board
Nina Baym, *University of Illinois, Champaign-Urbana*
Sacvan Bercovitch, *Harvard University*
David Levin, *University of Virginia*
Joel Porte, *Cornell University*
Eric Sundquist, *University of California, Berkeley*
Mike Weaver, *Oxford University*

A HOUSE UNDIVIDED

Domesticity and Community in American Literature

DOUGLAS ANDERSON
University of Virginia

The right of the
University of Cambridge
to print and sell
all manner of books
was granted by
Henry VIII in 1534.
The University has printed
and published continuously
since 1584.

CAMBRIDGE UNIVERSITY PRESS
Cambridge
New York   Port Chester   Melbourne   Sydney

Published by the Press Syndicate of the University of Cambridge
The Pitt Building, Trumpington Street, Cambridge CB2 1RP
40 West 20th Street, New York, NY 10011, USA
10 Stamford Road, Oakleigh, Melbourne 3166, Australia

© Cambridge University Press 1990

First published 1990

Printed in the United States of America

Library of Congress Cataloging-in-Publication Data
Anderson, Douglas R.

A house undivided : domesticity and community in American
literature / Douglas Anderson.

p.   cm – (Cambridge studies in American literature and
culture)

ISBN 0-521-38287-4

1. American literature – History and criticism.   2. Community in
literature.   3. Family in literature.   4. Home in literature.
I. Series.
PS169.C65A54   1990
810.9'355 – dc20   89–48373
                                                                CIP

British Library Cataloguing in Publication Data
Anderson, Douglas

A house undivided : domesticity and community in American
literature. – (Cambridge studies in American literature
and culture).

1. English literature. American writers – Critical studies
I. Title
810.9

ISBN 0-521-38287-4

For P.E.S.

CONTENTS

ACKNOWLEDGMENTS

Vassar College granted me a sabbatical during the course of which this book began to take shape, and offered a teaching environment in the first years of my career that permitted my scholarly interests to grow along unexpected (and, I hope, fruitful) lines. Two of my colleagues there – Robert DeMaria and Ann Imbrie – read portions of the text with care and generously gave their advice and encouragement. The librarians at Vassar – like librarians the world over, I am convinced – were unfailingly competent and energetic in their assistance. Donald Spicer at the Dartmouth College Computing Center arranged for the services of Dartmouth's optical scanning equipment in order to put the text on a computer disk for ease of editing. My wife's parents, Dr. and Mrs. John B. Shilton, cheerfully offered shelter, support, and the resources of their personal library on countless occasions when this book trespassed on family holidays. Mr. and Mrs. F. Russell Wade of Fillmore, California, made available to my own small family a beautiful writer's refuge on the South Fork of the Kaweah River in the shadow of Sequoia National Park. Albert Gelpi and the readers for Cambridge University Press provided the impetus for a reconsideration of the text that produced a more accurate, more readable, and more satisfying account of my purposes and meaning. All my life I have been fortunate in my teachers, but David Levin has guided my scholarly growth in general, as well as the evolution of this manuscript, with Franklinian wit and solicitude, setting me models of stylistic grace, editorial rigor, intellectual energy, and affectionate (and charitable) pedagogy that have become my standards of humane learning. Paula Ellen Shilton repeatedly edited the following chapters with a challenging and supportive intelligence that is unwavering in loyalty and in honesty, a loving critic, as Anne Bradstreet would have understood the phrase.

ix

INTRODUCTION

I propose to describe a remarkably durable imaginative tradition emerging from the work of some representative American writers between the early seventeenth and the early twentieth centuries. Over such a span of years any vital cultural or literary impetus must be expected to change form repeatedly and offer itself to us in various disguises suited to particular times and particular artists. But to a surprising degree the work in which I am interested maintains a close association with a group of images and ideas that first appears in John Winthrop's "A Modell of Christian Charity" (1630) and that continues to sustain the prose of the revolutionary period and the major artistic products of the nineteenth century.

The outlines of the ideas and images themselves are fairly simple to trace. In his speech to the *Arbella* emigrants, John Winthrop established the central importance, to the colonizing errand, of a communal bond that he understood in both traditional and radical forms. To endure in America the community must be "knit together" as a single body – an idea that was familiar to Winthrop's contemporaries from a number of sources.[1] But the degree of loyalty required was not fundamentally contractual or political in nature; it had to be familial. The guiding analogy, or model, of American life for Winthrop was to be the family, embodied for him most dramatically (and typologically) in the figure of Eve, transported by selfless love for her spouse and children. Winthrop's decision to employ Eve in such a striking role both reverses the inherited notions of sexual hierarchy of his day and transforms her from an agent of the Fall to an emblem of stable, sacramental marriage. Indeed, Winthrop assigns to Eve the paradigmatic founder's role that Genesis reserves for Adam.

The commitment to emigrate to Massachusetts Bay took on, in Winthrop's eyes, the shape of a selfless marriage, diffused as an ideal over the entire civil body. He summed up these extraordinary aspirations by offering to his fellow passengers on the *Arbella* a contemporary equivalent of Moses' choice of life or death from the closing chapters of Deuteronomy, affirming that "life" in America meant embracing the familial, sacramental model that he envisioned. Any compromise with such selflessness was "death."

Winthrop's dramatic vision illuminates the literary achievements of his Puritan contemporaries and casts, at the same time, a uniquely informative light on the work of many of the best American literary artists since his day. The three key elements of that vision were not original to Winthrop and are not unfamiliar to twentieth-century students of American culture, but they have seldom been identified as parts of a single, imaginative fabric that joins some of the oldest with some of the newest products of that culture. Those three key elements are the imaginative and moral primacy of marriage as both a subject and a metaphor, the corresponding preeminence of women and of domesticity as a privileged sphere of meaning, and the sense of the ongoing predicament in America of a choice between "life" and "death." My purpose here is to follow the interplay of these elements through a number of texts central to American literature in order to demonstrate the range and the power of the network that they comprise.

In doing so, I have tried to be sensitive, as well, to the range and influence of my historical and critical predecessors. The significance of the family in the Puritan community, as both an institution and an image, received careful attention in Edmund Morgan's pioneering study more than forty years ago.[2] In his account of the Puritan social order, Morgan (quoting Cotton Mather) confirmed that seventeenth-century Americans recognized the family as "the very *First Society*" among human beings, specifically sanctioned by God and used by him as the means and the model for forming all subsequent social institutions among His fallen creatures.[3] Morgan's description of the relations between husband and wife and the education of children in the Puritan household is the forerunner of more detailed, but in important ways less balanced, discussions by Philip J. Greven in *The Protestant Temperament* (1977) and David Leverenz in *The Language of Puritan Feeling* (1980). Both of these more recent books are interesting and valuable, but Greven is deeply committed to a view of what he calls the "evangelical household," in which the parents are "engaged in war with their children," breaking the wills of their offspring to conform to the dictates of an authoritarian piety.[4] Leverenz, however, gives a generous account of the Puritan practice of "household government," stressing the affection as well as the gravity of Puritan family life, but his psychoanalytic focus on the status of male identity as a defining condition of Puritan anxieties often leads him to judgments that seem clinical rather than historical or literary.[5]

In certainly the most thorough (and perhaps most controversial) treatment of the history of the family in seventeenth- and eighteenth-century England, Lawrence Stone appears to endorse both of these opposed positions on the climate of the Puritan household. Stone attributes to evangelical piety a ruthless emphasis on breaking the will, but he also repeatedly acknowledges the central role played by Puritan writers and thinkers in the evolution of what he calls the modern affective family and the companionate marriage. Particularly in the social classes that produced the most influential of the emigrants to New England, the family had become, certainly by the seventeenth century, the central focus of emotional and spiritual life among Puritans. Linda Pollock's recent critique of Stone's work, *Forgotten Children: Parent–Child Relations from 1500 to 1900* (1983), significantly reinforces this view of the importance of family bonds in seventeenth-century America. Winthrop's employment of the idea of the family in his speech both reflected and exploited this fundamental locus of human values.[6]

Michael Gilmore and Sacvan Bercovitch have both written books that trace important elements of the Puritan sensibility, and aspects of Puritan literary practice, through some of the major writers of the nineteenth century. In both cases John Winthrop plays a role in characterizing the Puritan example. Gilmore in *The Middle Way: Puritanism and Ideology in American Romantic Fiction* (1977) associates "A Modell of Christian Charity" with Arthur Dimmesdale's election sermon in *The Scarlet Letter,* identifying both speeches as warnings against too deep a commitment to worldly things.[7] The "middle way" of Gilmore's title reflects the devout Puritan's attempt to "live in heaven, while he lived on earth" – to live in the world but not of the world, as Edmund Morgan puts it in his biography of Winthrop – and the Puritan jeremiad (of which Gilmore's book itself is a modern example) grows out of the understandably common and acute sense of having failed to strike that balance. Gilmore finds such jeremiads convincingly reborn in the work of Hawthorne and Melville.

Bercovitch's more focused study, *The American Jeremiad* (1978), identifies Winthrop's speech as one of two prototypic American jeremiads, a genre he finds especially durable precisely because it posits a gap between rhetoric and history and not because it falls into one. Puritan New England, in Bercovitch's view, was "constantly 'betwixt and between,' forever at the brink of some momentous decision," just as Winthrop himself had made clear at the very beginning of the New England experiment in 1630.[8] Neither Bercovitch nor Gilmore, however, gives sufficient attention to the language of Winthrop's speech to permit them to link the key feature of the jeremiad tradition – the choice between "life" and "death" – to the accompanying emphases on marriage and domestic life that give Winthrop's speech its unusual scope and fertility.

Winthrop's communal vision has made him a central figure for the history of ideas in America at least since Perry Miller's emphasis on the role of "A Modell of Christian Charity" in forming the contractual theory of the Puritan community.[9] More recently, Loren Baritz and Wilson C. McWilliams have argued for Winthrop's conception of "organic community" or for the importance of the idea of brotherhood to his view of social obligations.[10] Philip Gura, in *A Glimpse of Sion's Glory* (1984), regards Winthrop as the definitive orthodox participant in an "emergent synthesis of religious and political ideology" that was "continuously revitalized by the challenge of radical elements."[11] Winthrop's "vision of the Kingdom of God in America," Gura argues, was not identical with New England Puritanism. It simply characterized a major element of New England's strikingly heterogeneous religious life. Amy Lang has recently examined "A Modell of Christian Charity" in the context of her study of the figure of Anne Hutchinson, *Prophetic Woman* (1987), identifying in Winthrop's text a "conflation" of election and good citizenship that the antinomians would come to repudiate.[12] What is finally most remarkable about Winthrop's fairly brief address to his fellow passengers on the *Arbella* is its ability to accommodate and sustain all of these subsequent views and arguments, and to identify a single metaphorical framework for fixing this supple vision in his audience's memory. The family, after all, is a contract with legal as well as organic elements. It is fraternal, as well as parental, and (like the wider social body) it must be able to withstand the kinds of stresses that arise from the intimate association of people who are, inevitably, of different minds. Winthrop's accomplishment is as much artistic, then, as it is political or ideological, and it has wide-ranging artistic consequences.

In *The Feminization of American Culture* (1977) Ann Douglas has described a process of sentimentalization in nineteenth-century America that was marked by what she calls the disenfranchisement of women and the clergy, followed by an impoverishment of theological and secular life. "America lost its male-dominated theological tradition," Douglas writes, "without gaining a comprehensive feminism or an adequately modernized religious sensibility."[13] From being producers and managers of wealth, women became consumers and articles of consumption. The theological doctrine of atonement evolved from its paternal, authoritarian framework into "maternal and affective" forms. Death was domesticated and trivialized into "a celestial retirement village."[14] Douglas laments these developments like the speaker of yet another impassioned, American jeremiad, and few readers would be inclined to quarrel with the broad outlines of her assessment of America's "Victorian" culture. But Winthrop's example suggests that American spiritual and intellectual life was "feminized" – or at least domesticated – long before the nineteenth century. Moreover, it was a conscious process of domestication, every bit as deliberate as the domestication of the image of Washington that George Forgie has described, or the maternal shawl that Abraham Lincoln appropriated at least partly as a dimension of his wartime image as the mourning national parent.[15]

These are features of American life that are deeply rooted in its history and ideals. They are responsible for some of the most troubling parts of our culture, as Ann Douglas has suggested, but they are also responsible for some of the most admirable. It is much too simple to continue to assume, for example, that Hawthorne, Thoreau, Melville, and Whitman constitute a canonical aesthetic tradition that is opposed in subject and style to the sentimental domestic spirit of their day. In fundamental ways their work is perfectly consistent with that spirit and helps to establish its complexity, value, and durability.[16] At least one benefit of returning to John Winthrop and then following the implications of his vision forward to the early twentieth century may be the restoration of a measure of unity to American writing. Increasingly that body of writing has seemed to break down into at least two antagonistic categories: the work of "serious artists" on the one hand, enshrined in our major anthologies, and what Mary Kelley identifies as the work of the "literary domestics" on the other.[17] Recognizing the common enterprise of these two groups of writers is a critical step toward reforming a single tradition along the lines of excellence rather than of gender.

A few notes on method and on the title I have chosen may help to clarify these purposes still further. It seemed that one way to call attention to the integrative hopes of the following chapters would be to associate them with Lincoln's famous reference to the American household and at the same time to modify his biblical allusion as a way of acknowledging that the cultural house of American writing is neither united nor divided but painfully suspended between those two states. Joyce Warren, for example, has forcefully argued the case that major elements of our literary heritage are callously dismissive of the "other" – women, blacks, Hispanics, Indians – whereas William Spengemann has suggested dividing American literary culture according to the competing appeals of opposed "muses," those of adventure and domesticity.[18] But both Spengemann and Warren readily admit that such a division into camps is far too clear-cut to account for the complex loyalties of the writers they examine. Hawthorne is the source of the most widely quoted dismissal of the efforts of women writers in the nineteenth century, yet he is Warren's exceptional case: the male American author who most successfully evades the influence of a sexist individualism. Melville clearly fits Spengemann's profile of the masculine adventurer, but his finest book is a critique of the questing and adventuring soul. Deep divisions may finally separate our canonical writers from one another and from their more popular, frequently female contemporaries, but deep affinities apparently drew them together as well. Some of the scope and nature of those affinities I hope to indicate here.

One obvious means of doing so would be to treat in detail the major work of some representative writers in the domestic tradition – Sedgwick, Child, Southworth, Cummins, Warner, Stowe – along with the more familiar figures of the eighteenth and nineteenth centuries: Crevecoeur, Franklin, Emerson, Thoreau, Melville, James. Out of such a joint consideration the picture of an undivided house could clearly emerge. I have not chosen this comparative course primarily because of the richness and variety of the recently emerging body of work by other scholars on the contributions of nineteenth-century women writers to American literature: Mary Kelley's examination of the tradition of woman authorship, Cathy Davidson's treatment of domestic fiction in the context of the early American novel, Nina Baym's descriptive account of the body of material produced by American women writers in the middle decades of the nineteenth century, Jane Tompkins's outline of the tradition of the "sensational" in American fiction and its application to Stowe and Warner.[19] I have comparatively little to add to the contributions made by these books, but I have much more to say concerning the parallel reconstructions of male identity in Franklin and Thoreau, the domestic ethic of Crevecoeur, the seventeenth-century resonances of *The Portrait of a Lady,* and Emily Dickinson's dialogue with John Milton – all of which bear directly upon the relationship between domesticity and community in American literature and culture. Accordingly I think of these chapters as self-contained and at the same time dependent upon the larger critical (and, one hopes, social) enterprise of which they are a part.

It should be clear, then, that I mean to explore an expressive continuity in American literature that is both more and less adversarial, with respect to mainstream culture, than Melville's proverbial "No! in thunder" has traditionally suggested. Jane Tompkins recently pointed out the surprising degree to which Melville's extraordinary review of *Mosses from an Old Manse* shares the prevailing sentimentalism of its day even as it celebrates Hawthorne's power of blackness.[20] My interest here is in the interplay between such sentimental affirmation and the blackness of darkness, not in choosing between them. Taken together, and in a wider historical context than Tompkins provides, they offer an unusually rich instance of what Michael Kammen has called the biformities of the American mind:

a sentimental blackness of the imagination, perhaps, or a dark sentimentalism, following the terminology that David Reynolds has recently offered as a characterization of the subversive tradition of "dark reform" in the American renaissance.[21] Nancy Cott isolates a particular version of this biformity in *The Bonds of Womanhood* (1977) when she notes the peculiar and paradoxical conjunction in American history between the appearance of a cult of domesticity and the emergence of an active, indigenous feminism.[22] The two developments should preclude one another, whereas in fact (Cott demonstrates) the emergence of American feminism depended to a significant degree on the ideology of domesticity as a means of developing a sense of the collective importance of women and a sense of their shared destiny.

These scholars take me further into social history than I finally intend to go, but they serve as an important foreground for a discussion of American literature that begins with John Winthrop's use of domesticity and of a representative woman as figurative versions of the community – metaphors that simultaneously bound the colonists to an exacting contract and sought to free them from older and ultimately destructive models of heroism. This was an experience of liberated identity that John Cotton recognized, and that Cotton Mather endorsed, in the former's eulogy of Winthrop with which Mather concluded his biography in *Magnalia Christi Americana,* identifying Winthrop not as the wall-builder or the founder or the father of Massachusetts Bay, but as its mother.[23] I do not mean to exonerate Winthrop, or any other established literary figure for that matter, from all charges that he failed to adhere to his finest principles. As I remind the reader in the first chapter, the structure of the jeremiad presupposes failure – and promise as well.

1

"THIS GREAT HOUSEHOLD UPON THE EARTH"

The Book of Deuteronomy, particularly its closing chapters, had an irresistible appeal for the first generation of New England Puritans because of the parallels they recognized between their own situation and that of the Children of Israel, poised upon the borders of the Promised Land. All of the Old Testament had typological significance, of course, and the New Testament was the source that the leaders of the emigrants would consult for guidance in shaping their communal institutions. But it was to Deuteronomy that John Winthrop turned when he sought a forceful conclusion for the discourse on Christian charity that he delivered at sea as the *Arbella* and her consort ships sailed west toward Massachusetts Bay.

The passage Winthrop chose partly to quote and partly to paraphrase was from Moses' "last farewell" to his people, after he had at length restored their laws and was preparing to die. This wonderfully dramatic moment was deservedly familiar to readers, playgoers, and congregations long before Winthrop singled it out. The medieval compilers of the *Gesta Romanorum* were influenced by Moses' words of farewell as they assembled their popular collection of monastic and chivalric tales. The same passage that Winthrop chose, and the chapter or two immediately following it, served as the source for some of the dialogue in the Exodus plays of the English *Corpus Christi* cycle, and William Shakespeare, drawing perhaps on all these sources, had incorporated elements of Moses' farewell into several scenes from *The Merchant of Venice* – most notably into Portia's memorable lines on the quality of mercy.[1] But Winthrop's treatment of his text is much more direct and, in its way, momentous than that of these literary predecessors. He uses it to capture in the form of a single choice the challenge facing the new colonists:

And to shutt upp this discourse with that exhortation of Moses that faithfull servant of the Lord in his last farewell to Israell Deut. 30. Beloved there is now sett before us life, and good, deathe and evill in that wee are Commaunded this day to love the Lord our God, and to love one another to walke in his wayes and to keepe his Commaundements and his Ordinance, and his lawes, and the Articles of our Covenant with him that wee may live and be multiplyed, and that the Lord our God may blesse us in the land whether wee goe to possesse it: But if our heartes shall turne away soe that wee will not obey, but shall be seduced and worshipp other Gods our pleasures, and proffitts, and serve them; it is propounded unto us this day, wee shall surely perishe out of the good Land whether wee passe over this vast Sea to possesse it:

> Therefore lett us choose life,
> that wee, and our Seede,
> may live; by obeyeing his
> voyce, and cleaveing to him,
> for hee is our life, and
> our prosperity.[2]

The images of a city on a hill and of a "speciall Commission" or covenant are the traditional metaphors that modern scholarship has focused on as the heart of Winthrop's speech, but the emphases of Winthrop's text itself suggest that this Mosaic choice was a central part of his message, the condensation of what he believed the Puritan errand signified. The idea of a special covenant was vital to the emigrants' sense of destiny, but in "A Modell of Christian Charity" Winthrop devotes only a paragraph to the implications of this contract, subordinating it (as he does in the passage above) as just one metaphor among others. Even the vision of a "Citty upon a Hill" is, in many respects, only a kind of conspicuous predicament in which, according to Winthrop, the emigrants simply find themselves. "[T]he eies of all people are uppon us," he observes in an interesting modification of the Sermon on the Mount (203), implying that New England will be exposed to considerable scrutiny, like it or not.[3] The choice between life and death, however, is at the center of what it means to be a deliberate participant in this dangerous enterprise. This is the master "modell" of Winthrop's title, and he set out in his discourse to identify the Puritan errand as closely as he could with the powerful appeal of life.

It may seem especially curious, then, that Winthrop chose to begin what he considered to be the "preface" of his speech with an explanation of the reasons why God had ordained that "in all times some must be rich some poore, some highe and eminent in power and dignitie; others meane and in subjection" (190). Where, one wonders, is the charity in this? Winthrop undertakes at the outset to explain to us nothing less than the reasons why such social divisions should exist. Perry Miller mistakenly identified this apparently complacent – and from Winthrop's point of view wholly traditional – acceptance of social stratification as Winthrop's main text and thought it called for "incessant brooding" on the part of all students of American history.[4] For Winthrop, however, these opening comments are not so much a bulwark for the rights of property, or a rehearsal of familiar aristocratic platitudes, but the beginnings of an assault upon ordinary notions of worldly ownership and worldly duty. His antagonist, in conformity with a rich tradition of Puritan thought, was the self, and he began "A Modell of Christian Charity" by boldly addressing the chief incitement to selfishness among his economically vulnerable listeners.[5]

God, quite simply, reserves all earthly property to himself. Its uneven distribution among men is no more than another manifestation of the familiar renaissance concept of plenitude. God multiplies his "Stewards counting himself more honored in dispenceing his guifts to man by man, than if hee did it by his owne immediate hand" (190). Winthrop reinforces the implications of this idea by examining the two primary rules that are to guide the lives of the emigrants, justice and mercy, and the two kinds of law to which they are subject, that of nature and that of grace. The import of these principles and laws is that "community of perills calls for extraordinary liberallity" (192). It was quite clear to Winthrop's audience – even before Winthrop himself explicitly confirmed it – that the voyagers in the *Arbella* stood to one another as in a community of perils and that, regardless of the objections of prudent self-interest (with which instinct Winthrop holds a small debate in the text of his speech), they must all conduct their affairs "with more enlargement towardes others and lesse respect towards ourselves" (195).

With Levitican scrupulousness, Winthrop is careful to discuss the various contingencies involved in lending, giving outright, and forgiving debts, but it is clear that he does not have in mind as the guiding virtue of his new community simply ordinary generosity:

> It is to be observed that both in Scriptures and latter stories of the Churches that such as have beene most bountifull to the poore Saintes especially in these extraordinary times and occasions god hath left them highly Commended to posterity . . . observe againe that the scripture gives noe causion to restraine any from being over liberall this way; but to all men to the liberall and cherefull practise hereof by the sweetest promises as to instance one for many, Isaiah 58.6: Is not this the fast that I have chosen to

loose the bonds of wickednes, to take off the heavy burdens to
lett the oppressed goe free and to breake every Yoake, to deale
thy bread to the hungry and to bring the poore that wander into
thy house, when thou seest the naked to cover them etc. then
shall thy light breake forthe as the morneing, and thy healthe
shall growe speedily, thy righteousnes shall goe before thee, and
the glory of the lord shall embrace thee, then thou shalt call and
the lord shall Answer thee. (195)

"A Modell of Christian Charity" in fact moves steadily toward a vision of
communal unity that is founded upon two "patterns," as Winthrop
would have called them, taken not from covenant legality but from apocalyptic vision and private life: the body and marriage. Both are traditional images, but that is precisely why Winthrop adopts them. He can
draw upon the familiar associations of the body of Christ and the marriage of Christ with his church to enhance the authority of his appeal for
community and his argument against the self.

For though he was in fact making a kind of argument, Winthrop knew
(as Shakespeare's Portia came to recognize) that people could not be
argued into "workes of mercy" toward one another (196). Mercy had to
emerge from within, and that emergence required a psychological and
spiritual transformation on the part of those who would found a new
community upon a spiritually regenerate basis. Winthrop concluded that
the "first mover or maine wheele" of mercy and justice in human life was
love, the "bond or ligament" that knits together human beings as firmly
as the parts of a single body are knit together in mutual dependence. In
conformity with the taste of his age, Winthrop was prepared to extend
this bodily conceit just as far as it could go in the service of his point,
delving into some of the particulars of digestion, for example, in order to
show that just as the mouth may "mince the food" for the whole body
and yet receive "a due proporcion" of nourishment in return, so affection
is always perfectly reciprocal in the kind of society he envisions for
America (200). This conceit, however, unlike those in the more strictly
secular verse of Winthrop's contemporaries, does not succeed or fail
purely on poetic grounds. Winthrop derives its authority from passages
in I Corinthians, Galatians, Romans, and John. Nor is such a literal and
spiritual view of their social "constitution" simply one desirable alter-
native among many. Winthrop is not discussing possible social options
but necessities.[6] The extraordinary nature of the colonizing enterprise
demanded that "wee must not content our selves with usual ordinary
meanes":

Whatsoever wee did or ought to have done when wee lived in
England, the same must wee doe and more allsoe where wee
goe: That which the most in theire Churches maineteine as a

truthe in profession onely, wee must bring into familiar and constant practise, and in this duty of love wee must love brotherly without dissimulation, wee must love one another with a pure hearte fervently wee must beare one anothers burthens, wee must not looke onely on our owne things, but allsoe on the things of our brethren, neither must wee think that the lord will beare with such faileings at our hands as hee dothe from those among whome we have lived. (202)

In its rhythmic sequence of binding exhortations ("wee must love . . . wee must beare . . .") this passage anticipates by a few paragraphs the culminating vision of Winthrop's speech, toward which he is building with both musical and argumentative care. The nature of Winthrop's message requires such orchestration, for in opposition to the stubborn claims of the self, Winthrop pits a social ideal more demanding and more rewarding (he suggests) than marriage (200). Yet it is to marriage, and to its extension in family, that he appeals as a model for how this binding love operates upon the inward lives of those who choose to "exercise" it.[7]

The loyalty of David and Jonathan is the second of the instructive instances of social beauty upon which Winthrop calls to give his ideal a dramatic life, but his chief example of the self-effacing power of human affection is Eve. And just as Milton has Eve recite the most beautiful hymn to human love in *Paradise Lost* (4, 635–56), so Winthrop elects to describe the psychological impact of love solely through an elaborate characterization of its effects on her. Strikingly – and it would certainly have seemed striking to Winthrop's biblically sophisticated listeners – he departs from scriptural authority and assigns to Eve the "fleshe of my fleshe" acknowledgment that Genesis attributes to Adam:

Now when the soule which is of a sociable nature finds any thing like to it selfe, it is like Adam when Eve was brought to him, shee must have it one with herselfe this is fleshe of my fleshe (saith shee) and bone of my bone shee conceives a great delighte in it, therefore shee desires nearenes and familiarity with it: shee hath a greate propensity to doe it good and receives such content in it, as feareing the miscarriage of her beloved shee bestowes it in the inmost closett of her heart, shee will not endure that it shall want any good which shee can give it, if by occasion shee be withdrawne from the Company of it, shee is still lookeing towardes the place where shee left her beloved, if shee heare it groane shee is with it presently, if shee finde it sadd and disconsolate shee sighes and mournes with it, shee hath noe such joy, as to see her beloved merry and thriveing, if shee see it wronged, shee cannot beare it without passion, shee setts noe boundes of

her affecttions, nor hath any thought of reward, shee findes rec-
ompence enoughe in the exercise of her love towardes it. (199)

It is no simple matter to describe the uses to which Winthrop has put
gender in this extraordinary passage. Despite the neuter pronouns with
which he has referred to the "soule" in his opening sentence, it is possible
to treat the insistent use of "shee" thereafter as a conventional gesture on
the part of any properly educated English gentleman who wished his
usage to conform to the gender of the Latin *anima* for soul. Even two
centuries later Emerson will continue to treat the mind, the intellect, and
the Reason as feminine, all the while insisting that living by the light of
Reason is "manly." Such a reassuringly traditional reading of Winthrop's
usage, however, does not square comfortably with the abruptness with
which Eve's appearance in his initial main clause immediately transforms
the pronouns. Nor can it account for the intensely sexual nature of the
soul's commitment, the conception of delight, the fear of miscarriage,
the maternal devotion to her "merry and thriveing" beloved. Winthrop's
purposes in fact seem quite complex: He undertakes both to feminize
Adam and to exalt Eve as the primary example of everyone who seeks the
well-being of others above that of themselves. Eve is his model citizen,
not his model wife, and she represents for Winthrop the conflation of the
ideas of election and good citizenship that Amy Lang has identified as one
of the critical accomplishments of "A Modell of Christian Charity."[8]

Part of the reason for Winthrop's uncharacteristic freedom with the
language of Genesis in this instance may well be his desire to impress
even more vividly upon his audience the revolutionary nature of their
undertaking. If the demands of the self must yield to the force of communal love, then the demands of sexual primacy cannot be entirely inviolable. If we must maintain as a truth what others merely profess, then our
domestic as well as our political relations call for careful examination.[9]
Eve's devotion in Winthrop's passage, after all, is both an acknowledgment of her exemplary power and a celebration of its domestic single-
mindedness. At the same time Winthrop is drawing on an old exegetical
tradition that identifies the figure of Eve both with her typological successor, Mary, and with the church.[10] Adam's typological associations are
with the inward process of election itself and with Christ, the Second
Adam, whose apocalyptic return to earth marks the climactic "marriage"
of Christian history but who is not readily available as a social presence in
human life until the end of time. The typological network of Eve, Mary,
and the church are, as Winthrop recognizes, "of a sociable nature," available in a way that Adam is not as a model for the operations of the human
"church" understood both exclusively and inclusively. The Eve of
Winthrop's passage is not occupied in distinguishing between the regene-

rate and the unregenerate in the objects of her affection; she is in pursuit of a "beloved" whose status seems to fluctuate between the confident joy of election and the disconsolate sorrow of doubt. She is capable of uniting the complete community of Massachusetts Bay, not simply (as Stephen Foster has suggested) those who "commune," in a network of affection that challenges the power of selfishness with a dramatic model of human, and female, generosity. This extraordinary capacity in Eve and in the typological network she embodies forms the connecting link between Milton's epics of the lost and regained Paradise. And as we will see in the last chapter, the range of Eve's appeal gave Emily Dickinson a model of female heroism upon which to shape the monologues of some of her boldest poems. This important modification of the hierarchal tradition is at the heart of Winthrop's model for the American community. The abrupt shift in focus from Adam to Eve with which his passage begins is only a condensed form of the shift in social focus that Winthrop proposes throughout "A Modell of Christian Charity": the shift from self to self-lessness, the shift from death to life.

It is, moreover, not only Eve's marital devotion but also her maternal zeal that Winthrop presents as images of the larger social union of community. She is simultaneously both terms in her typological identity, both Eve and Mary, spouse and mother. The neutral pronouns of the passage that celebrate her impassioned devotion generalize her self-lessness and blur the distinction between spousal and parental love. The "beloved" over whom she solicitously hovers in Winthrop's description might as readily be her "merry and thriveing" child as her husband. The result of this fusion of images is a far more complex and powerful presentation of the sociable nature, for Winthrop has not only employed his biblical figures in traditional typological ways, he has compressed the typological relationship into an extraordinarily rich and suggestive network of familial affection.

Winthrop's personal sense of the potency of the marital bond is perhaps one index of the meaning with which he, and no doubt many of his audience, invested the analogy between community and marriage. He was separated from his wife on the *Arbella*'s momentous voyage. She remained in England and planned to follow on a later ship. Winthrop's letters to her as he prepared to sail are a lively mixture of the latest news on his sailing arrangements, pious consolations for their separation, and domestic tenderness. "Mine owne, mine onely, my best beloved," he addresses her on March 10, 1630, and on March 28 writes in part to remind her of the pact that they had apparently made (in cheerful ignorance of the effect of distance upon time) to "meet in spiritt" on Mondays and Fridays "at 5: of the clocke at night" until they would be able to meet again in fact (186). For Winthrop, then, it meant a great deal to describe the emigrants' relationship to one another and their relationship to God as a "more neare bond of marriage" (202).[11]

The closing allusion in "A Modell of Christian Charity" to Moses and the choice of life emerges naturally from this discussion of the communal marriage and the communal body. If the bonds of contract alone were involved in the sanctifying of Massachusetts Bay, then it would be difficult to understand, except perhaps in a technical sense, why Winthrop and his companions found their enterprise so urgent and so moving. It would be particularly difficult to see how Winthrop intended to appeal to the always significant percentage of the emigrant population who were not literally covenanted, or contracted, to church membership. A sense of "contract" is deeply embedded in the origins of Puritan colonization, but even in the case of Winthrop's colleagues in the business-like Agreement at Cambridge, it was not contractual sanctity but a vision of life that urged them forward.

Like the Agreement at Cambridge, the Mayflower Compact, shaped by practical necessity though it was, shows evidence of the appeal of a similar visionary union. Its signers bound themselves into a "civil body politic" the very nature of which they had yet to agree upon and the laws of which they had yet to frame, even as they engaged themselves in advance to obey them. Such confidence looks more than a little imprudent from a modern standpoint, until we recall the sorts of implications that Winthrop would later draw from the traditional metaphor of the body as applied to human communities. Indeed, perhaps even more deeply than did Winthrop, William Bradford identified the founding of Plymouth and the trials of the separatists with the plight of a family. Bradford expressed the anguish of their original escape to Leyden by emphasizing the suffering of the husbands who were hurried away to sea by their Dutch captain as they watched their wives and children taken into custody on shore by a "great company, both horse and foot, with bills and guns and other weapons." The separatists' determination to leave Holland for America was motivated in some measure by their desire "for the propagating and advancing of the Gospel," but the reasons that seemed to carry the greatest weight with them – and that prompted the most moving prose from Bradford – were the strains of European exile upon their families: "As necessity was a taskmaster over them, so they were forced to be such, not only to their servants but in a sort to their dearest children, the which as it did not a little wound the tender hearts of many a loving father and mother, so it produced likewise sundry sad and sorrowful effects."[12]

The escape from this sadness and sorrow brought with it the terrible conditions of their first New England winter. But even in the grimmest circumstances, Bradford identified the devoted nursing of Miles Standish

and William Brewster as a dramatic instance of the sort of selfless tenderness that Winthrop was to invoke on behalf of his own community ten
years later. Standish and Brewster, among others, "spared no pains night
nor day" in their devotion to the sick,

> but with abundance of toil and hazard of their own health,
> fetched them wood, made them fires, dressed them meat, made
> their beds, washed their loathsome clothes, clothed and un-
> clothed them. In a word, did all the homely and necessary offices
> for them which dainty and queasy stomachs cannot endure to
> hear named; and all this willingly and cheerfully, without any
> grudging in the least, showing herein their true love unto their
> friends and brethren; a rare example and worthy to be remem-
> bered . . . And what I have said of these I may say of many
> others who died in this general visitation, and others yet living;
> that whilst they had health, yea, or any strength continuing, they
> were not wanting to any that had need of them. And I doubt not
> but their recompense is with the Lord.[13]

Some of the same fluidity of gender and sensitivity to typology that
Winthrop skillfully employs in "A Modell of Christian Charity" is present in the example of these maternal Pilgrim Fathers. Bradford had
begun writing *Of Plymouth Plantation* just at the moment when the larger
and better-financed expedition to Massachusetts Bay was about to super-
sede Plymouth in colonial history. But the shift in center of gravity from
Plymouth to Boston involved virtually no change at all in the relation
that leaders in both colonies hoped to maintain between the claims of the
self and the claims of the community. Winthrop gave that relation its
definitive expression in the closing sentences of "A Modell of Christian
Charity," drawing on the commanding image of the body and on the
verbal complexity of his portrait of Eve's restless devotion in order to
suggest the kind of vitality that he felt in his social ideal:

> For this end, wee must be knitt together in this worke as one
> man, wee must entertaine each other in brotherly Affection, wee
> must be willing to abridge our selves of our superfluities, for the
> supply of others necessities, wee must uphold a familiar Com-
> merce together in all meekenes, gentlenes, patience and liber-
> ality, wee must delight in eache other, make others Condicions
> our owne rejoyce together, mourne together, labour, and suffer
> together, allwayes haveing before our eyes our Commission and
> Community in the worke, our Community as members of the
> same body, soe shall wee keepe the unitie of the spirit in the bond
> of peace, the Lord will be our God and delight to dwell among

us, as his owne people and will commaund a blessing upon us in
all our wayes, soe that wee shall see much more of his wisdome
power goodness and truthe then formerly wee have beene ac-
quainted with, wee shall finde that the God of Israell is among
us, when tenn of us shall be able to resist a thousand of our
enemies, when hee shall make us a prayse and glory, that men
shall say of succeeding plantacions: the lord make it like that of
New England. (203)

Within a moment or two of this ringing forecast, Winthrop is quoting
Moses on the choice of life. To his listeners it must have seemed a
completely appropriate text with which to close, on metaphorical as well
as on typological grounds.

Winthrop's accomplishment in "A Modell of Christian Charity" is the
extraordinary degree of concentration with which he was able to express
a wide range of hopes and fears shared by his colleagues. Perry Miller
was among the first to recognize this representative property of Winthrop's discourse and to employ the speech in *The New England Mind:
From Colony To Province* as a fixed point of reference from which to
measure the dissolution of the Puritan errand as the eighteenth century
progressed.[14] Miller's influential treatment, however, has tended to ob-
scure the degree to which Winthrop's initial vision of the emigrants'
plight not only anticipated decline but absorbed the pattern of great
promise and great peril – a pattern inherited from the Puritan vision of
the plight of the individual soul and from their reading of the cyclical
history of the people of Israel – and accepted it not as a unique and
temporary predicament but as the ongoing condition of life. The Mosaic
choice that Winthrop describes seems resonant with finality, but in fact,
as he makes clear, it renews its terms constantly in the private, daily labor
of life, in the intimate bonds of marriage, in the obligations of a parent
and a neighbor.

The heroic, public work of Joshua or even of Nehemiah, the wall
builder, with whom Cotton Mather was much later to identify Winthrop, is not the sphere of activity that Winthrop himself evokes as central
to his new, American experience. He evokes instead a deeply domestic
and familial set of values, and he offers a wonderfully assertive and commanding vision of Eve as the most comprehensive embodiment of those
qualities necessary to avoid the figurative shipwreck that was all too
vividly present to the imaginations of his seaborne listeners.

The image of Moses and the choice of life with which Winthrop closes
is grand enough in its own right, but it has its roots in, and draws its
authority from, unusually modest sources in human experience. Nor is it

by any means clear that Winthrop saw this authority as the exclusive property of one sex. Indeed, though "A Modell of Christian Charity" begins in an apparent justification of the traditional structures of authority within the English community, that justification proves to be the preamble to a description of communal authority that is both more and less stable than the familiar three-way alliance of wealth, place, and masculinity. The comforting implications of the concept of divine plenitude give way to the necessity that people comfort one another, nurture one another, and delight in one another. Those are the values of the household, not of the Great Chain of Being, and authority is grounded in them much as the stature of Eve is grounded both in her typological identities and her power of affection, or that of William Brewster and Miles Standish is grounded in their nurturing strength during the first winter at Plymouth.

These are the central features, then, of the vision of life that Winthrop presents: the sense of the ongoing predicament of choice, the domestic center of meaning within which that choice takes place, the necessary identification of communal authority – of power – with the bonds and obligations of the family. It does not follow from the presence of these features in Winthrop's speech that he was binding himself always to act under their guidance. They simply represent his best description of those professed truths that the residents of Massachusetts Bay must strive to put into action in daily life. Like any good Puritan, Winthrop must have expected a great measure of failure on his own part as well as on that of others. The twin perceptions of impending failure and exhilarating opportunity are the definitive properties of Moses' choice, and these along with the other critical elements of Winthrop's discourse provide the context for the poetic achievements of Anne Bradstreet and Edward Taylor.

Anne Bradstreet – newly married and sailing to New England with a father and a husband each of whom would in turn succeed to Winthrop's position as governor – was among the listeners whom Winthrop addressed on the *Arbella* in 1630. Under the circumstances it would have been next to impossible for her to avoid feeling the pertinence of Winthrop's appeal to the models of the body and the family.[15] Indeed her domestic life was so intimately involved with the political life of the colony that she comes quite close to being a historical equivalent to the figure of Eve that Winthrop uses in his speech: the wife whose marital devotion is indistinguishable from a political act, and whose love transforms the remote relationships of power.

It is scarcely an exaggeration to trace the character of Bradstreet's work to the social vision that "A Modell of Christian Charity" embodies. Her loving, verse letters to her absent husband, for example, present themselves as expressions of a private affection that is peripheral to the serious masculine business of the state. In the context of Winthrop's model, however, Bradstreet's private affections and her celebration of them have public stature. Her own family appeared to recognize this fact and treat her poetry much like a public resource.[16] Bradstreet does, to be sure, complain in "The Prologue" to *The Tenth Muse* that men are prone to patronize her work, but men were also prone to conspire to publish it without the author's consent, and Nathaniel Ward wrote some cheerful introductory verses to Bradstreet's book in which he mocks the myopic incompetence of a sexist Apollo, "the old Don":

> Good sooth quoth the old Don, tell ye me so,
> I muse whither at length these girls will go;
> It half revives my chill frost-bitten blood,
> To see a woman once do ought that's good;
> And shod by Chaucer's boots, and Homer's furs,
> Let men look to't, lest women wear the spurs.[17]

Bradstreet apparently engaged in poetic exchanges with her father that Emily Dickinson would have found marvelous, and Simon Bradstreet, her son, wished particularly that his mother would leave him some written record from which he could continue to take counsel after her death.

Like Emily Dickinson, Bradstreet assembled private books of her poetry, but unlike Dickinson, she had clearly in mind an ultimate purpose for them, as she indicates in the six lines with which she prefaced the brief spiritual autobiography that she wrote for her children:

> This book by any yet unread,
> I leave for you when I am dead,
> That being gone, here you may find
> What was your living mother's mind.
> Make use of what I leave in love,
> And God shall bless you from above. (240)

These are characteristically simple couplets. Bradstreet obviously had no poetic aspirations for them. But even so they capture the sense of affectionate seriousness that she brought to her work. She leaves this book in "love," but she makes sure her children know that she does not intend it for reverent neglect. There is just enough of the benevolent, maternal taskmaster in her admonitory "make use" to leave the unmistakable impression of an authoritative, parental voice. Much of Bradstreet's most memorable poetry is tied, directly or indirectly, to this sense of her domestic role and to the events of domestic life. She and those around her, however, would not have considered this fact as evidence of a purely personal or limited sensibility.[18]

The extraordinary stature that Bradstreet was willing to claim for her domestic posture is generally couched in language that is, at least apparently, self-effacing. But this is much the same kind of self-effacement that Winthrop understands to be the central achievement of Christian charity. It does not happen in us naturally but must be actively sought and struggled for. As often as not, in Bradstreet's case, the struggle seldom achieves even a temporary resolution. Nor is the reader always perfectly certain of the relative merits of the antagonists. This sense of struggle is present even in a poem like "The Author to Her Book," which seems merely conventional in its modesty and resignation. Bradstreet adopts in these dedicatory lines the stance of a mother embarrassed by the flaws in her poetic child. She does her best to correct her offspring's "blemishes," but her own lack of skill and her child's stubborn imperfections defeat her best intentions. She finally dismisses her hobbling "work" with some cautious advice about avoiding critics and pleading the lowliness of one's parentage.

There seems, at first, little struggle here. Bradstreet solicits a bit of tenderness for her "rambling brat" and concocts one or two clever (if disturbing) puns on printing "rags" and on her offspring's crippled "feet," but only in the closing lines does she suggest the striking model for her creative zeal:

> In this array, 'mongst vulgars mayst thou roam;
> In critics' hands, beware thou dost not come.
> And take thy way where yet thou art not known.
> If for thy father asked, say thou hadst none;
> And for thy mother – she, alas, is poor,
> Which caused her thus to send thee out of door. (221)

These poems, Bradstreet claims, are perhaps imperfect, but they are also unfathered, created out of nothing but the author's "feeble brain," harshly judged for their failings yet forgiven by a mother whose nurturing hand seems at once affectionate and heavy with nearly an excess of formative power:

> I cast thee by as one unfit for light,
> Thy visage was so irksome in my sight;
> Yet being mine own, at length affection would
> Thy blemishes amend, if so I could:
> I washed thy face, but more defects I saw,
> And rubbing off a spot, still made a flaw. (221)

Bradstreet is both a chagrined parent and an analogue for God in these seemingly modest lines. She is apologizing for her artistic inadequacies and asserting an extraordinary potency all at once – a potency that both evokes and dismisses the figure of the absent father. At the same time, Bradstreet's omnipotent motherhood is marked by the typological network that Winthrop exploited in his portrait of an equally affectionate and powerful Eve. Like Eve, Bradstreet the author is implicated in the "defects" of her crippled verse. She, after all, has made it. But she is also a mother strangely independent of earthly fathers – like Eve's typological descendant – and prophetically sensitive to the fate she envisions her child will suffer once it falls into the hands of critics. The fusion of the tradition of authorial modesty with typological ambition in these lines is both unsettling and invigorating. It represents the "willed resignation" that Robert Daly has described as the characteristic mark of Bradstreet's best verse, and at the same time asserts the kind of communal authority that Winthrop identified with his sociable and selfless Eve.[19]

Bradstreet was capable of evoking Winthrop's metaphors quite directly, often in contexts that strike a modern reader as almost inconceivably unsophisticated. "In Reference to Her Children, 23 June 1659" is a fine example of such an exaltation of the domestic posture, working out of conditions that are less poetically promising than the witty conceits of "The Author to Her Book." Like most of Bradstreet's work, "In Reference to Her Children" is metaphorically and structurally straightforward, ninety-four lines in more or less regular couplets, built on the commonplace fiction of a mother bird reminiscing about her chicks: "I had eight birds hatched in one nest," the poem begins, "Four cocks there were, and hens the rest." The earthy savor of such language would have seemed quite familiar to contemporary readers. John Cotton had preached a farewell sermon to some of the earliest emigrants to Massachusetts Bay in which he urged his listeners to "forget not the wombe that bore you and the breasts that gave you sucke. Even ducklings hatched under an henne, though they take the water, yet will still have recourse to the wing that hatched them: how much more should chickens of the same feather, and yolke?"[20] Cotton's purpose was to encourage his listeners to remember England and it did not strike him as unseemly to do so in this simple way.

Bradstreet's metaphor is equally simple and traditional. She comments on each of her hatchlings in turn, from the eldest, who has now flown to "regions far," to the three youngest, who "still with me nest" but whose flight she already anticipates. The departure of her "brood" fills her with fear both because of the dangers of the world – fowlers, hawks, and untoward boys – and because her children are in want of wisdom. "O to your safety have an eye," she urges them, and after describing how she intends to pass her old age, singing "my weak lays" in a shady wood, she offers them her last piece of advice:

> When each of you shall in your nest
> Among your young ones take your rest,
> In chirping language, oft them tell,

You had a dam that loved you well,
That did what could be done for young,
And nursed you up till you were strong,
And 'fore she once would let you fly,
She showed you joy and misery;
Taught what was good, and what was ill,
What would save life, and what would kill.
Thus gone, amongst you I may live,
And dead, yet speak, and counsel give:
Farewell, my birds, farewell adieu,
I happy am, if well with you.   (234)

What is most interesting, and most characteristic, about these concluding lines is the way in which Bradstreet is able to infuse her almost insistently naive conceit with a surprising, and moving, degree of seriousness. The change is anything but heavy-handed, but if we are alert, then the three pairs of antonyms – joy and misery, good and ill, life and "kill" – seem unmistakably to echo the structure of Moses' farewell injunctions on "life and good, death and evil" to which Winthrop had attached such significance nearly thirty years earlier. Bradstreet certainly does not force the association upon us, but there is a great deal of difference between the distressed mother bird who had cried "O to your safety have an eye" just a few lines earlier and the quality of calm and stately wisdom that suddenly settles upon the poem's close. The shift in tone that occurs in these final lines suggests Bradstreet's desire to entice us along into a delightful and striking contrast. But even without such a formal hint, it is clear that one of the chief advantages of Bradstreet's childlike conceit of birds, chicks, and nests is what we might call its inherent poetic humility.[21]

As the rich fusion of tones in "The Author to Her Book" suggests, Bradstreet is engaged in a more or less steady struggle with the self. "The finest bread hath the least bran," she wrote in "Meditation 6," "the purest honey the least wax, and the sincerest Christian the least self-love" (273). The vocation of a poet, however, is almost inevitably an assertion of the individual sensibility, particularly as Bradstreet practiced it. She was the family elegist and spiritual counselor, the family solicitor with God in many of her verse prayers. Unless we are devoted antiquarians, we know very little indeed about those "public employments" for which Bradstreet's husband was so often absent, but Bradstreet's amorous verse letters to him are familiar to many modern readers. At some level she sensed the potential incitement to egotism that such power over feelings and over human memory could represent. Taking counsel with the chastened peacock of her "Meditation 5," she appears to have focused her own literary efforts not on the dramatic display of poetical "gay feathers," but rather upon a considered exposure of those embarrassing black feet: "So he that glories in his gifts and adornings should look upon his corruptions, and that will damp his high thoughts" (273). Bradstreet took some care to damp her own.

It is equally clear that accompanying this conventional, or corrective, humility of Bradstreet's is a genuinely religious sense of unworthiness, expressed most directly in the private verse laments that she left to her children, in which a succession of fainting fits, sicknesses, and periods of bodily weakness all conspire to remind her of her utter dependence upon God:

> My thankful heart with glorying tongue
> Shall celebrate Thy name,
> Who hath restored, redeemed, recured
> From Sickness, death, and pain.
>
> I cried, Thou seem'st to make some stay,
> I sought more earnestly
> And in due time Thou succor'st me
> And sent'st me help from high.
>
> Lord, whilst my fleeting time shall last,
> Thy goodness let me tell,
> And new experience I have gained
> My future doubts repel.
>
> An humble, faithful life, O Lord,
> Forever let me walk;
> Let my obedience testify
> My praise lies not in talk.
>
> Accept, O Lord, my simple mite,
> For more I cannot give.
> What Thou bestow'st I shall restore,
> For of thine alms I live. (259–60)

When Bradstreet's powers are fully engaged, her poetry manages to sustain an unusually effective balance between the genuine humility of these private laments and the kind of forthright self-confidence ("My praise lies not in talk") that conventional humility disguises. Even in these lines from a "thankful heart," Bradstreet cannot resist reminding God that his succor was something less than prompt, and she does indeed expect to encounter future doubts. Her gratitude and obedience are not inconsistent with an essential, human assertiveness, just as her authorial modesty is not inconsistent with a willingness to hint at her own, God-like powers of composition – of judgment and amendment. For Bradstreet (as Robert

Daly has again noted) man's relation to God was "familial," but that relation implied a degree of antagonism as well as intimacy that Bradstreet's own domestic roles permitted her to appreciate and dramatize.[22]

The brief dedicatory verses to her father that appeared in the posthumous, 1678 edition of her poems clearly overstate her modesty in the conventional manner when she characterizes her offered work as "this crumb." But other elements of the poem – the allusion to the parable of the talents, in particular, and to the necessity for "forgiving" debts that Winthrop emphasizes in parts of "A Modell of Christian Charity" – establish just as clearly both a sense of dependence and a sense of Bradstreet's own personal adequacy. Both the indebtedness and the stubbornness are deeply felt:

> Most truly honoured, and as truly dear,
> If worth in me or ought I do appear,
> Who can of right better demand the same
> Than may your worthy self from whom it came?
> The principal might yield a greater sum,
> Yet handled ill, amounts but to this crumb;
> My stock's so small I know not how to pay,
> My bond remains in force unto this day;
> Yet for part payment take this simple mite,
> Where nothing's to be had, kings loose their right.
> Such is my debt I may not say forgive,
> But as I can, I'll pay it while I live;
> Such is my bond, none can discharge but I,
> Yet paying is not paid until I die. (231)

The similarity between the language of Bradstreet's private lament (also a "simple mite") and this more public poem is another index of the complex interplay in her work between genuine and conventional selflessness, between self-effacement and self-confidence. "In Reference to Her Children" is built around a similar balance, offering at the same instant two versions of Bradstreet's maternal solicitude: one the implicitly patronizing view of the fretful mother bird, the other quite boldly identifying her parental concern with that of Moses for his people.

Bradstreet's apparently simple "Meditation 6" on self-love is in some measure a general admission of this characteristic mixture of boldness and modesty: "The finest bread hath the least bran, the purest honey the least wax, and the sincerest Christian the least self-love." The best bread may well have the least bran, but at the same time Bradstreet implies that all bread has some. Bees' wax may be an unwelcome intruder in one's honey, but its presence there is anything but unnatural. Accordingly, though the best Christian may have the least self-love, Bradstreet is more than prepared to take a forgiving attitude toward that residue of egotism, provided that it does not try to assert itself too openly. Like many of her best meditations, the analogies in this one have a benevolently corrective effect upon its dogmatic basis. Just as Winthrop recognized in his closing exhortations to "A Modell of Christian Charity," it is clearly desirable to struggle against the self, but it is entirely natural that the struggle should be at least a partial failure. "In Reference to Her Children" virtually enacts this struggle and dramatizes its fortunate failure. Without some sense of self there would, of course, be no poem at all. Without some potent restraint upon the self, the nature of the poem would change. The delicate allusion to Moses might harden into an unacceptably self-aggrandizing view of the speaker's role. Bradstreet intends that the emphasis fall where the title suggests: upon her children, not upon herself. She hopes simultaneously to enjoin "life" upon them and to embody the meaning of that injunction in her carefully balanced manner of giving it.

Not even the convention of poetic humility or a calculated simplicity, however, could disguise Bradstreet's immense satisfaction in her domestic roles. The images from "In Reference to Her Children," for example, are in one sense unsophisticated, but in the context of the whole poem – its seriousness of purpose as well as its simplicity of means – they are fondly playful. The innocence of its primary metaphor does not trivialize the emotions expressed but serves instead as a constant, gentle reminder of a parent's vulnerability through her children:

> O would my young, ye saw my breast,
> And knew what thoughts there sadly rest,
> Great was my pain when I you bred,
> Great was my care when I you fed,
> Long did I keep you soft and warm,
> And with my wings kept off all harm,
> My cares are more and fears than ever,
> My throbs such now as 'fore were never.
> Alas, my birds, you wisdom want,
> Of perils you are ignorant;
> Oft times in grass, on trees, in flight,
> Sore accidents on you may light.
> O to your safety have an eye,
> So happy may you live and die. (233–4)

These lines are solicitous and at the same time surprisingly blunt. Much as in the case of the typologically double identity of the speaker in "The Author to Her Book," Bradstreet assumes the role of a fussing mother bird, but she is also a demanding judge of her children's insufficient wisdom. It is clear that her sense of a mother's role (and voice) is anything but stereotypically simple. This same sort of complexity is present as well in the poems that reflect her status as wife.

The verse letters to her husband are among the most memorable of Bradstreet's poems, not only because of the enthusiasm with which they celebrate married love, but because of the nature of the love that they celebrate. Bradstreet always writes from the perspective of the home-bound wife who wants her busy partner to return; yet just as the vulnerability of "In Reference to Her Children" is mutual, so the dependence between husband and wife is mutual in Bradstreet's love poems. "I have a loving peer," she writes in one verse letter, making rather skillful use of the two meanings of "peer" to establish the double assertion: I have a loving lord, and I have a loving equal. Bradstreet's love poems take what appears to be unrestrained delight in acknowledging her dependence upon her husband, but the terms in which she expresses that delight almost always affirm, directly or indirectly, that the dependence is mutual – the perfect model for the mutual dependence of society at large that Winthrop envisioned for America.

Bradstreet's reference to her "loving peer," for example, comes in the midst of a poem that seems particularly extravagant in its images of wifely dependence:

> As loving hind that (hartless) wants her deer,
> Scuds through the woods and fern with hark'ning ear,
> Perplext, in every bush and nook doth pry,
> Her dearest deer, might answer ear or eye;
> So doth my anxious soul, which now doth miss
> A dearer dear (far dearer heart) than this. (229)

Bradstreet goes on to compare herself to a "pensive dove" mourning the absence of her "turtle true," and to "the loving mullet, that true fish" that leaps onto the bank to die with "her captive husband" rather than lead a lonely life. The poem draws to a close by heaping up these three identities in a way that draws attention to their hyperbolic nature but also discloses in the parallelism of the first two lines of the following passage the differences among them:

> Return my dear, my joy, my only love,
> Unto thy hind, thy mullet, and thy dove,
> Who neither joys in pasture, house, nor streams,
> The substance gone, O me, these are but dreams.

Of these three images of wifely desolation, only one is stereotypically passive and helpless: the dove, with whose "uncouth" moanings for "my only love" even Bradstreet herself is a bit impatient earlier in the poem. The loving hind is a restless, energetic searcher, as nimble as the puns that characterize her, and the mullet is "true" with a nearly fierce joy in self-sacrifice. It is a chivalric rather than a "feminine" loyalty, and it produces exhilaration rather than despair. The love in this poem is a complex passion that asserts its power as much as it laments its incompleteness.

"A Letter to Her Husband, Absent Upon Public Employment" explores the same kind of complexity. It is a scolding, witty, erotic poem, that may also acknowledge an indirect debt to the memorable portrait of Eve in "A Modell of Christian Charity." Bradstreet closes her "letter" with an allusion to Genesis that is a bit truer to the biblical text than Winthrop's but which is nevertheless a stern reminder that the bonds of marriage are not dependent upon metaphysical conceits for their power and ought not to be subjected to strain for routine causes:

> But when thou northward to me shall return,
> I wish my Sun may never set, but burn
> Within the Cancer of my glowing breast,
> The welcome house of him my dearest guest.
> Where ever, ever stay, and go not thence,
> Till nature's sad decree shall call thee hence;
> Flesh of thy flesh, bone of thy bone,
> I here, thou there, yet both but one. (226)

There is nothing merely "public" about Bradstreet's claim upon her husband. She openly reminds him, as Winthrop's Eve served to remind his listeners, of the relationship between marital devotion and the kind of apocalyptic imagery that these lines evoke: a loving "sun" united with his bride and forming a single being.[23]

"To My Dear and Loving Husband" brings this same, sobering force to bear even more directly, for though the title seems to express Bradstreet's confidence in her husband's affections, the text of the poem itself is more tentative in its claims of confidence and at the same time more emphatic about the momentous consequences of domestic loyalty:

> If ever two were one, then surely we.
> If ever man were loved by wife, then thee;
> If ever wife was happy in a man,
> Compare with me, ye women, if you can.
> I prize thy love more than whole mines of gold
> Or all the riches that the East doth hold.
> My love is such that rivers cannot quench,
> Nor ought but love from thee, give recompense.
> Thy love is such I can no way repay,
> The heavens reward thee manifold, I pray.

Then while we live, in love let's so persevere
That when we live no more, we may live ever. (225)

Bradstreet is "happy" in her husband and prizes his love, but these assertions fall ever so slightly short of confirming that his love equals the
resistless force of hers, and her direct address to the community of wives
establishes that masculine affection is in general less satisfactory than it
might be. The poem is a celebration of the Bradstreets' particular relationship and at the same time a plea for recompense and a reminder that
earthly love and loyalty are the critical symbols of "covenanted" love, the
basis upon which John Winthrop had established the Puritan community.[24] They exert a momentous claim upon human attention. These messages are potentially so antagonistic to one another that their mixture in
thirteen lines of poetry is an unusual achievement. Bradstreet's sense of
the psychological richness and import of domestic life called for both
extraordinarily exuberant and extraordinarily politic expression.

　She is similarly politic and tender with her children. The "Meditations" that she prepared for her son Simon are, as we have seen, both
reflections of sound doctrine and ameliorations of that doctrine to accommodate Bradstreet's sense of human limitation. Indeed, some of the most
beautiful of these "Meditations" cast God in the role of a "prudent mother" who has a fund of good sense to draw upon in rearing her children.
"Meditation 39" is the finest example of this domestic analogy. No wise
mother, Bradstreet observes, will give her little child "a long and cumbersome garment," for that would only result in falls, bruises, or worse.
Similarly, God recognizes that generous earthly endowments are likely to
prove too cumbersome for weak Christians: "Therefore God cuts their
garments short to keep them in such a trim that they might run the ways
of His Commandment" (279). The message of this meditation is both
reassuring and discouraging. We might have preferred that God be more
generous with earthly wealth and honor and let us take our chances with
stumbling. But Bradstreet's understanding of maternal solicitude is not
sentimental. Her sense of the role has a priestly quality to it that is both
fond and stern. Her dedication of the "Meditations," for example, displays at once her care for Simon's well-being, her desire to respond to his
request for something in writing by which to remember her, and her
gently expressed suspicion that he might, after all, need just this sort of
guidance and spiritual support. "I could think of nothing more fit for you
nor of more ease to myself," writes Bradstreet, than these incitements to
spiritual thinking. That motherly observation itself might well serve as
Simon's first topic of meditation.

　The prose memorial that she left to her children is similarly solicitous
and stern. Bradstreet wished to share with her children a generous record

of her own struggle with doubt and of her own assurance of God's ultimate provision for "this great household upon the earth" (243). At the same time she casts these reflections as a deathbed speech – not unlike Moses' last farewell – which she hopes will "sink deepest" and give useful guidance: "I have not studied in this you read to show my skill, but to declare the truth, not to set forth myself, but the glory of God" (240). This document is personal – Bradstreet meant it to remain private – but its voice is also public and, in its way, remote:

> I knowing by experience that the exhortations of parents take most effect when the speakers leave to speak, and those especially sink deepest which are spoken latest, and being ignorant whether on my death bed I shall have opportunity to speak to any of you, much less to all, thought it the best, whilst I was able, to compose some short matters (for what else to call them I know not) and bequeath to you, that when I am no more with you, yet I may be daily in your remembrance (although that is the least in my aim in what I now do), but that you may gain some spiritual advantage by my experience. I have not studied in this you read to show my skill, but to declare the truth, not to set forth myself, but the glory of God. If I had minded the former, it had been perhaps better pleasing to you, but seeing the last is the best, let it be best pleasing to you. (240)

The same mixture of maternal solicitude and power that gave such richness to the texture of "The Author to Her Book" is responsible for the interplay of confidence and doubt, authority and affection in this striking paragraph. It is probably inadvisable to place too much emphasis upon the artful significance of seventeenth-century syntax. But Bradstreet's long first sentence in this passage – twice interrupted by dramatically contrasting asides – captures in a single unit of expression the complexity and importance of the domestic role as Bradstreet understood it. She captures as well the characteristic alternation between security and insecurity that Winthrop identified so deeply with the predicament of the *Arbella* emigrants. "Downy beds make drowsy persons," Bradstreet wrote in "Meditation 8," "but hard lodging keeps the eyes open; a prosperous state makes a secure Christian, but adversity makes him consider" (273). It was precisely to foster such considered living in her children that Bradstreet took on her authoritative role, but it was an authority that she naturally derived from the roles linking her to Winthrop's emblematic Eve and to the potent, mediating figure of Mary, whose sorrows Bradstreet also took up in the elegies she wrote for three of her grandchildren and for a daughter-in-law who died in childbirth.

Bradstreet's power as an elegist consists in her ability to dramatize what Robert Daly names the "weaning" process by which a Puritan learns to be resigned to the loss of earthly beauty. But in the best of these poems it is not entirely as an earthly speaker that Bradstreet presents herself anymore than she presents herself in the memorial to her children as an earthly presence or defends her poetic children in "The Author to Her Book" as an earthly creator. Her command over the powers of consolation does not really seem to derive from the traditional, natural metaphors of which the poems are composed. These, in fact, are curiously out of harmony with the deaths of children, as Bradstreet quietly shows us in "In Memory of My Dear Grandchild Elizabeth":

> Farewell dear babe, my heart's too much content,
> Farewell sweet babe, the pleasure of mine eye,
> Farewell fair flower that for a space was lent,
> Then ta'en away unto eternity.
> Blest babe, why should I once bewail thy fate,
> Or sigh thy days so soon were terminate,
> Sith thou art settled in an everlasting state.
>
> 2
>
> By nature trees do rot when they are grown,
> And plums and apples thoroughly ripe do fall,
> And corn and grass are in their season mown,
> And time brings down what is both strong and tall.
> But plants new set to be eradicate,
> And buds new blown to have so short a date,
> Is by His hand alone that guides nature and fate.   (235)

The first stanza begins with three formulaic laments that the poet seems able to put aside, in the fifth line, with a serenity that makes even one lament seem superfluous. The child is "blest," and Bradstreet does not require the consolatory metaphor of fair flowers to reach her state of inward peace, as "settled" apparently as that of the infant's soul itself. Nor does the second stanza make more use of its more elaborate, natural parables of mutability. The child was neither grown nor ripe, not strong and tall. The lessons of nature simply encumber a relationship to the divine will that is direct and confident – that of a mother who recognizes that she had received her child directly from the same hand that now claims it. This is a posture that is not easy to credit in a human speaker, but neither is it easy to credit the complex posture that Bradstreet adopts in "The Author to Her Book" until one recognizes that Bradstreet is speaking (as a Puritan might put it) "typically" as well as humanly, face to face with God in a relation that Emerson would later recognize and envy as the mark of his Puritan ancestors.

In perhaps the finest of her poems envisioning her own death, Brad-street made it clear just how deeply her imagination responded to the network of associations and images that Winthrop summoned up in his vision of Eve as the redemptive model for life in Massachusetts Bay. "As Weary Pilgrim" offers the reader a description of two figures, one the poet in a state of perplexity and glorious anticipation, the other a hypothetical traveler through life to whom the poet compares herself in the simile that the title suggests. This first pilgrim, however, is disturbingly content to die. He "hugs with delight his silent nest" in a selfish parody of Winthrop's vision of social delight, and "blesses himself" to think that his earthly trials are over and the grave's "safety" awaits. Bradstreet's own earthly pilgrimage is quite different, marked by the domestic tempera-ment, by the vitality of the image of marriage, and by the thirst for life. Her "clay house" decays, but it is an existence "among the blest" that she counts upon after death and not a self-indulgent and isolated escape. The grave is a place of preparation, of urgency, leading to an apocalyptic marriage with Christ and the replacement of human weakness and dis-honor with human power:

> What though my flesh shall there consume,
>   It is the bed Christ did perfume,
> And when a few years shall be gone,
>   This mortal shall be clothed upon.
> A corrupt carcass down it lays,
>   A glorious body it shall rise.
> In weakness and dishonour sown,
>   In power 'tis raised by Christ alone.
> Then soul and body shall unite
>   And of their Maker have the sight.
> Such lasting joys shall there behold
>   As ear ne'er heard nor tongue e'er told.
> Lord make me ready for that day,
> Then come, dear Bridegroom, come away. (295)

Bradstreet clearly chooses "life" in this poem, whereas the first weary (and, not incidentally, male) pilgrim chooses death. Her last two lines are characteristically retiring and bold, insecure about her personal worth-iness and at the same time startlingly confident in her own powers of appeal. Christ too is an absent spouse, with whom Anne Bradstreet is willing to assert her erotic claims. "As Weary Pilgrim" progresses, then, from a depiction of the Old Adam of selfish contentment to an embodi-ment of an ecstatic and visionary Eve who is, at the same time, the community as Bride, the Church welcoming her "Bridegroom." Brad-street's poetic exploration of Winthrop's typological triad from "A Modell of Christian Charity" is in its way the artistic midpoint between Winthrop's purposeful prose of 1630 and Edward Taylor's ecstatic meditations on the Eucharist and on Canticles, in which he celebrates at the outset of the eighteenth century the same communal and individual marriage.

The relationship between Edward Taylor's proliferation of images and the handful of metaphors assembled in "A Modell of Christian Charity" is both more and less direct than Anne Bradstreet's relationship to that same, fruitful speech. Nowhere does Taylor echo Winthrop as closely as Bradstreet does, for example, in the final lines of "In Reference to Her Children." Nor does he identify as closely as Bradstreet does with the fabric of domestic metaphor that links private with public life. It would be surprising if he did so, for Taylor is nearly two generations removed from the founders of Massachusetts Bay, arriving at Boston in his early twenties almost forty years after the *Arbella* and almost certainly with no access to the text of Winthrop's discourse.

At the same time, however, Taylor's poetry is dominated, to a far greater extent than is Bradstreet's, by the overriding subject of the soul's journey from death to life. Taylor has dozens of ways of describing the journey and of voicing the soul's aspiration toward God. He exhorts his Maker repeatedly to blow on the coal of his smoldering faith, to feed his spirit on heavenly food, to root up his "henbain," chokewort, and ragwort and plant him with honeysuckle, sage, and savory, to dress him in the bright garments of grace, to "screw" him up, to oil his rusty lock, to sharpen his dull pencil or brighten his dim ink, to fill his earthly bottle with heavenly liquor, to redecorate the "Flesh and Blood bag" of his soul and make it a shining temple. Extravagantly conceived and extravagantly mixed metaphors are the characteristic (and traditional) expressions of Taylor's pious zeal and spiritual exuberance, but they all focus on the contrast between what he called the "lifeless Life" or "Living Death" of sin and the spiritual life of grace.[25]

To some degree, it is a disservice to Taylor to single out only one set of images from his lively multitude, since the experience of reading him is so decisively marked by the pleasure of tumbling along a stream of figurative language. But as Karl Keller has observed, the significance of this inventive and eclectic richness for Taylor himself was its intensively focused interest in the great Puritan drama: the soul's preparation for grace, the exchanging of death for life.[26] In a single stanza, Taylor is quite capable of touching on four or five distinct, and to some degree competing, metaphors, all of which converge toward the central subject of life, even though that critical word itself may be present only implicitly in one or two modifiers, or in the contrast between withered and "frim" (or flourishing) fruits:

> Lord, make my Faith thy golden Quill wherethrough
>   I vitall Spirits from thy blood may suck.
> Make Faith my Grinders, thy Choice Flesh to chew,
>   My Witherd Stock shall with frim Fruits be Stuck.
> My Soule shall then in Lively Notes forth ring
>   Upon her Virginalls, praise for this thing.[27]

As in Winthrop's image of the mouth that minces food for all the body, Taylor's "grinders" very nearly carry the idea of a conceit too far. Like Thoreau, however, Taylor himself seems to have feared only that he would not be extravagant enough. That such metaphorical diversity could tend to such spiritual unity is an underlying subject in most of Taylor's work, particularly in the "Preparatory Meditations," which are by their very nature diverse poetic approaches to a single spiritual goal: the sacrament of communion.[28]

From what we might call a doctrinal standpoint, then, Taylor's application of the scriptural contrast between life and death is more explicit than Bradstreet's even as his figurative language is more lavish and more daring. In many ways they scarcely seem comparable except as extreme instances of opposite tendencies within the tradition of Puritan poetry.[29] But Bradstreet and Taylor share a number of assumptions, in addition to the devotion to spiritual "life," that govern their work, the most important and most obvious of which is the context of familial discourse within which they understood their verse to be operating:

> My Lord I fain would Praise thee Well but finde
>   Impossibilities blocke up my pass.
> My tongue Wants Words to tell my thoughts, my Minde
>   Wants thoughts to Comprehend thy Worth, alas!
>   Thy Glory far Surmounts my thoughts, my thoughts
>   Surmount my Words: Hence little Praise is brought.
>
> But seing Non-Sense very Pleasant is
>   To Parents, flowing from the Lisping Child,
> I Conjue to thee, hoping thou in this
>   Will finde some hearty Praise of mine Enfoild,
>   But though my pen drop'd golden Words, yet would
>   Thy Glory far out shine my Praise in Gold. (1.34)

In recent years the most acute and thorough of Taylor's readers have tended to agree that the self-deprecation expressed in stanzas such as these fairly mild ones (by Taylor's standards) reflects a genuine contempt on Taylor's part for his own poetic efforts.[30] Anne Bradstreet's gentle dismissals of her verse seem almost vain by comparison to the depths of spiritual and artistic self-loathing to which Taylor repeatedly seems to sink, but even the most strongly stated of these depictions of human corruption – sometimes in their very extravagance – evoke the innocence of the lisping child and the image of parental solicitude that sustains the lines above. Taylor may well envision himself as a leper "all o're clag'd" with running sores and scabs, with "Stinking Breath," corrupted lungs, and a "Scurfy Skale" encrusting his entire body like the "Elephantik Mange," but the extremity of the description itself calls attention to its own conventional nature in a way that prevents the reader from taking such descriptions very seriously (2.27). The more highly wrought they get, the more childlike they seem, and the more plausible and more tender, in turn, seems the Lord's careful "springeing" and "besprinkling" that cures the leper's malady with His blood.

The personal usefulness of the "Preparatory Meditations" was, after all, to prepare and not to incapacitate. Taylor employed these poems as a means of readying himself for what he perceived as the momentous role he played administering and receiving the sacrament. The biblical quotations accompanying all but one of the meditations are the texts upon which he had chosen to preach on each communion Sunday, and all the meditations except the first one are dated. These poems are rooted just as deeply in Taylor's life as Bradstreet's domestic poems are rooted in hers, and their repetitive nature (like that of Bradstreet's laments) was from Taylor's perspective their primary meditative asset. They were meant to transform the mere repetitions of life into exalted occasions, all of the same fundamental kind to be sure but as diverse as the most heterogeneous natural imagery could make them. Collectively these poems also provide an extraordinary portrait of the ongoing interplay between security and insecurity in the Puritan imagination. William Scheick is only partly right when he states that the meditations nowhere depict "any sense of comfort on the poet's part."[31] In fact the strategy of virtually every one of the poems is to enact the recovery of a degree of personal assurance sufficient to make the ceremony of communion possible both for Taylor as the priestly celebrant and for the reader. They are, as Scheick elsewhere perceptively notes, acts of preservation, however inadequate their language may have been to Taylor's vision and however incomplete the process of reassurance might remain. No orthodox Congregational sacramentalist – as Taylor was – would have felt comfortable laying claim to an absolute certainty of personal election. But the church as a social entity had to accommodate itself to irresolvable metaphysical uncertainty, and in one sense that act of accommodation is what the meditations perform, much as the figure of Eve accommodated the strict demands of election to the social necessities of Massachusetts Bay in "A Modell of Christian Charity."

The particular ways in which Taylor sought to make his poetry useful confirm his participation in the tradition of the believing self's inadequacy and at the same time suggest his own peculiar softening of that tradition. The "Preparatory Meditations" repeatedly assert the unaided soul's incapacity properly to praise or to serve God, but they do so in a remarkably homely, very nearly forgiving, fashion.[32] One cannot escape the implication throughout Taylor's diction that even at their worst man's sins are not so serious after all. The cajoling attitude of the "Crumb of Dust" with which Taylor opens the "Prologue" to his meditational series represents the consistent tone of his poetic persona:

> Lord, Can a Crumb of Dust the Earth outweigh,
>   Outmatch all mountains, nay the Chrystall Sky?
> Imbosom in't designs that shall Display
>   And trace into the Boundless Deity?
>   Yea hand a Pen whose moysture doth guild ore
>   Eternall Glory with a glorious glore.
>
>   . . . .
>
> I am this Crumb of Dust which is design'd
>   To make my Pen unto thy Praise alone,
> And my dull Phancy I would gladly grinde
>   Unto an Edge on Zions Pretious Stone.
>   And Write in Liquid Gold upon thy Name
>   My Letters till thy glory forth doth flame.
>
> Let not th'attempts breake down my Dust I pray
>   Nor laugh thou them to scorn but pardon give.
> Inspire this Crumb of Dust till it display
>   Thy Glory through't: and then thy dust shall live.
>   Its failings then thou'lt overlook I trust,
>   They being Slips slipt from thy Crumb of Dust.

Taylor's posture throughout the poems that follow reflects both the humility and the assertiveness of these prefatory lines. These are clearly the words of a fallen speaker, aware of his diminished status in the universe, but aware as well of the larger typological design that makes a measure of bemusement at his own "Slips" something other than a gesture of theological impertinence. On occasion, to be sure, Taylor will revile man's corrupt condition, but it is nevertheless clear that he is prone to exercise a kind of poetic "grace" upon his human sinners, alleviating their afflictions in a way that anticipates, and to some extent symbolizes, the operations of genuine grace upon the genuinely corrupted spirit.[33]

At times, in his joy at God's care for His erring and undeserving creatures, Taylor can approach a sort of elation in his lines that suggests both stark surprise and a kind of durable innocence on the part of the awe-struck speaker:

> Oh! Good, Good, Good, my Lord What more Love yet!
>   Thou dy for mee! What am I dead in thee;
> What, did Deaths arrow shot at me thee hit?
>   Didst slip between that flying shaft and mee?
>   Didst make thyselfe Deaths marke shot at for me?
>   So that her Shaft shall fly no far than thee? (2.112)
>
>   . . . .
>
> Oh!, Thou, my Lord, thou king of Saints, here mak'st
>   A royall Banquet, thine to entertain
> With rich and royall fare, Celestiall Cates,
>   And sittest at the Table rich of fame.
>   Am I bid to this Feast? Sure Angells stare,
>   Such rugged looks, and Ragged robes I ware. (2.62)
>
>   . . . .
>
> Who is the Object of this Love? and in
>   Whose mouth doth fall the Apple of this tree?
> Is Man? A Sinner? Such a Wormhole thing?
>   Oh! matchless Love, laid out on such as Hee!
>   Should Gold wed Dung, Should Stars wooe Lobster
>   Claws,
>   It would no wonder, like this Wonder, cause. (2.33)

Stanzas like these are not particularly unusual in Taylor's work, ingenuous as they are, and it would be a mistake to ascribe their peculiar charm either to the author's lack of poetic sophistication or (as Robert Daly suggests) to an extremely sophisticated suspicion of all metaphoric speech. One indirect way of asserting the inadequacies of the self – as we noted in Bradstreet's verse – is to make certain that one's imagery reflects the "inadequacy" of human vision in general. That, in part, is the purpose of Taylor's nearly comic pursuit of preposterous images. At the same time, in Taylor's work such language has the effect of convincing us that unregenerate man is not really a very great redemptive challenge. Taylor's generic sinner does not fall into the glorious metric apostasy of Milton's Satan, but into a kind of childish "naughtiness" in which the value of human life remains very much apparent despite its temporary state of degradation:

> A Bran, a Chaff, a very Barly yawn,
>   An Husk, a Shell, a Nothing, nay, yet worse:

A Thistle, Bryer prickle, pricking Thorn,
   A Lump of Lewdeness, Pouch of Sin, a purse
   Of Naughtiness I am, yea, what not, Lord?
   And wilt thou be mine Altar? and my Lord?

Mine Heart's a Park or Chase of sins: Mine Head
   'S a Bowling Alley: sins play Ninehole here.
Phansy's a Green: sin Barly-breaks in't led.
   Judgment's a pingle; Blindeman's Bluff's plaid there.
   Sin playes at Coursey-park within my Minde;
   My Will's a Walke in which it aires what's blind. (2.18)

In her recent treatment of Taylor's typological poetics, Karen Rowe finds in these lines a "scathing self-denunciation" of the "sin-riddled soul's empty frivolities," a point of view that seems, at best, unjustifiably sober.[34] Barley-breaks and Coursey-park are, like Blindman's Bluff, innocent games. A state of sin that can be characterized in this manner is already well on the way toward being forgiven.

Taylor wrote, of course, from the perspective of one of the elect. In the opening poem of "God's Determinations," he makes it clear that even in the full panic of their sense of sin, such elected souls resemble a "Child that fears the Poker Clapp," who falls to earth and "lies still for fear least hee – Should by his breathing lowd discover'd bee" (389). The errors of such children invite gentle treatment and that is precisely the sort of treatment that they receive both in the drama of "God's Determinations" and in the lines of the "Preparatory Meditations." Presumably a cycle of poems and meditations describing the inner life of the damned would be considerably more grim, but Taylor's interest in their fate is quite perfunctory, and his portrait of the elect has sufficient variety in it to allow almost any reader to identify with the saved souls rather than with the lost ones. Ezra Stiles, Taylor's grandson and a temporary custodian of his papers, once occupied himself in calculating quite seriously the numbers of resurrected souls involved at Judgment Day. How crowded would Christ's courtroom be and how might the verdicts go in proportion of saved to lost souls? Stiles estimated that about 120 billion souls would be involved altogether, of which 90 billion would be saved and 30 billion damned.[35] These are, by strict Calvinist standards, rather good odds. More importantly, perhaps, they seem consistent with Edward Taylor's own tendency to weight the human predicament in favor of election and then to focus his imagination upon the benevolence of that process of salvation.

Taylor's depiction of the anxieties of the insecure human soul is detailed and sincere; he is by no means complacent in his vision of the operations of grace. Even the saved are filled with a sense that they "have long ago deserv'de Hells flame," that God's "abused Mercy" could only "burn and scald" them, that Justice and Vengeance "Run hotly after us our blood to spill" (429). Such accounts of the genuine terror of human life, however, are almost always followed by descriptions of our mortal plight that subtly, but decisively, relieve the strain and imply our ultimate rescue:

> Who'le with a Leaking, old Crack't Hulk assay
> To brave the raging Waves of Adria?
> Or who can Cross the Main Pacifick o're?
> Without a Vessell Wade from shore to shore?
> What! wade the mighty main from brim to brim,
> As if it would not reach above the Chin?
> But oh! poor wee, must wade from brinck to brinck
> With such a weight as would bright Angells sink.
> Or venture angry Adria, or drown
> When Vengeance's sea doth break the floodgates down.
> If Stay, or Go to sea, we drown. Then see
> In what a wofull Pickle, Lord, we bee. (429)

To be saved from hell's flames and from an aroused, bloodthirsty Justice seems scarcely possible. But even a deeply shaken believer might reasonably expect to escape from a "wofull Pickle." In the dialogue poems from "God's Determinations" that prepare the soul to resist Satan's temptations and to achieve church fellowship, the "Saint" assures the "Soul" that God dispenses grace to human beings only gradually, for good psychological reasons:

> You think you might have more: you shall have so,
> But if you'd all at once, you could not grow.
> And if you could not grow, you'd grieving fall:
> All would not then Content you, had you all.
> Should Graces Floodgate thus at once breake down,
> You most would lose, or else it you would drown.
> He'l fill you but by drops, that so he may
> Not drown you in't, nor cast a Drop away. (441)

Equipped with this kind of reassurance, even the most reluctant of Taylor's elect souls, the second and third "rancks" that originally had fled God's presence and held their breath waiting for the poker-clap, are filled with "holy Raptures" and able to capture the entire heavenly strategy in a single couplet:

> Sin sincks the Soul to Hell: but here is Love
> Sincks Sin to Hell: and soars the Soul above. (451)

The sense of great peril and great promise that marks Winthrop's description of the American plight is present to Taylor's imagination in this sense of a carefully nurturing God, releasing His grace with all the cautious circumspection of a mother watching over her child's slow but steady growth. Taylor never explicitly manipulates God's gender, as Bradstreet is willing to do in her "Meditation 39," for example. He takes his images from emblem books and from the Bible, with very little of the kind of provocative modification that Winthrop himself was willing to employ in his treatment of the figure of Eve. But it is equally clear that Taylor is firmly grounded in the imaginative heritage of Winthrop's "modell," and in the preeminence that model had given to domestic settings and domestic instincts.

What finally gives Taylor's work its distinctive, infectious energy is the earnestness with which he takes to heart his own poetic version of this tradition, operating in the experience of election: Even in our degraded state, we are still children; even in his inconceivable majesty, God is still our parent and takes a parent's interest in us. The household metaphor that was so formative for Anne Bradstreet is critical to the sense of intimacy that Taylor feels with his attentive and forgiving Maker. It is possible to tease, to cajole, to "tweedle" praise, to fill one's address to God with the most humdrum domestic metaphors, to offer Him "wagon loads" of love and glory, to dedicate one's services as a spinning wheel, an organ pipe, a liquor bottle, a writer. The fullness and to some degree the very unevenness of Taylor's poetic discourse is a substantial part of its meaning. One does not attempt to polish or revise for God's benefit, any more than the compilers of the *Bay Psalm Book* would have attempted to polish God's altar. One simply opens one's humanity to God, and to the greatest extent possible one celebrates it. Taylor's confidence in God's closeness is at least as critical to the shape his poetry takes as is his awe at God's power. In this sense he is in perfect agreement with Milton, whose God is strikingly at ease in Paradise and much more at home there than among His marshaled ranks of militarized angels.[36] Taylor's own wonderfully comfortable relations with God are by no means paradisal. He remained a crumb of dust, a bag of botches, a purse of naughtiness. But in this colloquial vocabulary of degradation, the intimacy of the family thrives.

2

"TO BE GREAT AND
DOMESTIC"

The familial vision with which John Winthrop identified the Puritan errand finds complex ways of asserting its influence even within the single intellectual and spiritual tradition of New England Puritanism. What Winthrop understood as a public sacrament – the choice of a particular conception of community – Anne Bradstreet and Edward Taylor both adapted to personal poetic concerns. For Taylor the adaptation was fairly straightforward; he was, after all, a minister, and the sacrament for which his "Preparatory Meditations" prepared him was the most conspicuous visible analogy to the choice of life that Winthrop hoped all the inhabitants of Massachusetts Bay would make. Bradstreet's relationship to the tradition involves more subtle exploitation of the domestic metaphors upon which Winthrop based his model, but Bradstreet too is able to turn the dramatic nature of Moses' farewell and the typological posture of Eve into the substance of a personal drama the outcome of which – like the fate of Winthrop's own appeal to his people – is invested with a potent mixture of hope and uncertainty.

This peculiarly intense degree of insecurity, compressed into a domestic setting, is very much the hallmark of Puritan experience and writing, but it continues to appear in a surprising array of forms throughout the work of the nonecclesiastical writers of the eighteenth century. The central images of the first two books of *Gulliver's Travels,* for example, employ the shifting status of Gulliver himself, as giant or as pygmy, for many of the same purposes that the shifting status of his own soul had served for Edward Taylor. In Lilliput man is a giant, more naive, certainly, but in many ways more noble than the petty community that surrounds him and emblematically binds him to earth with hundreds of slender threads. In Brobdingnag, on the other hand, he is contemptibly tiny, powerless, and correspondingly small in spirit. Yet the giants among whom he lives occasionally remind the reader, if not Gulliver himself, of man's breathtaking potential.

Within this broad contrast Swift's intelligence is always at work, disturbing the clear duality he seems to establish. Gulliver is indeed grand in Lilliput, but his grandeur is all too often of the flesh, measured in excremental terms that recall the tradition of self-deprecation so vividly depicted in Taylor's meditations. He is physically insignificant in Brobdingnag, to be sure, but he is also courageous and ingenious. The self-assurance that Gulliver himself displays amid these fluctuations in status and attributes is only the most obvious of the devices Swift employs to ensure that the reader's sense of spiritual and intellectual confidence in human nature remains deeply troubled. The communities among which Gulliver lives during his first two voyages are every bit as unstable as Gulliver himself in the moral weight that we are able to attach to them. And forever at the back of the reader's mind is the growing family that Gulliver repeatedly abandons in his thirst for travel and whose loyal affections he finally repudiates in his mad devotion to the Houyhnhnm ideal. Gulliver finally enacts a pattern of parental indifference of which even the repulsive Yahoos cannot be accused and which establishes decisively the complex link between domestic experience and the larger question of the status of human nature that constitutes the meaning and the appeal of *Gulliver's Travels*. This is the same link that Winthrop identified as critical to the success of Massachusetts Bay and that Benjamin Franklin took up when he set out to advise his fellow citizens on the management of the Revolution.

When Benjamin Vaughan counseled Franklin to complete his *Autobiography,* he made clear that its purposes were not only private (as Franklin had originally claimed) but quite urgently public:

> I am earnestly desirous then, my dear Sir, that you should let the world into the traits of your genuine character, as civil broils may otherwise tend to disguise or traduce it. . . . For the furtherance of human happiness, I have always maintained that it is necessary to prove that man is not even at present a vicious and detestable animal; and still more to prove that good management may greatly amend him; and it is for much the same reason, that I am anxious to see the opinion established, that there are fair characters existing among the individuals of the race; for the moment that all men, without exception, shall be conceived abandoned, good people will cease efforts deemed to be hopeless, and perhaps think of taking their share in the scramble of life, or at least of making it comfortable principally for themselves.[1]

Franklin's *Autobiography* seemed to Vaughan an indispensable aid to establish the fair character and the amendable nature of human beings, to prevent life from deteriorating into a scramble among animals that would be consistent with the darkest visions of the Brobdingnagian king. The weight of "present" evidence, moreover, seemed anything but encouraging about the future. Vaughan's letter of 1783, in other words, places Franklin's *Autobiography* both in and against the long tradition of hortatory warfare with the self that motivates Winthrop in "A Modell of Christian Charity," that underlies the fierce indictment and the complex affirmations in Swift's prose, and that prompted Franklin's own uncle Benjamin to remind his four-year-old nephew and namesake, in a birthday acrostic from 1710, that "man's Danger lyes in Satan, sin and selfe."[2]

No seventeenth-century Puritan, or eighteenth-century revivalist, would have been capable of placing the kind of absolute confidence in human nature that Vaughan places in Franklin's "genuine character," but Franklin is clearly exemplary rather than representative in Vaughan's view. And Franklin's own intention to print both Vaughan's letter and his uncle's acrostic in the finished *Autobiography* suggests the extent to which he grasped this exemplary position as a mediator between the Puritan and the revolutionary communities.[3] Vaughan's "good people" in the passage from his letter quoted above face the same choice offered to the passengers on board the *Arbella* in 1630: between self and selflessness, death and life. Franklin's narrative role under such circumstances is in many ways analogous to the typic role of Eve in Winthrop's speech: he is a dramatic embodiment of communal values, both a typical identity and an individual one, whose function is in part to accommodate the meaning of political events to human understanding. The status of the American Revolution, as Vaughan implies, would depend on the nature of the people who had made it. Had they chosen death or life? Had they made a new community in which professed truths would become truths in practice, or had they simply exchanged one earthly empire for another? In the last quarter of the eighteenth century, American writers attempted to discern or to proclaim which of these choices they had made. In the work of Thomas Jefferson, Hector St. John de Crevecoeur, and Benjamin Franklin that self-scrutiny focuses most intensely on the nature of the family and on its capacity to vivify images both of the future success and the future failure of the Revolution.

Despite the apparent modesty of his title, Jefferson clearly means to offer much more than "notes" in *Notes on the State of Virginia*.[4] He very quickly establishes that he thinks of his own state as essentially synonymous with the whole of America – with the continent itself, as well as with the coastal colonies. Circumstances favored this extended vision, for at the

time Jefferson wrote, Virginia claimed territory all the way from the
Atlantic seaboard to the Mississippi. At the close of his opening paragraph, he cannot resist reminding his reader that the total area of Virginia
alone is one-third greater than that of the combined "islands" of Great
Britain and Ireland.[5] The prefatory "Advertisement" that Jefferson wrote
for the 1787 edition of the *Notes* declares his determination not "to open
wounds which have already bled enough," but Jefferson himself can
scarcely resist reminding the English how far their imperial reach had
exceeded their grasp in trying to subdue such a vast country. In his
response to Query 2, which asks rather modestly for a review of Virginia's rivers and "rivulets," Jefferson provides an overview of the entire
Mississippi watershed, including the Missouri, the Ohio, and the Illinois
rivers, and all the country from the Great Lakes to New Orleans, closing
with a brief comparison of the commercial potentials of the Potomac and
the Hudson.

The anxieties and the triumphs of the Revolutionary period, during
which Jefferson wrote the *Notes,* led him to draw encouragement from,
and finally to exult in, his country's size.[6] This kind of geographical
patriotism, of course, is not the only sign of the tumultuous circumstances under which Jefferson wrote. His lengthy and spirited reply to
Buffon's theories of natural degeneracy in the New World is a counterat-
tack of its own peculiar sort in the civilized wars of science. His bitterly
concise definition of the term "tory" at the beginning of Query 16 – "a
traitor in thought, but not in deed" (281) – is a reminder of how immediate and how intense the passions of the Revolution remain in Jefferson's
text. On one remarkable occasion even the landscape becomes a symbolic
vocabulary for political events. Jefferson describes the passage of the
Potomac River through the Blue Ridge as a "war between rivers and
mountains" the signs of which serve as metaphorical reminders both of
the destructive force of the Revolution itself and of Jefferson's hopes for
the peace that follows: "For the mountain being cloven asunder, [nature]
presents to your eye, through the cleft, a small catch of smooth blue
horizon, at an infinite distance in the plain country, inviting you, as it
were, from the riot and tumult roaring around, to pass through the
breach and participate in the calm below" (143). A "breach" in the mountains and a breach between peoples are both on Jefferson's mind here,
permitting his prose to tell two complex stories at once.

Nor is it simply politeness that leads Jefferson to couch this contrast in
landscapes as a choice confronting the human viewer. One can either
remain in the region of "riot and tumult" or one may pass through and
"participate" in the peace of the "plain country," a curious phrase that has
the effect of turning the geographical term into a kind of pun for American simplicity. Jefferson is not by nature an allegorist or a maker of adroit
puns, but he constructs here an unusually telling version of Winthrop's

Mosaic choice in language that is true to the descriptive purposes of the *Notes* and at the same time unusually sensitive to the national predicament.

Jefferson's fiercely partisan politics and his optimism about the American future suggest that, in Winthrop's terms, he viewed the Revolution as a clear triumph of life over death, of plainness and simplicity over riot and tumult. But he shares with Winthrop, too, the acute sense of a mixture of peril and promise. The calm that is faintly visible through the breach in the Virginia mountains is but a "small catch . . . at an infinite distance." It invites human participation but at the same time hints at the fundamental insecurity of human hopes. As the *Notes* unfold it becomes increasingly clear that Jefferson sees great cause for worry about the future. The Revolution is at best incomplete and may at any moment, for a variety of reasons, deteriorate into a social compact indistinguishable from those of European states – what Benjamin Vaughan might have called a scramble for life among vicious and detestable animals. Peace itself is a threat, bringing with it a complacent population and a relaxation of republican vigilance and virtue. "It can never be too often repeated," Jefferson warned, "that the time for fixing every essential right on a legal basis is while our rulers are honest, and ourselves united" (287). War had brought honesty and unity, he believed, but "from the conclusion of this war, we shall be going down hill. . . . The shackles, therefore, which shall not be knocked off at the conclusion of this war, will remain on us long, will be made heavier and heavier, till our rights shall revive or expire in a convulsion" (287). The apocalypticism that one usually associates with the Puritan jeremiad tradition – with Winthrop's warnings about the consequences of failing in a covenanted enterprise, for example – is by no means foreign to Jefferson. The geographical metaphor of the Potomac running peacefully into the plain country could also foretell a downhill course to social collapse. The life of the Revolution could lead to a convulsive death.[7]

Manufacturing might develop in America, Jefferson feared, and undermine the foundations of agrarian virtue (290–1). Immigrants from the absolutist countries of Europe might flood the United States, bringing with them characters degraded by life in a monarchy that could "warp and bias" the direction of legislation in a democracy (211). An international commerce might draw the country into wars that would weaken the social fabric. Jefferson thought it might be better to give up oceangoing commerce altogether, rather than risk the costs of war (300). Defects in the current government of the new state seemed to Jefferson so serious that he devoted the bulk of Query 13 to enumerating them in the hope of arousing his fellow citizens to action. "Our situation is indeed perilous," Jefferson concluded. Only a constitutional convention could save Virginia, and perhaps the whole country, from a series of rebellions to correct injustices in the design of government (254–5).

By far the most serious menace to the survival of the country was slavery. Jefferson returned to the subject repeatedly, expressing his hope for its gradual disappearance, voicing his own, anguished prejudices and doubts about the viability of a multiracial society, and perhaps most memorably describing the psychological corruption that slavery inflicted upon masters and anticipating a fearful retribution:

> The whole commerce between master and slave is a perpetual exercise of the most boisterous passions, the most unremitting despotism on the one part, and degrading submissions on the other. Our children see this, and learn to imitate it; for man is an imitative animal. This quality is the germ of all education in him. From his cradle to his grave he is learning to do what he sees others do. If a parent could find no motive either in his philanthropy or his self-love, for restraining the intemperance of passion towards his slave, it should always be a sufficient one that his child is present. But generally it is not sufficient. The parent storms, the child looks on, catches the lineaments of wrath, puts on the same airs in the circle of smaller slaves, gives a loose to his worst of passions, and thus nursed, educated, and daily exercised in tyranny, cannot but be stamped by it with odious peculiarities. The man must be a prodigy who can retain his manners and morals undepraved by such circumstances. . . . Indeed I tremble for my country when I reflect that God is just: that his justice cannot sleep for ever: that considering numbers, nature and natural means only, a revolution of the wheel of fortune, an exchange of situation, is among possible events: that it may become probable by supernatural interference! The Almighty has no attribute which can take side with us in such a contest. (288–9)

Jefferson writes in this passage like a scientist of human nature and at the same time like a Puritan connecting the judgments of God with the sins of His people. Indeed, he is drawn to provide a glimpse of the operations of slavery within a particular domestic setting, much as Winthrop illustrated the operations of communal love, at somewhat greater length, in his treatment of Eve. The point is not that Jefferson knew of Winthrop's example, or that he consciously evoked the Puritan tradition. It is unlikely that he did either. But his understanding of the dangers of slavery is based upon the same grasp of the importance of domestic life that Winthrop exploited in "A Modell of Christian Charity." The family is less a metaphor for Jefferson than it is an educational institution, but it is an education that is uniquely, perhaps catastrophically, spiritual. Its importance for Jefferson rivals the metaphorical stature it possesses for Winthrop and leads, ultimately, to precisely the kind of cosmic implications that Winthrop drew in his choice of life.

Slavery corrupts the most vital bond in the community – the same one that Anne Bradstreet celebrated so memorably – the bond between parent and child. At no point in the *Notes* does Jefferson seem less certain of the future, or less confident that he and his fellow citizens can chart some course of action that will prevent the collapse of the American social experiment. Only one of the purposes of Jefferson's *Notes* was to satisfy the curiosity of foreigners. In important respects the book was directed to an American audience who, like Winthrop's emigrants, were about to embark upon a great enterprise involving momentous choices.

Like Jefferson's *Notes,* Crevecoeur's *Letters from an American Farmer* straddles the point of transition from a revolutionary to a postrevolutionary society. Almost certainly Crevecoeur wrote much of the book during the Revolution itself; his final letter in particular, "Distresses of a Frontier Man," reads very much like a dispatch written in the heat of conflict:

> The hour is come at last that I must fly from my house and abandon my farm! But what course shall I steer, inclosed as I am? The climate best adapted to my present situation and humour would be the polar regions. . . . Once happiness was our portion; now it is gone from us, and I am afraid not to be enjoyed again by the present generation! Whichever way I look, nothing but the most frightful precipices present themselves to my view, in which hundreds of my friends and acquaintances have already perished; of all animals that live on the surface of this planet, what is man when no longer connected with society, or when he finds himself surrounded by a convulsed and a half-dissolved one?[8]

This fervent impression of topical immediacy, however, is as deceptive as the modesty of Jefferson's title. Crevecoeur excluded from the *Letters* his most explicitly topical writing about the Revolution.[9] The *Letters* themselves present a much more general view both of the promise of American life and of the forces that threaten it. Even the "frightful precipices" to which Crevecoeur refers in the passage above are more generic than specific. Indeed, Crevecoeur constructs his book around a fable of life and vision of death that correspond closely to the stark biblical choices which Winthrop invoked in 1630.

Crevecoeur's introductory "letter," like Swift's prefatory material to *Gulliver's Travels,* both establishes and undermines the realistic pretense of the book. The advertisement to the 1782 edition insists that the letters are the "genuine production" of an American farmer and "the actual result of a private correspondence" (35). James, the narrator, urgently repeats this claim in the second letter ("Believe me, what I write is all true and real"), but though Crevecoeur is indeed an American farmer, this correspondence is completely fabricated, and James's protests of veracity are only rendered more suspicious by the distinction he himself invokes between the true and the "real." James's introduction is clearly designed to promote in Crevecoeur's audience precisely the kind of wariness with which James's skeptical wife approaches the idea of holding correspondence with an educated Englishman. She entreats James to "read [their correspondent's] letter over again, paragraph by paragraph, and warily observe whether thee canst perceive some words of jesting, something that hath more than one meaning" (41). Crevecoeur's own words contain little jesting, but his letters are clearly meant to be meaningful in a very special sense.

The most conspicuous sign that all is not as it seems in the *Letters* is the pronounced disparity between James's claims of provincial simplicity and his markedly formal prose: "Pray do not laugh in thus seeing an artless countryman tracing himself through the simple modifications of his life" (54). Such a disclaimer is, if anything, too obvious in the double message it conveys. The quite artful voice of James is not a serious attempt at the creation of character but the first and most pervasive of several signs that Crevecoeur intends his book to be unsettling from the very outset.[10] If the spiritual vocabulary of the Puritans can be used as a critical terminology, then it makes perfect sense to describe James's language as "insecure." This fundamental quality of Crevecoeur's book becomes more pronounced as his narrator cuts himself loose even from the slender mooring of his opening role. James's perspective in the *Letters* swiftly expands to correspond to the elevated language he employs. He is scarcely a farmer at all but a roving inquirer into the state of "prosperous families" all over the colonies (86), a forerunner of Tocqueville, who undertakes what he calls "my review of the component parts of this immense *whole*," the whole of America (107).

In the course of that review, James acknowledges that he expects to find the same mixture of good and evil that characterizes all societies (51). The picture of America that initially emerges from his report, however, is so exclusively characterized by "good" that the unwary reader is likely for a time to forget the mixed nature of human experience, rejoicing instead in the images of harmony and peace that James at first evokes. The introductory letter begins the idealization of American life chiefly through the confident words of James's minister, whom he consults about the propriety of exchanging letters with a learned foreigner:

> Do not you think, neighbour James, that the mind of a good and
> enlightened Englishman would be more improved in remarking
> throughout these provinces the causes which render so many
> people happy? . . . In Italy, all the objects of contemplation, all
> the reveries of the traveller, must have a reference to ancient
> generations and to very distant periods, clouded with the mist of
> ages. Here, on the contrary, everything is modern, peaceful, and
> benign. Here we have had no war to desolate our fields; our
> religion does not oppress the cultivators; we are strangers to
> those feudal institutions which have enslaved so many. Here
> Nature opens her broad lap to receive the perpetual accession of
> newcomers and to supply them with food. I am sure I cannot be
> called a partial American when I say that the spectacle afforded
> by these pleasing scenes must be more entertaining and more
> philosophical than that which arises from beholding the musty
> ruins of Rome. (42–3)

The ironies in this passage are sufficiently broad to make an impression
upon even the least vigilant readers, particularly in an England still offi-
cially at war with its colonies when Crevecoeur's *Letters* were published.
Crevecoeur himself soon subjects such partiality to sharp criticism.

He establishes his American farmer in the Quaker colony of Pennsylvania and has James report extensively on the Quaker communities of
Nantucket and Martha's Vineyard partly to foster this already dubious
identification of America with a peaceful, latitudinarian spirit. The gentleness of Nature and the benign quality of his existence are James's main
subjects in his second letter, in which he portrays himself less as an
industrious farmer than as a benevolent steward of all life. He contemplates his family, his bees, his livestock, birds, and insect life in general,
indulging himself in philosophical speculation. When he ploughs, he
fastens his infant son to the plough beam and muses on the responsibilities of parenthood while the motion of the horses and the "odorif-
erous furrow" bring a bloom to the child's cheeks (55). In winter he
shelters the harmless quail and provides them with a bed of chaff "to
prevent their tender feet from freezing fast to the earth" (57). He maintains peace and equity among his cows and horses, interferes benevolently in the quarrels of nesting birds, and marvels at the industrious
hornets, who live in the middle of his parlor and pluck the flies off the
eyelids of his children (63).

This picture of rural harmony is immensely attractive and completely
unbelievable.[11] Indeed, at the close of the introduction, James's wife expresses her acquiescence in the plan of the letters in language that decisively undermines the vision of America that James and the minister

offer. She continues to regard writing, rather suspiciously, as the avocation of Englishmen, who can live upon bank notes and who have "no trees to cut down, no fences to make, no Negroes to buy and to clothe" (49). But if James wishes to write, she is willing that he do so:

> However, let it be a great secret; how would'st thee bear to be called at our country meetings the man of the pen? If this scheme of thine was once known, travellers as they go along would point out to our house, saying, "Here liveth the scribbling farmer." Better hear them as usual observe, "Here liveth the warm substantial family that never begrudgeth a meal of victuals or a mess of oats to any one that steps in. Look how fat and well clad their Negroes are." (49)

One need not be a particularly wary reader to sense the ugly contradictions here. James and his minister concur that "we are the most perfect society now existing in the world" (67). Together they take considerable satisfaction in noting the absence of "the hostile castle and the haughty mansion" (67) from the American landscape, and both of them anticipate Emerson's stirring diction in *Nature* when they assert democratic prerogatives: "Why should not a farmer be allowed to make use of his mental faculties as well as others; because a man works, is he not to think, and if he thinks usefully, why should not he in his leisure hours set down his thoughts?" (46). This considerable confidence, however, and the many genuine advantages of America are deeply compromised in Crevecoeur's view by slavery. Indeed the rhetoric of equality that the minister applies to farmers can quite readily form the basis of an appeal for the equality of races.

The language with which James describes the agreement with his European correspondent is calculated to suggest to the reader a far more momentous contract at issue in the book: "I flatter myself, therefore, that you'll receive my letters as conceived, not according to scientific rules to which I am a perfect stranger, but agreeable to the spontaneous impressions which each subject may inspire. This is the only line I am able to follow, the line which Nature has herself traced for me; this was the covenant which I made with you and with which you seemed to be well pleased" (50). James is attempting to excuse his intellectual deficiencies, but Crevecoeur's conspicuously biblical language unavoidably, even clumsily, reminds the reader of the kind of moral and communal deficiencies that John Winthrop feared might threaten the future of the colony at Massachusetts Bay. From the very beginning of the *Letters,* then, Crevecoeur openly encourages us to see James's idyllic view of America in the context of an impending, catastrophic failure.[12]

Crevecoeur, in fact, does everything in his power to exaggerate the intensity of the American contradiction. The highly idealized character of James and his equally idealized descriptions of his life on the farm sharpen the reader's sense of the grave disparity between the image of America cherished by James and his minister on the one hand and the fact of slavery on the other.[13] But the chief means that Crevecoeur employs for describing America's internal conflict involves appropriating the minister's conventional view of America's difference from Europe and applying that simple dualism to America itself. This, quite simply, is the same dualism with which Winthrop confronted the emigrants to Massachusetts Bay in 1630. Italy, James's minister affirms, is a place of ruins, "the vestiges of a once-flourishing people now extinct," a scene of death and decay. America, on the other hand, is the seat of life. Specifically, it is a place where "the embryos of societies" may be observed at the very outset of the cycle of life, where a kind of social and personal infancy thrives as opposed to the tombs and "putrid fevers" of the Campania.[14]

Crevecoeur extends this social embryology – founded upon the quite commonplace metaphor of American "infancy" – throughout James's celebration of national promise, both with specific references to the image of the embryo itself and with a more general emphasis upon the states of infancy and childhood, the processes of growth and education. As most readers have noticed, Crevecoeur employs developmental images of all kinds, but this rhetorical pattern suggests more than just a habit of mind. His allusions to America's "strong vegetative embryos" (46), to "that precious embryo of life" that insects miraculously preserve through winter (58), to the "embryos of all the arts, sciences" and European ingenuity springing up in America – all reflect Crevecoeur's determination to identify James's idyllic vision with the life-giving powers of gestation. His emphasis upon James's careful observations of birds incubating their eggs, of wasps meticulously shaping the oblong cells of their nests, of the "dawning tempers" of his own children, are part of the same determination.

Indeed, the domestic and familial sensibility so prominent in Anne Bradstreet's poems and prose meditations is the governing force in Crevecoeur's *Letters* as well. The rich psychology of parent and spouse, however, is not Crevecoeur's central interest. James does not struggle with God and with his own soul so much as he addresses himself to the subject of "family" in America and finds to his surprise that he is describing not an enviable situation, but, once more, a predicament. The reassuring "embryology" of eighteenth-century rhetoric implies that out of such promising beginnings a great, adult future is to be expected. James celebrates that future with a kind of scientific rapture, up to the point where the new determinism of natural law breaks down, and Crevecoeur's narrator is thrust back upon older categories of meaning –

categories that had been implicit all along in the increasingly resonant insecurities of his book.

With his account of the transformation of a representative immigrant and of the establishment of a representative community, James both sums up the embryological vision of America and begins the process of discrediting it. Crevecoeur has James describe the new immigrant's introduction into America as a species of birth. Under the influences of American institutions and opportunity, the new arrival "begins to feel the effects of a sort of resurrection; hitherto he had not lived but simply vegetated; he now feels himself a man because he is treated as such" (82). Over the course of several pages, Crevecoeur fuses the ideas of botanical transplantation, dormancy, and familial adoption into a single fabric of imagery suggesting that even adults come to America in a kind of embryonic state and gradually emerge into new life. When James's exemplary immigrant, Andrew the Hebridean, has finally established himself on a farm, the joy of the occasion reduces him virtually to the status of a newborn. He is completely unable to assist in the labor of raising his house but instead occupies himself by carrying his cheerful bottle about, "smiling, laughing, and uttering monosyllables" (103).

This helplessness is both comically delightful and vaguely disquieting. James's own devotion to the critical ideals of industry and sobriety seems quietly and inexplicably relaxed in this image of the tipsy, ineffectual, and infantile Andrew. Andrew's house, moreover, is not raised upon his own land but upon leased property that Andrew and his family have agreed to take up on terms that James professes to find generous. Even allowing for the diversity of arrangements by which land was actually acquired in the eighteenth century, it is curious that the figure of a "landlord" should enter into James's description of the remarkable advantages of America over Europe. The country that rejoices in the absence of haughty castles and mansions has apparently preserved the economic conditions that will, in time, defeat James's compelling, egalitarian biology.

When James turns his attention to the island community of Nantucket, he begins to sound like a precursor of Walt Whitman with the pleasure he takes in the Nantucketers' bodily health, their unimpaired "digestive powers," the marvelous constitutions they receive "from parents as healthy as themselves, who in the unpolluted embraces of the earliest and chastest love conveyed to them the soundest bodily frame which nature could give" (150). Nantucket, it would seem, is a place of remarkable embryonic health. Moreover, Nantucket children receive, in James's view, a superb education once they are out of the womb, beginning from the first moments that they hear the sound of the sea, and gradually acquire boldness "by early plunging in it" (144). Parental example and practical experience in seafaring and household management finish the training that the environment itself had begun. Indeed, Nantucket as a whole is a complex system of gestation producing the island's most valuable "crop": Nantucketers. The inhabitants, James reports, "are all in some degree related to each other" and treat one another as members of a single, large family (160). For Crevecoeur's purposes, the prolific power and familial intimacy of the Nantucketers give concentrated expression to the idyllic view of America as the seat of life.

Against this dreamlike evocation of health and life, Crevecoeur poses the example of Charles Town and the culture of slavery. But it is not Charles Town alone that undermines the complacent satisfaction that James seems to take in Nantucket. Throughout James's celebration of America's gestative powers, Crevecoeur had planted hints of the terrible inadequacy of such a view. The satisfaction that both James and his wife take in their "fat and well clad Negroes" is the first such hint, of course, but even in the abolitionist community of Nantucket, Crevecoeur finds signs of the brutality of power in the whale hunt that James describes at great length. The hardy Nantucketers think it a "favorable circumstance" when they can stalk a female whose attention is distracted by the safety of her calf (135). The "ardour" with which they approach their female prey and the anxiety with which the hunters contemplate the cord that binds them to the stricken mother whale cannot help but suggest a new set of biological metaphors in which the Nantucketers are not the products of healthy gestation but its destroyers. James puzzles over what he calls the "singular custom" of opium addiction among Nantucket women, but the wary reader once again is less likely to be surprised at the necessity for some opiate among a people whose pacific ideals are so at odds with their violent commercial practice.[15] According to Crevecoeur the island itself, for all its virtues, is located in a fabulous geography, like Swift's Brobdingnag, 80 miles north of Boston and 800 miles south of Bermuda, northeast of Cape Cod and northwest of Woods Hole (110). Crevecoeur seems to suggest that such a community as this one can have no genuine connection with the earth.[16]

In Charles Town itself James discovers that slavery corrupts precisely the same sources of life upon which he had built his American optimism. Just as Jefferson noted the effects of slavery on the master's family, Crevecoeur describes its impact upon the family of the slave. Pregnancy becomes, to the slave, "a fatal present" rather than a source of joy (169). Fatherhood is a "fatal indulgence." Husbands cannot protect their wives, and parents cannot care for their children. The result is a terrible mutilation of the human spirit that finally drives James to a magnificent outburst not so much against American slavery in particular as against all the manifestations of power in human history.

Suddenly the psychology and sociology of the *Letters* are completely reversed. Human nature is no longer the precious embryo that it had seemed in earlier pages but an extensive collection of monstrous passions. The "principles of action in man," James declares, are "poisoned in their most essential parts" (174). Honesty and simplicity are always victimized by "force, subtlety, and malice." The planet itself grows hellish. Where Nature seems most benevolent, "the poison of slavery, the fury of despotism, and the rage of superstition are all combined against man!" (176). Most of the globe only produces vices unique to local climates, or the tortures of heat or cold. Against the vision of American life, James poses an image of death as graphic as the finest hellfire sermons, complete with raging volcanoes "pouring forth from several mouths rivers of boiling matter which are imperceptibly leaving immense subterranean graves wherein millions will one day perish!" (175).

The violence of this outburst is a direct result of James's encounter with a slave hung up in a cage in the South Carolina countryside and left to die a horrible death for the crime of having killed his overseer. But though the provocation for James's despair is particular and shocking, Crevecoeur makes it clear that this suffering slave stands for all men and not just for the plight of blacks in the American South.[17] This figure is the individual image of death, as Andrew the Hebridean, with his joyful monosyllables, was the individual image of life. Crevecoeur underscores the comparison by having James's first hint of the slave's presence be the "few, inarticulate monosyllables" he utters in his pain (177). Human slavery – a horrible sort of emigration by force – and the gestative emigration process exemplified by Andrew are an American expression of the choice between death and life that characterizes the grim history of the world as James describes it in his angry prose.

The last of the *Letters* emphasize the insistent nature of the choice, and its nearly allegorical clarity. Immediately following his encounter with the dying slave James composes a seemingly routine report on American snakes and on the hummingbird, many details of which were, in fact, cribbed from the work of Crevecoeur's patron, the naturalist Abbé Raynal in his *Histoire Philosophique*.[18] But the hummingbird's combination of extraordinary beauty with "lacerating" behavior (Crevecoeur's adjective, not Raynal's) echoes the contrast between the beauty of James's initial vision of America and the lacerations of the slave master's whip (184). The rattlesnake, whose bite (according to James) "is not mortal in so short a space," and the copperhead, whose poison is swift and deadly, are clear emblems for the distinction that James tries vainly to draw between benign Northern slavery and brutal Southern slavery: Both poisons will kill, Crevecoeur suggests, but one is swift while the other is merely insidious.[19]

In the letter describing "Bertram the botanist," Crevecoeur returns once more to the idyll of life in the American countryside, but this time it is an idyllic vision that is conscious of its greatest flaw. John Bertram (Crevecoeur's consistent spelling of Bartram) has attempted to reverse the effects of slavery and to recover America's lost moral ground, just as he recovers pasture land from the encroaching waters of the Schuylkill. Over his greenhouse Bertram has engraved a couplet from Pope's *Essay on Man* evoking much of the beauty in human nature that the images of Charles Town had denied:

> Slave to no sect, who takes no private road,
> But looks through nature, up to nature's God! (191)

It is certainly no accident, however, that Crevecoeur has James encounter the dying slave as he is walking down a quiet, "private" road in the South Carolina countryside, looking up through nature to the slave's hanging cage. Even Pope's optimistic couplet, then, reawakens the anxieties of the American predicament, just as a sense of the inherent justice of nature's God leads Jefferson to tremble for the perils of his country. When one "looks through nature," as James has done in his letters, one finds even in the smallest living creatures or in the apparently most innocuous agricultural practices the kind of metaphorical commentary on human behavior that the Puritans would have read as Divine Providences. One must indeed read warily, as James's wife suggested, in the tradition of considered living that Anne Bradstreet urged upon her son. Pope's ideal vision beckons out of his lines, but the careful reader of Crevecoeur's book must fall despairingly short of Pope's exaltation, as the new residents of Massachusetts Bay must often have fallen short of Winthrop's.

The same pattern of despair and hope, death and life, is renewed in Crevecoeur's final letter, "Distresses of a Frontier Man," in which James himself is first an innocent victim of power and finally a refugee among a tribe of Indians, whose community he plans both to join and in some measure to modify along slightly civilized lines in the hope that he can prevent the minds of his children from being influenced too greatly by the "savage" example. In his introductory letter James had promised to let his reader into the "primary secrets" of his text (49). For James and his minister those secrets involved the celebration of American life. For Crevecoeur himself, however, the issue was far more clouded. More primary still than the glorious promise of America was the inescapable choice between death and life.

Jefferson and Crevecoeur concern themselves more or less directly with the corrupting influences of power upon the postrevolutionary community. Each in his way writes a contemporary version of the seventeenth-century jeremiad.[20] Benjamin Franklin's attitude toward the challenges of what George Forgie has called postheroic life in America is quite different.[21] Like Jefferson, Franklin played a central role in the formative events of the Revolution. He participated directly in shaping the circumstances to which Crevecoeur was compelled to respond. Had he lived to finish his *Autobiography* he would certainly have given a full account of this role. But even in its unfinished form, the *Autobiography* suggests that Franklin's literary concerns are both narrower and broader than those of Crevecoeur or Jefferson. Franklin is in no sense surveying the nation, as those two writers in some measure do. Only one life engages him – however remarkable that life may have been – and the motives for writing that he acknowledges in his opening paragraphs are private and even a bit self-indulgent (he confesses) rather than national in their implications.

Franklin's decision to include Benjamin Vaughan's extraordinary and lengthy letter in his text, however, confirms that his scope is anything but limited. Vaughan's own sense of the importance of Franklin's example, not only as a representative American but as an advocate for human nature, immediately establishes a much wider context within which to judge Franklin's performance. In keeping with his own self-effacing strategy for promoting community projects, Franklin is able to assert this representative status by having someone else claim it for him. Vaughan concurs with Abel James's conventional judgment of the didactic (and civic) value of Franklin's habits, but for Vaughan himself Franklin's narrative had a fundamental significance. The *Autobiography* offered, Vaughan believed, a "key to life" rather than simply a key to prosperity. It was a secular wisdom book explaining "many things that all men ought to have once explained to them," regardless of whether or not Franklin's character proved influential in changing the world.[22]

Franklin offered, in other words, not a lament but a guide on the conduct of life in specifically postheroic times. When Lemuel Gulliver's attempts to reform the English people along Houyhnhnm lines proved ineffectual, Gulliver himself grew bitter and withdrew into a misanthropic isolation that was close to madness. Franklin's testament to human possibility, however, seemed to Vaughan so vitally interesting that even its failure as a means of public reform would not affect its importance, its capacity to give pleasure, to enhance for all its readers "the fair side of a life otherwise too much darkened by anxiety and too much injured by pain" (140). This surprisingly private, enhancing function begins, appropriately, with Franklin's approach to form.

More interesting, perhaps, than any of Vaughan's comments alone is the fact that Franklin apparently meant to endorse them even though Vaughan himself, at the time he wrote his letter, had read none of the actual *Autobiography*. Clearly Franklin hoped to appropriate Vaughan's claims, but he also intended to call attention to an aspect of his book that is consistent with Vaughan's characterization of it as a key to life and at the same time one of the most distinctive of the *Autobiography*'s features. To some degree Franklin had determined to make the interruptions in his writing process, and the resulting fragmentation of his narrative, a part of his subject.[23] The reason for this decision, and its consequences, are part of the rhetoric of privacy that Franklin is attempting to reestablish after the necessarily public business of politics and war.

The *Autobiography* (as every reader must recall) begins fortuitously, rather than deliberately, as a letter to Franklin's son written in an unusual week of "uninterrupted Leisure" in Franklin's busy schedule. Interruptions are the rule rather than the exception thereafter, and Franklin calls attention to them in the brief memorandum that precedes the James and Vaughan letters, in the letters themselves, and in the opening sentences of Parts 2 and 3 of the *Autobiography*. He notes the length of each interval since he last wrote, his new whereabouts, the difficulties caused by his absence from home or by the loss of his papers. Only the very brief Part 4, written in the last months of his life, is without some formal acknowledgment of narrative discontinuity, and even so its very brevity suggests that Franklin had to steal from his last illness the time and energy to write it.

Of course, this fragmentation can be directly and solely attributed to historical circumstances.[24] Franklin himself coyly notes that the "affairs of the Revolution" delayed the writing of Part 2. But rather than attempt to smooth over such gaps, Franklin prefers to incorporate them, giving every indication that he meant these rather rough seams to remain in his final version. Robert Sayre has argued that Franklin's book gives the impression of being a multiple exposure largely because Franklin himself made three distinct tries at composing his material in some unified way.[25] The result, Sayre contends, adopting the vocabulary of Henry Adams, is "the first example of twentieth-century multiplicity" in prose, embodied in Franklin's failure to find a single, secular model that could supply the organizational purposes that religious conversion served for Saint Augustine's *Confessions*. But Franklin's failures and errors, when he makes them, usually receive a warm welcome into his text. Moreover, Franklin enjoyed the support, in his formal eccentricities, of the candid example of John Locke. In the prefatory letter to *An Essay Concerning Human Understanding,* Locke cheerfully acknowledges the haphazard circumstances of his own composition – circumstances that, for Locke, merely underscore the natural handicaps under which the mind functions at the best of times and which ought to foster humility in all the products of human intelligence.[26] Franklin clearly had in mind a similar, corrective relation between literary form and the natural vanity of authors.

Almost certainly Franklin would have given his final text a higher polish than the remaining manuscript possesses. But it seems equally certain that he intended to retain the Vaughan and James letters, the informal and digressive style, as well as the close association he establishes with place and time of composition in each distinct section. His book takes its shape directly from the life that it narrates, identifying at the outset the inevitable antagonism that exists between the natural desires of parents, or talkative old men, and the demands of the kind of public life that insistently intrudes on Franklin's story.

A key result of this version of imitative form is the sense that Franklin's book conveys of being an unusually intimate document. At one point early in Part 4 he apologizes for his digressive tendencies by noting that "one does not dress for private company as for a public ball" (57). Part 1 is the most personal of the *Autobiography*'s sections, but the entire book has the informal air of a work written for private company, by a man whose deepest loyalties were to private life.[27] Benjamin Vaughan once again calls attention to this fundamental paradox of Franklin's character. In contrast to the examples of statesmen, warriors, and other "distinguished men" in history, Vaughan notes, Franklin's life will provide important evidence of "how compatible it is to be great and *domestic; enviable and yet good-humored*" (136). Vaughan's emphasis falls not on the significance of Franklin's public achievement but on the origins of that achievement in domestic character, and the *Autobiography* itself bears out Vaughan's judgment. Franklin keeps his public stature consistently in the background, even when he is writing primarily about public affairs. The unifying principle of the *Autobiography,* like the conceptual basis of "A Modell of Christian Charity" or the central subject matter of Anne Bradstreet's poetry, is domesticity.

It seems, at first, incongruous to think of Franklin as a domestic writer. After the early pages of the *Autobiography* that describe his childhood in Boston, he appears to devote little direct attention to his family life. Deborah Franklin receives a fuller treatment than any woman in the book, but beyond the courtly references to "Miss Read" in Part 1 and a few, brief anecdotes from their marriage later on, her role is at best peripheral. Franklin himself spent the last ten years of Deborah's life in England as an agent for the colonies, leading the life of a rather worldly bachelor. He is not, on the face of things, a very promising candidate for the role of recording and celebrating domestic sentiments. But it is not the sentimental side of domesticity that moves him so much as it is the parental, or more particularly the paternal, side. And the rather striking absence of women in the autobiography of a man who relished, and even exulted in, female companionship serves in part as a means of focusing attention upon the "womanly" virtues that are proper, even desirable, in men – most especially upon the womanly virtues of Benjamin Franklin.[28]

In this emphasis, too, Franklin may well have in mind a model that ties him both to the Puritan tradition in general and to the specific strand of that tradition that we are tracing here. Charles Sanford noted some years ago the broad affinities between Franklin's *Autobiography* and a book for which Franklin expressed his particular affection, *The Pilgrim's Progress*.[29] But Sanford's view of Franklin's self-portrait as a secularized "Christian" neglects some of the most suggestive details of Bunyan's fable. The family is both an impediment to and a symbol of Christian's allegorical journey to the Celestial City. He must flee his wife and children in order to embark on his momentous pilgrimage – plugging his ears to shut out their appeals and crying aloud, "Life, Life, Eternal Life." But at the Interpreter's house, where Christian receives vital instruction for his journey, he sees a painting of Christ whom the Interpreter describes in the hermetic tradition as being both man and woman, father and mother, capable of begetting children and of travailing in childbirth.[30]

This extraordinary parent is the spirit who presides over Christian's journey, whose sacrifice frees him of his sins, and who finally makes possible his entry into Heaven. Christiana and her children will later follow in her husband's footsteps to the Celestial City, but to Bunyan it was scripturally important that the worldly family be divided and replaced by an otherworldly figure of parental care that transcended human limitation and human sexuality. It would, of course, be inaccurate to claim such a thoroughgoing, metaphysical significance for Franklin's self-portrait in the *Autobiography;* in any event the motherly qualities of Bunyan's Christ allude to his powers of promoting the rebirth of grace and not to a genuine androgyny. But just such a bold application of domestic metaphor marked Winthrop's treatment of sexuality in "A Modell of Christian Charity" and influenced his ideal of a domestic, and maternal, heroism founded upon the typologically apprehended figure of Eve. Although it is important not to credit Franklin with too great a degree of allegorical artfulness, it is also important to recognize that his fascination with parenthood and his adoption of a complex attitude toward gender were not strictly secular phenomena. The work of Jefferson and Crevecoeur reflects more closely than does that of Franklin the anxieties of Bunyan's pilgrim, fleeing from the City of Destruction and crying out for life. Franklin as he portrayed himself in the *Autobiography* is not so much the harried and desperate pilgrim as he is the knowing Interpreter, or perhaps even the grave parent in the Interpreter's "private room," with a mother's and a father's combined concern for the plight of his children.

Franklin's interest in parenthood begins with his portrait of his father, Josiah, and his doting Uncle Benjamin, whose poetic missives to his young nephew Franklin apparently cherished all his life. Uncle Benjamin's value as a guide and preceptor – as an interpreter of sorts – seems to have been largely confined to these occasional acrostics and admonitory verses. Josiah's influence was much more pervasive, for the most part indirect, and astutely applied so as to take advantage of the natural course of his son's interests and habits.[31] Indeed, it is not much of an exaggeration to say that Franklin's own ways of exercising political influence later in life directly reflect Josiah Franklin's unobtrusive style of parenting.

Franklin himself invites this comparison when he comments on the upbringing of Robert Hunter Morris, a proprietary governor of Pennsylvania and Franklin's first antagonist in the Pennsylvania Assembly's struggle to tax the proprietary estates. Morris, Franklin notes, had been brought up to a life of conflict and turmoil by a father who taught his children "to dispute with one another for his Diversion while sitting at Table after Dinner" (213). No reader can miss the allusion here to the way in which Josiah Franklin conducted his more humble family dinners, as often as possible with "some sensible Friend or Neighbor" present with whom Josiah "always took care to start some ingenious or useful Topic for Discourse, which might tend to improve the Minds of his Children" (55). In the Franklin household children listened, learned, and if possible grew philosophically indifferent to the quality or quantity of the food before them. This kind of domestic education, in Franklin's experience, proves to be a far better preparation for public life than Morris's training in discord.[32]

Josiah Franklin was similarly opportunistic in his efforts to instruct his son in the finer points of prose style or to find some form of employment that would engage Franklin's interest sufficiently to keep him from running off to sea. There is little or no exercise of parental power in his childhood for Franklin to record or to rebel against. James Franklin, his older brother, plays the role of tyrant. Even when a young, enterprising Benjamin gets in trouble for stealing construction stones, and when Benjamin's boyish accomplices are sternly "corrected" by their own fathers, Josiah Franklin rather modestly "convinces" his son "that nothing was useful which was not honest" (54). It seems unlikely that this instance of "convincing" is a euphemism for punishment, particularly when we recall that, even when Franklin first signed his articles of apprenticeship in James Franklin's print shop, he was apparently free to make his own decision without any undue coercion from Josiah and "stood out some time," at the rather tender age of twelve, before being "persuaded" to become his brother's apprentice.

In each of these instances Josiah's conduct is less singular once we recognize its sources in John Locke's popular and influential book, *Some Thoughts on Education* (1693), which goes to great lengths to describe the proper way for parents to shape children's character without tyrannizing over them. It is part of Locke's program to favor the growth of mutual respect between parent and child rather than the exercise of parental authority, to match education as closely as possible to the inclinations of the child, to foster habits of virtue rather than to rely on the imposition of great numbers of arbitrary rules. Both Franklin and his father share this indebtedness to Locke; Josiah and Uncle Benjamin in fact are two of the earliest and most prominent examples in the *Autobiography* of the pattern of nurturing men who take a fatherly interest in Franklin and do their best to smooth his path in life in ways that give dramatic extension to Locke's parental principles. The tradesman Matthew Adams, patron of James Franklin's print shop and owner of "a pretty collection of books," singles out the young apprentice Franklin and invites him "very kindly" to make use of his library (59). Crafty old William Bradford, the New York printer, directs Franklin to his son's shop in Philadelphia and, upon meeting Franklin there, escorts him to Samuel Keimer's shop, where Franklin got his first job. Samuel Vernon, a friend of John Franklin in Rhode Island, kindly and quietly ignores the substantial sum of money Franklin was empowered to collect for him, treating it for years as an unspoken loan until Franklin was able to pay it back to him. Thomas Denham served as a kind of surrogate father for Franklin when he was stranded in England, hired him as a clerk with a promise to set him up as an independent merchant, brought him back to Philadelphia, and continued to display a fatherly concern for Franklin until his sudden death sent Franklin back to Keimer's print shop.

The world that the *Autobiography* describes sometimes seems to abound with fathers who are solicitous for the welfare of their sons, or (in a closely related pattern) with older men on the lookout for young men whom they might advise and encourage. Andrew Hamilton, for example, takes up Franklin's cause with the Pennsylvania Assembly and helps to secure him the public printing contracts for reasons that apparently have little to do with self-interest (121). Dr. John Browne, an innkeeper, befriends a rather bedraggled young Franklin on his way to Philadelphia, and the two strike up an acquaintance for life (73). Sir William Wyndham, in England, learns of Franklin's prowess as a swimmer and tries to secure him as a teacher for his sons before they embark on a tour of the continent (105). Hugh Meredith's father agrees to set up Franklin in business, hoping that Franklin's good example will help cure his own son of the habit of dram drinking (111). Increasingly, as he ages and grows more settled in his circumstances, Franklin himself takes on the fatherly role that Hugh Meredith's actual father had prematurely thrust upon him, assisting in the education and the establishment of young printers all over the colonies, taking his brother James's son into his house and helping him prepare to run his father's business, adopting the persona of Father Abraham in his almanac of 1757 and giving paternal advice one of its most memorable and widely published forms in "The Way to Wealth."

This atmosphere of benevolent paternity makes all the more conspicuous those figures in the book who, in one way or another, abuse such a trusting relation. Governor Keith, with his empty promises of support and credit for the young Franklin's printing business, is the most conspicuous example of this sort of human failure. In some respects so are the conniving "old folks" who offend the rather sensitive young Franklin during his first courtship negotiation. Both of these instances of disappointment, however, elicit from Franklin the writer a degree of retrospective gentleness and understanding that is itself paternal in quality. Governor Keith's deceit, in particular, seems far less forgivable to the reader than it proves to be for Franklin himself, who attributes Keith's duplicity to a kind of misdirected generosity and, on the whole, rather approves of Keith's politics:

> But what shall we think of a Governor's playing such pitiful Tricks, and imposing so grossly on a poor ignorant Boy! It was a Habit he had acquired. He wish'd to please every body; and having little to give, he gave Expectations. He was otherwise an ingenious sensible man, a pretty good Writer, and a good Governor for the People, tho' not for his Constituents the Proprietaries, whose Instructions he sometimes disregarded. Several of our best Laws were of his Planning, and pass'd during his Administration. (95)[33]

It is quite likely that Franklin meant this emphasis upon the paternal instincts to have a political as well as a personal dimension. One of the commonplace metaphors of political rhetoric during the Revolutionary period involved the characterization of the king as a father to his people, both in England and in the colonies, an image that lent itself to arguments both for and against the necessity for revolution. Franklin does not directly evoke this rhetorical tradition in the *Autobiography,* but his emphasis upon the pervasiveness of parental behavior in the colonies has the effect of isolating all the more dramatically those elements of the English colonial system that do not display such generous care: the proprietors of Pennsylvania and their governors, Lord Loudoun in his high-handed mismanagement of colonial affairs, the accusatory language of Lord Granville in Part 4, the fatal military arrogance of General Braddock.[34]

Franklin's emphasis on paternity is by no means the only instance of the prevailing domesticity of his book. From the outset he quietly and indirectly claims for himself a range of personal qualities that were, by the standards of his day and to some degree of ours, homelike or housewifely in nature. Nancy Cott has established that most of the key elements of what nineteenth-century Americans came to recognize as a cult of domesticity and of the "woman's sphere" were already in place by the last decades of the eighteenth century, with many features of the division of spheres dating to the late seventeenth century and to the publication of Rousseau's widely influential *Emile* (1762).[35] Franklin's selection of personal traits in his self-portrait draws quite purposefully on this emerging social pattern. In Franklin's case the traits he chooses to emphasize include his attention to matters of diet and cookery, as well as his sensitivity to domestic economy in general and his careful cultivation of the useful habits of modesty and (in appearance at least) passivity. The most important of these traits do not come to Franklin naturally. He has to achieve them, overcoming in the process his native inclinations for verbal aggression and dogmatic self-assertion. But so impressed is he with the utility of a modest and self-effacing demeanor that twice in his *Autobiography* he goes into detail explaining how he modified his speech and behavior so as to avoid offense and ingratiate himself with his listeners by his personal reticence and modest manners. The Junto adopted Franklin's policy of personal deportment and imposed fines for dogmatic speech, "which might prevent our disgusting each other" (118). In some sense Franklin's public life began with the assumption of female identities – the Silence Dogood letters, and later those of Martha Careful and Caelia Shortface – and as he moved more openly into public affairs his preferred modes of procedure were invariably discreet, polite, private to the degree that he could manage, and deferential whenever he could be so without compromising a principle.

It is important to emphasize that Franklin did not simply disguise an exuberantly masculine character in a protective, feminine coloration. He quite deliberately criticized what we would call today the patterns of socialized behavior associated with being male, and he embraced opposite patterns. A simple illustration involves his approach to the beer-guzzling habits that prevailed among his fellow printers in London. Franklin noted that one primary justification among his London colleagues for their drinking was that "strong Beer" made men "strong to labour" (100) – a set of assumptions perfectly consistent with contemporary American advertising. Against this recognizably self-serving masculine myth, Franklin opposed the force of reason and good example to no avail. His colleagues continued drinking and Franklin continued his policy of thrifty and healthful abstention. This is the sort of incident in the *Autobiography* that led Mark Twain to view Franklin as a natural ally of Sid Sawyer or Miss Watson, and Franklin does indeed get along quite well with widows and pious maiden ladies, particularly in his London lodgings. But it is also the sort of incident that establishes Franklin as an antagonist of the brutalizing habits of Pap Finn. Of primary importance to Franklin is not the integrity of sexual myth but whatever nourishes life.

By nature Franklin was by no means retiring, and his capacity to engage in verbal combat – to be a formidable "Riggite" as his English colleagues admiringly said – stood him in good stead in the Pennsylvania Assembly's struggles with the proprietors, and in the pamphlet wars that preceded the Revolution. But he is also careful in the *Autobiography* to portray himself as a serviceable participant in affairs rather than as an initiator, even when he does, in fact, initiate. The formation of the voluntary association for defense in Pennsylvania is a fair example of the way Franklin could mix the roles of active leader and passive follower in a project for the public good. In the absence of any defense initiative from the Assembly or the governor during King George's War in 1747, Franklin notes with some vigor, "I determined to try what might be done by a voluntary Association of the People" (182). His first act is to write the pamphlet *Plain Truth,* in which he promises shortly to propose a plan for meeting the colony's defense needs. This promise alone is enough to transform Franklin from leader to follower, for the people are so aroused by his arguments that they immediately demand to hear his proposals. During a mass meeting that follows, Franklin briefly takes the stage again to "harangue" the crowd and explain his plan of association. No sooner are copies of the plan distributed, however, than the whole operation takes on a momentum of its own and Franklin himself is occupied in designing the colors that the women are making for the new militia companies and declining the office of colonel, "conceiving myself unfit" (183).

In these events, indeed, Franklin is unusually assertive. His customary mode of influencing his contemporaries is simply to write out his ideas, consult a few friends, and then accommodate himself to the whirlwind of public activity that follows. Seldom, if ever, does the *Autobiography* present us with a picture of Franklin exercising the means of political power: making speeches, managing legislation through assembly or committee, forming parties. In this respect it is quite the opposite of Thomas Jefferson's *Autobiography,* for example, which does go lovingly into the details of assembly and committee work, of speeches, drafts, and compromise.[36] Franklin's book presents political life as an extension of private life, and the preferred sphere for Franklin's political activity was private. He loved to record the details of private consultation, of conversation on public matters that was off the record, and to give only the most cursory descriptions of public action and his own public role.[37]

Although he was active in conducting the official opposition to Pennsylvania's proprietary governors, Franklin records with much greater detail and much more satisfaction his private defense, over dinner, of the Assembly's rights of taxation, or his private resistance to Governor Denny's blandishments, for example, over a decanter of Madeira (247). When Franklin's efforts to organize a Pennsylvania militia seemed to threaten his position as Assembly clerk by offending the powerful Quakers, he records his spirited self-defense as a private reply to the officious "young Gentleman" who sought to displace him:

> It was thought by some of my Friends that by my Activity in these Affairs, I should offend that Sect, and thereby lose my Interest in the Assembly where they were a great Majority. A young Gentleman who had likewise some Friends in the House, and wished to succeed me as their Clerk, acquainted me that it was decided to displace me at the next Election, and he therefore in good Will advis'd me to resign, as more consistent with my Honour than being turn'd out. My Answer to him was, that I had read or heard of some Public Man, who made it a Rule never to ask for an Office and never to refuse one when offer'd to him. I approve says I of his Rule and will practise it with a small Addition; I shall never *ask,* never *refuse,* nor ever *resign* an Office. If they will have my Office of Clerk to dispose of to another, they shall take it from me. I will not by giving it up, lose my right of some time or other making Reprisals on my Adversaries. I heard however no more of this. I was chosen again, unanimously as usual, at the next Election. (185)

This answer is, in fact, a short speech, complete with a preamble, a body, evidence of verbal emphasis and a sharply pointed (but decorously phrased) conclusion. And Franklin takes a great deal of pleasure in recording, indirectly, the speech's impact. But it is such a speech as is consistent with the *Autobiography*'s domestic character, delivered in private to an audience of one, in all likelihood in the humble surroundings of Franklin's print shop.

A special manifestation of this sense of privacy in the *Autobiography* is the educational importance that Franklin attaches in his life not so much to heroic predecessors or to vivid human examples as to books – the educational medium of a post-heroic age. The most familiar of such instances, perhaps, involve the copies of Addison's essays that Franklin uses to teach himself how to write and the copy of Bunyan's *The Pilgrim's Progress,* from which Franklin claims to have learned to appreciate narrative method. Bunyan, once again, is Franklin's model in this conduct of the private experience of reading, for reading is the dominant activity in Bunyan's own spiritual autobiography, *Grace Abounding to the Chief of Sinners* (1666). The long process of personal redemption that Bunyan

records there begins with his marriage and with the two popular religious manuals that his wife brings him, *The Plain Man's Pathway to
Heaven* and *The Practice of Piety,* both distinctly (if anachronistically)
Franklinian titles.[38] Like Franklin, Bunyan gradually learns to speak
more civilly and to avoid the contentious verbal habits of his sinful days.
As the senses of sin and of salvation alternate in Bunyan's life, he experiences these states of soul through literary means. Certain passages of
scripture alternately terrify and reassure him. He returns to his Bible
habitually to assess "the natural force and scope" of key verses and gauges
his spiritual wakefulness by the impact of his reading: "I have sometimes
seen more in a line of the Bible then I could well tell how to stand under,"
Bunyan confesses, "and yet at another time the whole Bible hath been to
me as drie as a stick."[39]

When Bunyan begins to feel some of the operations of grace, they take
the form of newfound powers of reading, as well as of an ability to be
stimulated by the negative example of the Quakers, whose peculiar stubbornness would provide a similar stimulus for Franklin. Just as Franklin
cherishes Bunyan's literary example, so Bunyan singles out Martin
Luther's commentary on Galatians "before all books that ever I have seen,
as most fit for a wounded Conscience" (43). Most dramatically, perhaps,
Bunyan stages in his mind a wrestling match, first between two passages
of scripture, and then between himself and Satan over possession of a
particularly consoling verse in John: "Oh, what work did we make!"
Bunyan exclaims as he reports this memorable tug-o'-war, "he pull'd and
I pull'd; but God be praised, I got the better of him, I got some sweetness
from it."[40] Some of the intensity with which Franklin as well extracted
the sweetness from reading derives from these private spiritual exercises
with "the Word" that Bunyan exemplifies in his own homely and informal prose.[41]

The prevailing influence of the model of domestic life in Franklin's
book has still other subtle but important effects on Franklin's language.
With surprising frequency Franklin casts his activities in a diminutive
mode, as if he were chronicling the interests of a child, emphasizing even
well into his adulthood the "littleness" of his affairs. This delicate, diminutive pressure begins with the book's opening reference to the "little"
anecdotes of his ancestors that Franklin enjoyed collecting, and continues
rather plausibly into his description of the "little" wharf he and his
friends set out to build and into his account of how he spent "all the little
money" he could get hold of on "separate little Volumes" of books (57).
By the time he is established in Philadelphia, Franklin is a fairly independent young man, but he still provides Governor Keith with "the invento-
ry of a little printing house" that he would like to set up, and later still he
opens a "little stationer's shop" to supplement his printing business. At

the end of the military expedition that Franklin leads to build forts on the Pennsylvania frontier, he gives his troops a "little exhortation," and in London on his first mission for the colonies he reflects on the "little advantages" that have so much more influence upon the happiness of life than do great turns of Fortune (207).

The most intensely diminutive passages of the book occur in Part 2, in which Franklin describes the methods he used to discipline himself in his thirteen virtues. Clearly determined to avoid the appearance of "a kind of Foppery in Morals," Franklin practically bombards the reader with associations of innocence. "I made a little book," he notes, for the recording of his failures in virtue with a "little black spot." He writes a "little prayer" for himself and takes another equally "little" one from Thomson's *Seasons* and never fails to carry his little book with him even after he had ceased putting himself through his course of instruction. The older Franklin who is writing about this episode in his life is able to treat it very much as if it were a well-intentioned grammar school project. At the same time, however, Franklin makes clear that these virtues and the method for mastering them have his warmest, adult endorsement. The effect of being both detached from and yet committed to an enterprise is really quite remarkable, and Franklin is able to achieve it almost entirely by establishing a quietly paternal relationship with his own past self: The man, in this case, is father to the child. He is attached to his younger self by the strongest bonds of affection, but he is wise enough to recognize the mismatch between youthful earnestness and human nature.

This complex mixture of points of view is embodied in the actual list of virtues. Each of the cardinal thirteen announces itself with youthful zeal and absoluteness: Temperance, Silence, Order, Tranquility, Chastity, Humility. But the mottoes that Franklin attached to each of them function in a manner quite similar to the humane and forgiving meditations of Anne Bradstreet. Each motto to some degree tempers the demands of its particular virtue, taking what seems at first to be a rather rigid list and bringing it into closer conformity with the limitations of life. Temperance, the motto acknowledges, has a certain latitude in its demands: "Eat not to Dulness. Drink not to Elevation." The motto for Resolution permits us to adhere to half of the virtue even if we are unequal to the whole of it: "Resolve to perform what you ought. Perform without fail what you resolve." The motto for Sincerity is willing to tolerate a measure of necessary deceit in human life, as long as it is not hurtful, and does not require that we earnestly mean everything we say but that we "Think innocently and justly." The motto for Humility – "Imitate Jesus and Socrates" – enforces in its exalted models the virtue it describes and at the same time rather ruefully acknowledges that our best approach to such a standard can only be the weakest kind of imitation. The mottoes, in other words, are almost invariably more complicated, wiser, older in some sense, than the virtues they describe, giving to Franklin's list much of the meditative richness that Bradstreet obtained in her prose homilies. [42]

Indeed, Franklin's perception of Providence itself was precisely the view that an enlightened child might take of the strictures imposed upon it by a concerned, rather than authoritarian, parent. What finally cured his deism, Franklin twice explains, was his sudden realization that Providence did not forbid some actions and command others simply arbitrarily, "yet probably those Actions might be forbidden *because* they were bad for us, or commanded *because* they were beneficial to us, in their own Natures, all the Circumstances of things considered" (115). The thoroughly considering entity here is the "bountiful Father" whom Franklin addressed daily in his little prayer and whose pattern of non-authoritarian guidance (as Franklin conceives it) has so much in common with the thoughtful manner in which Josiah Franklin managed the growth of his youngest son. The central implication of this brand of familial piety is that human nature – the communal self – is not so much an antagonist to be ruthlessly subdued as it is a kind of child to be subtly (on occasion cunningly) molded. Franklin's conception of the relationship between mankind and God is, in its essential features, very similar to that of Edward Taylor, whose God is watchfully engaged in dispensing his grace "by drops" so that his infant creatures might grow and profit under his care. Moreover, Franklin himself chose to adopt something like this manner of divine procedure on his own part, addressing human weakness with just the sort of charitable attitude that is consistent with the role of a responsible, affectionate parent.

This quality to the *Autobiography* is clear from the very beginning, when Franklin announces his intention to give "fair Quarter" to his own vanity, not quite welcoming its presence in his character but being "persuaded" nevertheless that it often has good effects (44). When James Ralph takes Franklin's name so that he might pursue the low business of teaching without damage to his reputation, Franklin is careful to imply only a sense of mild amusement at this expedient on Ralph's part. He is in fact a bit harder on himself for having attempted "familiarities" with Ralph's paramour than he is on Ralph for having treated Franklin's name with less delicacy than he treated his own. The behavior of Governor Keith is another instance of Franklin's decision to display his capacity for understanding rather than to exercise his right of making reprisals. Franklin records in some detail the expedients to which the Quakers were frequently driven in their efforts to strike a balance between the colony's need for defense and their own pacific ideals. But at no point does Franklin appear to gloat over their discomfort. Quite the contrary, he admired the ingenuity they sometimes showed in compromising with their beliefs and admired as well the determination some of his Quaker friends expressed to break with their principles, if need be, in the interest of the public welfare. The affectionate relations that Franklin maintained with prominent Quakers like James Logan and Abel James suggests that Franklin's sympathetic attitude toward the Quaker predicament paid the kind of friendly dividend that Franklin was fond of claiming for those who refuse to dogmatize.[43]

In describing the Quakers, however, and later the equally pacific Moravians, Franklin is invariably pleased when the demands of human nature force the modification of an absolute ideal. Just as with his list of thirteen virtues, the necessity for flexibility and compromise imposed by actual life seemed to Franklin far more compelling, far more pleasing, than ideological or ethical purity. He is, if anything, less gentle with the Moravians than with the Quakers when the Moravians find themselves taking to arms after the massacre at Gnaddenhutten: "Common Sense aided by present Danger," Franklin notes rather curtly, "will sometimes be too strong for whimsicall Opinions" (232). Unlike the Quakers, however, the Moravians had not had to struggle with the conflict between civic duty and private belief. They had simply sought a colonial military exemption from the English Parliament and then gone complacently about their business. Franklin makes this distinction clear. It is the complacency that draws his criticism, not the fact that the Moravians were unequal to their convictions.[44]

The military expedition that he leads into Moravian country proves to be one of the richest instances in the *Autobiography* of Franklin's capacity to preserve the even temper of his domestic life in the midst of a public pursuit – in this case, to practice war as peaceably and with as much regard for life as is humanly possible. Franklin was lucky in his one venture into frontier command. The Indians, who were (Franklin notes admiringly) "dextrous in Contrivances" for keeping their powder dry, massacred most of a party of farmers, whose sodden guns would not go off, on the same day that Franklin and his men were marching to Gnaddenhutten and sleeping in a friendly German's barn, "as wet as Water could make us" (232). There is genuine danger on this expedition, to which Franklin and his men, "all huddled together" in the rain and cold, are quite as vulnerable as if they were simply stranded travelers rather than a company of militia. On the other hand, there is not much of a military flavor to Franklin's leadership. Indeed, judged by the *Autobiography* he scarcely leads at all. The men themselves carry out the work, fell the trees, haul the logs, dig a trench, and plant the palisades. Franklin stands mildly by and times how long it takes two men to fell a fourteen-inch-thick pine, admiring the speed with which they work and the skill with which "our Carpenters" put up a firing platform on the inner wall of the stockade.

He notes that the men are happiest when they work and grow mutinous when the winter rain forces them to be idle, but he records these phenomena as if he were observing a family's shifts in mood rather than the serious morale problems of "Colonel" Franklin. The one intervention in the lives of his men that he does record is his devious expedient for getting them to attend the Chaplain's services by coordinating morning and evening prayers with the twice-daily ration of rum. "He lik'd the Thought," Franklin reports of the chaplain, "undertook the Office, and with the help of a few hands to measure out the Liquor executed it to satisfaction; and never were Prayers more generally and punctually attended" (235). In characteristic fashion Franklin deflects our attention from the cleverness of his own expedient to the cheerful pragmatism of this anonymous chaplain. Even the Indians become something akin to colleagues in this defensive enterprise – like Franklin, observing the proceedings from their hillside outposts. On the whole Franklin is rather impressed, in a grandmotherly sort of way, with the clever arrangements the Indians make for keeping their feet warm in charcoal pits on the cold January nights.

In short it is impossible to imagine a military expedition more completely the opposite of General Braddock's ill-fated march on Fort Duquesne. On two occasions in the *Autobiography* Franklin cannot resist a small pun that emphasizes the special nature of this experience. No sooner had he and his men arrived at "Gnaddenhut," Franklin notes mischievously, than they "hutted" themselves. And at the end of his frontier sojourn, Franklin complains of the difficulty of sleeping in a good bed: "It was so different from my hard Lodging on the Floor of our Hut at Gnadden, wrapt only in a Blanket or two" (236). These puns – rather conspicuous ones, as puns go – are both the amusement of an old man reflecting on experiences that are long past and at the same time reminders that, like the Moravians who named the settlement, Franklin and his men lived in "huts of Grace," the literal rendering of the settlement's name, rather than in a military encampment. They buried the dead, by good luck avoided battle, and at the end of his expedition Franklin attended a church service at Bethlehem, not with the Moravian brethren, who had proven so surprisingly forward in military affairs, but with the Moravian children, about whom Franklin recorded some parental concern, for they seemed pale, as if they had been kept too much indoors. In this passage the *Autobiography* comes quite close to the sort of sacramental symbolism that William Blake explored in his earliest poems, and that John Winthrop touched upon when he envisioned a community maintaining through labor, suffering, sorrow, or joy, "the unitie of the spirit in the bond of peace."

The Moravian expedition perfectly embodies the paradox of character that Benjamin Vaughan identified when he declared Franklin to be an example of the harmony between greatness and domesticity. Franklin clearly saw himself in that light and wrote the *Autobiography* so that his readers would grasp the domestic basis underlying even his most public acts. The relationship between familial models and public life in Franklin's book is suggestively similar to the relationship described by John Winthrop in "A Modell of Christian Charity." Being knit together as one did not necessarily mean that the human community would experience no friction. As writers both Franklin and Winthrop simply chose to characterize that friction as a domestic rather than a geopolitical phenomenon.

In the *Autobiography* the business of the state maintains its fundamental identity with the business of the household, a fact that Franklin never tires of emphasizing, even in the few pages that he was able to write of Part 4, describing his first diplomatic mission to England. There Franklin manages to offend the prickly lawyer of the Penn family, Fernando John Paris, with his "want of Formality" and mediates one conflict with the proprietors not in the august chambers of the Privy Council but in a private talk with Lord Mansfield, where it is Franklin's personal pledge rather than any ambassadorial formality that settles the issue. If, as John Adams reported, Franklin sometimes slept through the general sessions of the Continental Congress in 1776, it was probably because Franklin wisely chose to reserve his dwindling energies for those private, household meeting places where the familial business of arriving at consensus would be conducted.[45]

3

AZADS IN CONCORD

No American writer after Franklin would ever enjoy the same representative status that Franklin's political and intellectual achievements secured for him. Indeed, recognizing Franklin's singular position, Henry Adams framed his own autobiography as a deliberate contrast to Franklin's, characterizing himself as a young man born to prominence but achieving obscurity in a world dominated by impersonal scientific forces rather than by the cozy electrical apparatus of the late eighteenth century. It is very tempting to describe the course of American writing in institutional terms as a gradual descent from the vigorous centrality of Franklin's position to the entropic isolation of Adams, in which the communal values and familial metaphors invoked by Winthrop and deployed by Bradstreet, Crevecoeur, or Franklin himself would slowly lose their efficacy as the nineteenth century progressed.

The perception of such a fundamental discontinuity is consistent in many respects with the doubts that recent students of English and American writing have begun to express about the assumptions behind the idea of "tradition" itself. Adams's analysis of the conflict between multiplicity and unity is both a successor to Emerson's absorption in the "one" and the "two" and the forerunner of Marilyn Butler's recent argument with the concept of unifying traditions in English poetry and of Philip Gura's criticism of continuity studies in general and the tyrannous "novanglophilia" that prevails in American literary scholarship.[1] The dangers of too great an emphasis on continuity and tradition are serious: an oversimplification of the complex relationship between a given literary work and its predecessors, the presentation of modern biases as if they were historically authoritative, the subordination of important literary work that does not lend itself to the smooth continuities a given critic or period desires to celebrate. These perils alone warrant a considerable degree of caution in anyone trying to apply a common descriptive language to work written across a wide span of time. In the face of such considerations, the troubled issues of tradition and continuity might be put aside for the time being in favor of a pragmatically limited but more manageable inquiry. Can a rhetoric of domesticity that has already metamorphosed from the typological Eve of Winthrop's model to the exemplary parent of Franklin's *Autobiography* be useful in exploring work as distinct as *Walden, The Portrait of a Lady,* or Dickinson's lyrics? The chapters that follow take this question as a starting point. Henry Adams argued that old imaginative forms were not adequate to the task of understanding a new age of force, but the example of his own artistic generation and its immediate predecessors suggests that key imaginative tools that served John Winthrop remained vital two hundred years later.

At the end of "Economy" Henry Thoreau concludes his observations on the subject of philanthropy by quoting from one of the exotic sources he loved and often drew upon throughout *Walden,* "the Gulistan, or Flower Garden, or Sheik Sadi of Shiraz." The quotation concerns a question posed to a wise man, asking why it is that among all trees only the cypress, which bears no fruit, is called azad, or free. The wise man replies that the cypress is like the azads, or religious independents, fruitless but always flourishing: "If thy hand has plenty," he advises, "be liberal as the date tree; but if it affords nothing to give away, be an azad, or free man, like the cypress."[2]

Thoreau quite clearly invites a comparison between the peculiar freedom of the azad and his own, austere existence at Walden Pond. He too has "nothing to give away"; appeals to his philanthropic generosity will be of little use. But the concept of the azad is not limited in its pertinence just to the reflections on charity with which Thoreau introduced it. Thoreau himself is a religious independent in the broadest sense, not simply in the context of the final paragraphs of "Economy." The idea of a life without fruits and free suggests, in the same way, a series of broader applications to *Walden.* Though the book is the harvest of all of Thoreau's adult years, it too is paradoxically fruitless. Though Thoreau speaks to us in a vigorously principled way, he has (he insists) no program of principles to offer and provides not even an example for others to follow. *Walden* impresses its readers with the eloquence of its call to reform, yet Thoreau has little use for reformers and admires instead the response of the woodcutter Therien when asked by a "distinguished wise man and reformer . . . if he did not want the world to be changed": "No, I like it well enough" (148).[3]

Thoreau, by and large, likes it well enough too, and *Walden* is the record of this curiously adversarial contentment. The freedom of the

azad is both joyless and joyful. It is not liberal or fertile. It cannot re-
produce itself, but neither are its energies spent in a sexual cycle that
generates life without having the leisure or the capacity to appreciate it. In
one respect this human model is the antithesis of Winthrop's selfless
marriage in "A Modell of Christian Charity." Thoreau, indeed, enjoys
baiting the proponents of the narrower "charity" of his own day, but he
does so from the perspective of the recipient and the practitioner of a
wider charity, an older one, having affinities with Winthrop's that are not
immediately apparent but that influence the prevailing temper of *Walden*.
"There is nowhere recorded a simple and irrepressible satisfaction with
the gift of life," Thoreau complained. And so in *Walden* Thoreau himself
prepared to make such a record, to rectify that error. He is charity's
irrepressible object, and in the process of fulfilling that role he extends his
apparently narrow household at Walden Pond to include a remarkably
generous cross section of his neighbors, just as Winthrop envisioned the
extension of household intimacy to the wider community of Massachusetts Bay.[4]

This sociability notwithstanding, it is perilous to approach Thoreau in
a scholarly context, for he did not think much of scholarship and other,
secondhand enterprises. The success of the scholar, he observed, is
"courtier-like success, not kingly, not manly" (15). Yet Thoreau was a
scholar of himself as well as of others, and *Walden* is a scholarly work,
carpentered together out of the experiences of two years, requiring the
literary labor of eight, drawing on the journal reflections of fifteen and on
the reading of a lifetime.[5] It is a researched book as much as an experienced one. The writing of it required Thoreau to consult heavily the
indexes he made to his own journal volumes. Indeed, the very idea of
indexing one's journals – of imposing such a degree of bibliographic
system upon one's experience – suggests the extent to which Thoreau is a
temperamental heir of Benjamin Franklin, who undertook to store his
moral performance in a very similar fashion and for much less pragmatic
reasons than Thoreau. Franklin never bothered, or never had the leisure,
to write his *Art of Virtue,* but Thoreau bothered a great deal to write his
"Art of Virtuous Life" and to write it in such a way that it might seem
other than what it was, a painstakingly constructed book.[6]

The idea of life as a construction runs deep in both Thoreau and
Franklin, though in Thoreau it takes on the grander, romantic accents of
the nineteenth century: "Every man is tasked to make his life, even in its
details, worthy of the contemplation of his most elevated and critical
hour" (90). Franklin would surely concur in the attention to detail,
though this intensely self-directed contemplation might strike him as an
inadvisable indulgence of vanity. Thoreau, indeed, is almost strident in
his determination to "live deliberately," to "front" life, to drive it into a

corner, to "reduce it to its lowest terms," and "give a true account" of its nature (91). It is not difficult to find evidence in *Walden* of the preeminent importance of "life" as a transcendent value to Thoreau's imagination. But it is very easy indeed to mistake the character of Thoreau's inquiry, as Emerson did, who faulted him for failing to engineer for all America, for failing, in other words, to be for the nineteenth century what Franklin was in fact for the eighteenth.

Public service and public ingenuity of that sort was of no more interest to Thoreau than it was to Emerson himself.[7] And yet Thoreau is in the closest sympathy with the domestic Franklin in the prevailingly gentle nature of his treatment of human imperfection. Stridency is not the dominant tone of *Walden*. "The finest qualities of our nature," Thoreau observed in one of his most memorable sentences, "like the bloom on fruits, can be preserved only by the most delicate handling" (6). Thoreau sets out to handle life just that delicately, to preserve the bloom, not merely of his own private qualities but of all life that intersects with his.

In this sense, then, the distinctive features of Thoreau's imagination, as it is embodied in *Walden,* are precisely the liberality and the charity that he seems to scorn, a charity ranging in application from the smallest features of the environment to the most potent institutions of the day. Thoreau relished conversation that gave him an opportunity "to utter the big thoughts in big words" (140), but an understanding of the appeal of *Walden* must begin with its special reverence for the movements of squirrels and mice, the independent ways of hunting dogs, the habits of partridges. These are the neighbors who elicited much of the finest writing in the book and who permit Thoreau to display in its most intimate form his satisfaction with life. "Brute Neighbors," for example, begins by gently mocking the Hermit's pretensions to lofty thought and substituting a fishing expedition for what had begun as Thoreau's brief recapitulation of the contentious social themes of "Economy":

> Let me see; where was I? Methinks I was nearly in this frame of mind; the world lay about at this angle. Shall I go to heaven or a-fishing? If I should soon bring this meditation to an end, would another so sweet occasion be likely to offer? I was as near being resolved into the essence of things as ever I was in my life. I fear my thoughts will not come back to me. If it would do any good, I would whistle for them. (224)

This form of whimsical self-sabotage is quite common in *Walden*. "Higher Laws," for example, never truly lives up to the exalted promise of its title, for Thoreau acknowledges almost immediately in that chapter his fondness for taking "rank hold" on the primitive life (210).[8] As a kind of postscript to "Economy" Thoreau printed some verses by Thomas

Carew on "The Pretensions of Poverty" that appear to argue directly against the status that Thoreau had just claimed for the simplified life:

> Thou dost presume too much, poor needy wretch,
> To claim a station in the firmament,
> Because thy humble cottage, or thy tub,
> Nurses some lazy or pedantic virtue
> In the cheap sunshine or by shady springs,
> With roots and pot-herbs . . . (80)

In "Brute Neighbors" the collapse of the Hermit's speculations leads immediately to the brief record of Thoreau's acquaintance with a particularly bold mouse:

> Why do precisely these objects which we behold make a world? Why has man just these species of animals for his neighbors; as if nothing but a mouse could have filled this crevice? I suspect that Pilpay & Co. have put animals to their best use, for they are all beasts of burden, in a sense, made to carry some portion of our thoughts.
>
> The mice which haunted my house were not the common ones, which are said to have been introduced into the country, but a wild native kind (*Mus leucopus*) not found in the village. I sent one to a distinguished naturalist, and it interested him much. When I was building, one of these had its nest underneath the house, and before I had laid the second floor, and swept out the shavings, would come out regularly at lunch time and pick up the crumbs at my feet. It probably had never seen a man before; and it soon became quite familiar, and would run over my shoes and up my clothes. It could readily ascend the sides of the room by short impulses, like a squirrel, which it resembled in its motions. At length, as I leaned with my elbow on the bench one day, it ran up my clothes, and along my sleeve, and round and round the paper which held my dinner, while I kept the latter close, and dodged and played at bo-peep with it; and when at last I held still a piece of cheese between my thumb and finger, it came and nibbled it, sitting in my hand, and afterward cleaned its face and paws, like a fly, and walked away. (225–6)

This language captures, quite literally, a piece of delicate handling on Thoreau's part that is the more impressive for the indelicacy with which the passage itself begins. *Mus leucopus,* or the white-footed mouse, at first engaged Thoreau simply as an interesting specimen, a particular kind of beast of burden that Thoreau (like Pilpay & Co.) is willing to supply for his "distinguished naturalist" in a compliant spirit quite unlike that of the cheerful Therien in his own encounter with the distinguished reformer. A kind of cold taxonomy prevails here – much as it does in the structure of *Walden* itself – until Thoreau begins discussing the construction of his house. At that point even the translation of the apparently uninviting Linnaean name develops a striking degree of metaphorical appropriateness to this unusually nimble and fastidious visitor. The nature of Thoreau's interest changes once he is fully "domesticated" and the result is a dramatization, on a suitably small scale, of some of those finer qualities in our nature and in nature in general to which the Walden experience is most deeply committed.

Thoreau's cabin can easily serve as the chief symbol of his detachment from Concord life, as a concise expression of all the sharp judgments of "Economy" upon the desperate materialism of the nineteenth century. But the cabin itself, as Thoreau notes, also has an effect upon the apparently caustic intelligence it has come to symbolize. This is his third house, as Thoreau observes in "Where I Lived and What I Lived For," if one counts the boat in which he and his brother voyaged on the Concord and Merrimack rivers, but the Walden cabin is surely the most significant of his domestic "crystallizations," and it "reacted" on the builder in mysterious ways (85). Once Thoreau set up his household on the pond it became, in some respects, the new "Concord," the new harmony, and not even nature's apparent invitations to resume a judgmental rhetoric have much effect on Thoreau's sense of household bliss. His celebrated account of the battle between the red and the black ants on his woodpile contains a range of troubling allusions to the discordant, human world – Concord Fight, Austerlitz, Bunker Hill, the Fugitive Slave Bill – but all of these serve mainly to heighten the sense of miraculous quietude at Walden, an effect Thoreau underscores when he carefully transports three of the insect warriors on a single woodchip inside his cabin and places them under a glass tumbler on his windowsill.

In his description of the young of the partridge, Thoreau once again enacts the metaphor of delicate handling and connects it to the domestic sensibility that his cabin has begun to foster in him. Within a few sentences of his game of bo-peep with the hungry mouse, Thoreau begins an elaborate account of the defensive measures that a mother partridge will take to distract the attention of a human observer from her young: trailing her wing as if she were wounded, calling and "mewing" warnings to her concealed chicks, rolling and spinning on the ground "in such a dishabille," Thoreau writes almost gallantly, "that you cannot, for a few moments, detect what kind of creature it is" (226). All the while the chicks themselves remain hidden among the sticks and leaves, which "they so exactly resemble . . . that many a traveller has placed his foot in the middle of a brood" without detecting their presence: "You may even tread on them, or have your eyes on them for a minute, without discovering them."

As a rule, of course, Thoreau is a much more careful traveler than this. He is not only able to find the camouflaged chicks but he has held them in his hands and admired the instinct that instructs them to keep perfectly still even when concealment is no longer possible. "The ignorant or reckless sportsman," Thoreau concludes, "often shoots the parent at such a time," leaving the unnoticed chicks to be eaten by predators "or gradually mingle with the decaying leaves which they so much resemble." "These were my hens and chickens," he writes. Such a passage draws much of its impact from its power to remind us of what Thoreau's life did not contain, either in his cabin in the woods or elsewhere in Concord.[9] The absence, or the displacement, that he gently points up here in his whimsical reference to hens and chickens is an absence of just the sort of domestic experience that Anne Bradstreet consistently made the basis of her poetry. Thoreau's partridges serve him much as the image of the anxious mother bird and her chicks served Bradstreet in "In Reference to Her Children." Thoreau, of course, does not identify with the mother, but neither is he quite the unwary traveler or reckless sportsman whose distinctly masculine clumsiness or brutality threatens these little families. Even a careful observer might accidentally tread on one of the chicks, but with patience and luck you may hold them in your hand, note the comic discipline with which they obey their mother's warning even under awkward circumstances, reflect on their precise and oddly soothing resemblance to fallen leaves.

The interplay of sympathy, amusement, and regret in this language is remarkably satisfying, particularly given the smallness of the subject. Like Bradstreet, Thoreau explains what will save life and what will kill, reminding us at the same time of the costs and the rewards of his loneliness. He is not directly involved in this struggle, as an advocate of either life or death: The tenderness of the observer is matched by his detachment. Thoreau never permits himself or his readers to forget that his nonhuman subjects are all transacting their private business just as he is transacting his. His relations with them are sufficiently close for a degree of familiarity to develop but sufficiently distant for the requirements of dignity and independence.[10] Like the nighthawk that Thoreau sees "sporting" in the April sky, "mounting again and again with its strange chuckle . . . turning over and over like a kite, and then recovering from its lofty tumbling" (316), they come near enough to display their private satisfaction with life but keep a careful interval between themselves and even the most sympathetic of observers.

In some measure this respectful balance reflects the social ideal that Thoreau sought to establish in all the relationships of his life, but it is important to note that Thoreau's intimacy with these neighbors is suggestively deeper than the kind of simple cordiality that sometimes prevails among men and women. Notwithstanding his detachment, he is part of a living household at Walden and is close to household events: the rearing of young, the building of nests, the squirrels' flirtatious self-consciousness, the ants' bitter hostilities, and the private (perhaps sexual) "mounting" joys of a nighthawk in breeding season. The interplay between intimacy and distance in these passages is subtle and familial.

In many respects the pond itself is the principal figure in this eroticized nature – an equivalent in the landscape for the veiled goddess, Isis, whose myths served Thoreau as a particularly rich source of allusion.[11] He studies the "circling dimples" on its surface, "the gentle pulsing of its life, the heaving of its breast" with the attentiveness of a lover whom the pond herself had boldly solicited with the first inviting days of Thoreau's residence:

> For the first week, whenever I looked out on the pond, it impressed me like a tarn high up on the side of a mountain, its bottom far above the surface of other lakes, and, as the sun arose, I saw it throwing off its nightly clothing of mist, and here and there, by degrees, its soft ripples or its smooth reflecting surface was revealed, while the mists, like ghosts, were stealthily withdrawing in every direction into the woods, as at the breaking up of some nocturnal conventicle. (86)

This is a peculiarly seductive dawn, of course, rather than a nightfall, but Thoreau's reversal of the traditional chronology of sexual promise is consistent with his attitudes toward the traditions of civil men. Walden is the closest physical approximation to Hebe, "daughter of Juno and wild lettuce," whom Thoreau worships as "the only thoroughly sound-conditioned, healthy, and robust young lady that ever walked the globe" (139). The sexual candor of Thoreau's relationship with Walden – even his mischievous pun on Walden's "bottom" – reflects what Thoreau considers the unembarrassed freedom of Nature in the presence of those who live with rather than study her: "She is not afraid to exhibit herself to them" (258).

The boldest of such exhibitions, and the boldest use of a corporealized landscape in *Walden,* are the celebrated passages from "Spring" describing the sands of the thawing railroad embankment. Michael West has taught us to see this section of the book in the context of Thoreau's preoccupation with his health, but the excremental resemblances in the flowing sand are more than balanced by the explicitly uterine ones.[12] Rebirth is the traditional subject of "Spring," and Thoreau is quite explicit about positioning himself in the "laboratory of the Artist who made the world and me," at first a vigorously male creator "strewing his fresh designs about," but then suddenly and vividly the imagery turns to a description of gestation. The use of gender is quite complex in these passages – as complex as Winthrop's transformation of genders from Adam to Eve in "A Modell of Christian Charity" – but Thoreau is clearly in Nature's womb, rather than its cloaca, watching the formation of leaves, trees, fingers, blood vessels, the "great central life" to which "all animal and vegetable life is merely parasitic" (309). The strong vegetative embryos that in Crevecoeur had served simply as metaphors for American promise become strikingly literal in *Walden*. Thoreau is no longer a new Actaeon, or Osiris, but a kind of midwife to the season's fruitful goddess, touched by a measure of the goddess's own immunity. In "Winter Animals" he had concluded his account of hounds and hunting on the shores of Walden Pond by identifying himself not with the masculine hunters but with Diana, the goddess of the hunt and of childbirth, whose moonlight oversees his passage home: "At midnight, when there was a moon, I sometimes met with hounds in my path prowling about the woods, which would skulk out of my way, as if afraid, and stand silent amid the bushes till I had passed" (280). The critical passages of "Spring" give this sense of immunity and intimacy extraordinary extension. Under any circumstances it is difficult to imagine a more sensitive set of images handled with more suggestive power or more delicacy.[13]

By and large the delicate handling that is so often literal in Thoreau's treatment of his nonhuman neighbors at Walden also characterizes his handling of the human presence there. "I am naturally no hermit," he observes at the beginning of "Visitors," but that confession scarcely does justice to Thoreau's capacity for a special sort of graciousness in his relationships. The fact that his cabin was always open and his hearth always available reflects more than simple indifference to property. Part of the system of "beautiful housekeeping" that he established at Walden involved a kind of hospitality in absentia. Thoreau welcomed the signs left behind that his home had been used in his absence: a pile of whittlings by the fire, the scent of a pipe, a message written on a leaf and left on the table. The "cheering visitors" far outnumbered the bores and reformers, Thoreau reports, and he left tributes to some of his guests that are remarkable for their capacity to suggest the pleasures of companionship: to the poet with whom he made "that small house ring with boisterous mirth" (268) and to the philosopher who paid him a call during his last winter in the woods:

> Having each some shingles of thought well dried, we sat and whittled them, trying out knives, and admiring the clear yellowish grain of the pumpkin pine. We waded so gently and reverently, or we pulled together so smoothly, that the fishes of

thought were not scared from the stream, nor feared any angler on the bank, but came and went grandly, like the clouds which float through the western sky, and the mother-o'-pearl flocks which sometimes form and dissolve there. . . . Ah! such discourse we had, hermit and philosopher, and the old settler I have spoken of, – we three, – it expanded and racked my little house; I should not dare to say how many pounds' weight there was above the atmospheric pressure on every circular inch; it opened its seams so that they had to be calked with much dulness thereafter to stop the consequent leak; – but I had enough of that kind of oakum already picked. (269–70)

A good conversation could reliably elicit Thoreau's love of full-blown hyperbole, most memorably perhaps in the opening sentences of "Visitors," in which (much in the fashion of Melville's Ishmael) he playfully exaggerates the space required for really serious talk: "You want room for your thoughts to get into sailing trim and run a course or two before they make their port. . . . I have found it a singular luxury to talk across the pond to a companion on the other side" (141). In *Walden* Thoreau is particularly adept at finding images that fuse his appetite for contact with his appetite for isolation.

In some measure, for example, the rhythm of Thoreau's prose continually reproduces the flux of conversation, from great subjects to small ones, from moments of passion to moments of easy discourse. A look at his use of punctuation suggests the degree to which he loved to reach out to his listener with questions and exclamation, sometimes interjecting imaginary replies to his observations to keep the sense of exchange alive. These strategies aren't original with Thoreau by any means. He would have encountered all of them in his study of Pope's *Essay on Man,* in particular the pose of dialogue in what is in fact a monologue. But Thoreau's application of the social fiction in written discourse is a fundamental rather than conventional ingredient of *Walden*'s form. His authority always presents itself as companionable, even when it impresses readers as dangerously judgmental.

A severe test of Thoreau's treatment of his human neighbors comes during his visits to the homes of James Collins and John Field. The Collins shanty provided the boards for Thoreau's cabin at Walden. He records the inspection and the purchase in "Economy." John Field and his family occupied the hut where Thoreau took shelter from a thunderstorm in "Baker Farm." In each case Thoreau exposes the poverty of these Irish laboring families clearly and bluntly in what seems at first to be a spirit of accuracy mixed with distaste rather than with sympathy, noting the "dank, clammy, and aguish" atmospheres of these dwellings, the dirt floors, the meager possessions, the chickens that invariably co-habit with the family.

But having presented such a bleak picture of their predicament, Thoreau invariably treats the people themselves in a way that quietly stresses their superiority to their circumstances.[14] Though "Mrs. C" (as Thoreau calls her with neighborly familiarity) doesn't have much of a house to show, she shows it with pride, inviting Thoreau in, lighting a lamp, and observing as they go, "good boards overhead, good boards all around, and a good window" (43). Thoreau notes the list of furnishings without comment not because these items embody the Collinses' poverty but because they suggest something of the complexity of the life that can be lived in such unpromising surroundings: "a stove, a bed, and a place to sit, an infant in the house where it was born, a silk parasol, gilt-framed looking-glass, and a patent new coffee mill nailed to an oak sapling, all told" (43). These details do indeed "tell," as Thoreau punningly intended that they should, especially the stately setting of an infant in the house where it was born, grandly indifferent to the jumble of vanity and poverty into which it has been introduced.

Thoreau's description of "John Field's poor starveling brat" in "Baker Farm" is a more elaborate and perhaps more disturbing version of this same juxtaposition of human dignity and squalor, emphasizing as Thoreau does there "the wrinkled, sibyl-like, cone-headed infant that sat upon its father's knee as in the palaces of nobles, and looked out from its home in the midst of wet and hunger inquisitively upon the stranger, with the privilege of infancy, not knowing but it was the last of a noble line, and the hope and cynosure of the world" (204). This passage even in so short a space seems to move from irony very subtly into admiration. There is a sharper edge to this description than there is in the list of the Collins furnishings, but even so some of the fearless innocence of the partridge chicks is present in this sturdy, infant curiosity.

Indeed, a close observer like Thoreau would have expected his reader to recognize that John Field's "brat" is a newborn with the characteristic signs and shape of its age and condition: the wrinkled skin and misshapen head. On the title page of *Walden* he had announced his determination not to write an ode to dejection, and in his description of the Fields family he seems more than usually mindful of the poetic dialogue out of which his own allusion and Coleridge's ode emerged: The "privilege of infancy" that Thoreau recognizes in the Field baby corresponds to the privileged vision that Wordsworth had associated with childhood in the "Intimations Ode," and that age progressively dims into what Wordsworth called "the light of common day," just as this half-amusing, half-dignified baby dims into the figure of the father who is holding the child on his knee. The Field family are clearly (and punningly) among the meanest flowers that blow, and although Thoreau does not view them with Wordsworth's heightened pathos, he does invoke for them a context that enriches our sense of their plight and identifies them, quite surprisingly, with the central enterprise of *Walden*.

James Collins and his neighbor Seeley both possess a bold indifference to dejection that distinguishes them from the beleaguered Field family. Virtually all we learn of Collins himself is that he saw fit to give Thoreau warning of "certain indistinct but wholly unjust claims" against the Collins property and to caution the new owner to take possession of his boards and nails promptly (43). But even this little is sufficient to suggest that Collins has a certain guileful charm. Thoreau has only admiration for the aplomb with which Collins's neighbor Seeley is able (one supposes) to settle those claims by stealing some of Thoreau's nails even as he lingers sociably about the scene of the crime, "with spring thoughts" passing the time of day with his victim. John Field is not as resourceful as his two countrymen, but what he lacks in quickness he compensates for in what Thoreau recognizes as his bravery. Thoreau is openly critical of Field's way of life and harsh in his judgments on him ("The culture of an Irishman is an enterprise to be undertaken with a sort of moral bog hoe"), but he also goes to great lengths to try to reform him, in the process ridiculing his own officious naiveté. The reform is unsuccessful, though Thoreau is careful to note that Field has heard him out thoughtfully and is willing to make a brief experiment at a new way of living before slipping back to his bogging.

Even in their defeat, however, the Field family resemble Thoreau himself in their determination: "Therefore I suppose they still take life bravely, after their fashion, face to face, giving it tooth and nail, not having skill to split its massive columns with any fine entering wedge, and rout it in detail; – thinking to deal with it roughly, as one should handle a thistle" (206). This language is reminiscent of Thoreau's description of his own relentless pursuit of life in "Where I Lived, and What I Lived For." He exults in the differences between his own freedom, ingenuity, and knowledge in contrast to the burdensome existence of the Field family, but he also acknowledges through this verbal parallel the common human bond. Mrs. Field's face, for all the discouragements of her situation, is "glistening and hopeful" (206).[15]

This propensity to identify with the people whom he describes takes its most curious form in the most extensive of Thoreau's portraits of his neighbors: the detailed account he gives of his interviews with the woodcutter Therien in "Visitors." The same complex of attitudes that characterizes his treatments of John Field and the Collinses finds even fuller expression here. He is frank in his conviction that Therien represents only "the animal man" and that his mind remained "primitive and immersed in his animal life" (150), but these judgments, harsh as they are,

have surprisingly little effect on the generosity with which Thoreau
quotes Therien's words, comments on his virtues or his innocence, records the zest with which he talked, the care with which he observed his
surroundings and reasoned skillfully from what he knew. Therien was
precisely Thoreau's own age at the beginning of the Walden experiment,
with a little of Thoreau's own coloring and appearance. It seems quite
likely that some of Thoreau's comradely fascination with him was a kind
of curiosity about this rougher version of himself, a parallel that Thoreau
hints at in his description of the elusive nature of Therien's character – a
description cast in the idiom of a man looking into a mirror: "I sometimes saw in him [Therien] a man whom I had not seen before, and I did
not know whether to suspect him of a fine poetic consciousness or of
stupidity. A townsman told me that when he met him sauntering through
the village in his small close-fitting cap, and whistling to himself, he
reminded him of a prince in disguise" (148). This sauntering, self-sufficient, paradoxical figure might easily be Thoreau himself, who took
some satisfaction in being equally an item of curiosity among his towns-
men and equally a paradox.[16]

Indeed, even Therien's purely animal spirits have something in common with the resolution Thoreau offers at the close of "Higher Laws" in
the fable of John Farmer: "to let his mind descend into his body and
redeem it, and treat himself with ever increasing respect" (222). To descend into the body, to handle oneself and others delicately, seem to be, in
large measure, the mottoes of *Walden*. One senses these principles at
work too in the opening passages of "Economy," in which Thoreau cites
his six exotic Brahmin penances in a wonderfully exaggerated and gentle
attempt to chide his neighbors into treating themselves with a little more
care than their current, desperate lives permit. Thoreau participated quite
intimately in these lives, both as a critical observer of their desperate
moments and as a neighbor who shared in their occasional capacity to
shed that desperation in innocent release.[17] His recollection of a famous
Concord fire is a measure of that participation. In the course of this
account, Thoreau himself springs out of a spiritual torpor that is a comic
version of the spiritless life of his neighbors:

> Breed's hut was standing only a dozen years ago, though it had
> long been unoccupied. It was about the size of mine. It was set
> on fire by mischievous boys, one Election night, if I do not
> mistake. I lived on the edge of the village then, and had just lost
> myself over Davenant's Gondibert, that winter that I labored
> with a lethargy, – which, by the way, I never knew whether to
> regard as a family complaint, having an uncle who goes to sleep
> shaving himself, and is obliged to sprout potatoes in a cellar
> Sundays, in order to keep awake and keep the Sabbath, or as the

consequence of my attempt to read Chalmers' collection of English poetry without skipping. It fairly overcame my Nervii. I had just sunk my head on this when the bells rung fire, and in hot haste the engines rolled that way, led by a straggling troop of men and boys, and I among the foremost, for I had leaped the brook. We thought it was far south over the woods, – we who had run to fires before, – barn, shop, or dwelling-house or all together. "It's Baker's barn," cried one. "It is the Codman Place," affirmed another. And then fresh sparks went up above the wood, as if the roof fell in, and we all shouted "Concord to the rescue!" (259–60)

By Thoreau's more earnest standards this passage is playful – even a bit garrulous. The puns ("Nervii," leaping the "brook") are deliberately of a lowbrow order and the parenthetical aside on his uncle is almost gossipy. It is not customary to think of Thoreau in this kind of company, adding his voice to the triumphant cry "Concord to the rescue" and, later in this passage, standing around the idle fire engine swapping yarns about great fires of the past and bragging with his neighbors. But in its way *Walden* is a neighborly book. Along with his Puritan aspirations to simplify, Thoreau retained as well the sense of being "knit together" in community that Winthrop announced as the indispensable requirement of American life.[18]

If Thoreau is anywhere likely to have indulged in rough handling, it would surely be in his discussions of the social and economic institutions with which he found himself surrounded, even at Walden Pond. The Fitchburg Railroad touched there, merchants came to harvest the pond's emerald ice, the sounds of the village church and of the local militia could be heard in his bean field, and at one point an anonymous village wife seems to have stopped by and looked into the condition of Thoreau's sheets. Thoreau, indeed, never made any claims for the serene isolation of his cabin. He seems chiefly to have valued his situation for the points of contact it offered him with the varied business of the community and the similarities it shared with other huts (like the ill-fated Breed's) that had played some role in Concord's history.

It is only with the slightest seasoning of irony that Thoreau writes "I have always endeavored to acquire strict business habits" (20). At least in his exuberantly ideal vision, business becomes a supremely exhilarating challenge, involving the overseeing of countless details, buying, selling, keeping accounts, reading letters, visiting ports, "unweariedly sweeping the horizon, speaking all passing vessels" (20), studying charts, logarithms, universal science: "It is a labor to task the faculties of a man, – such problems of profit and loss, of interest, of tare and tret, and gauging of all kinds in it" (21). "Commerce," wrote Thoreau in "Sounds," "is unexpectedly confident and serene, alert, adventurous, and unwearied" (119). The wonder of economic life reimagined in these grandly geographic terms was not lost on him. His genuine celebrations of "business" take a great deal of the sting out of the most astringent passages of "Economy," much as the wry quotation of Carew's verse at the end of that chapter takes liberties with Thoreau's celebration of his own "pedantic virtue."[19]

Versions of this sort of compensatory admiration mitigate many of Thoreau's most sharply expressed views. There is very little in *Walden,* for example, to suggest the depth of rancor he felt toward the war with Mexico. His night in jail for failure to pay the poll tax occupies part of a paragraph at the end of "The Village," in which Thoreau characterizes his arrest as a more or less ordinary inconvenience, interrupting an errand to the village cobbler to pick up a mended shoe. As he is hoeing in his bean field, he hears the sounds of a "military turnout" like "some sort of itching and disease on the horizon," but within a few sentences these same offensive sounds remind him of a distant hum of swarming bees or of a "slight tantivy and tremulous motion of the elm-tree tops which overhang the village" (161). His focus is not on the ignoble purposes behind this military activity but on the comically patriotic effect that martial music could have even on such a skeptical listener as himself. When the tunes grew "really noble and inspiring," Thoreau confesses, even he "looked around for a woodchuck or a skunk to exercise my chivalry upon."[20] Elsewhere Thoreau spoke much more forcefully on war and government, but *Walden* is in many senses his book of life, so inviolable (as he suggests at the conclusion of "Spring") that nature might rain flesh and blood and still not threaten his faith in "universal innocence" (318).

The most vivid instance of Thoreau's accommodating intelligence in *Walden* is his treatment of the Fitchburg Railroad. Its sounds disturb his meditations, its appetite for wooden ties has stripped the surrounding hills of their trees, it is in most respects the central symbol of "this restless, nervous, bustling, trivial, Nineteenth Century" toward which Thoreau felt such antagonism (329). But it is a symbol as well for the exhilarating change Thoreau associated with new generations and for the impressive energies of commerce. It seems to him both a "bloated pest" and the most remarkable figure in a new collection of near-mythological beings called into existence by technology: "When I meet the engine with its train of cars moving off with planetary motion . . . it seems as if the earth had got a race now worthy to inhabit it" (116).[21]

With the very next sentence Thoreau expresses his own reservations about this grand picture. The "ends" of the railroad, the deeds that it does, fall short of its imposing appearance. But Thoreau's sense of this disparity is not in any way conclusive. If there is some failure here, then it is only a provisional one. The railroad continues to incite wonder, just as martial music continues to stir the spirit, just as the ideal of a college remains alive in Thoreau's vision of "the uncommon school" (110), and housekeeping and farming remain capable of sustaining their peculiar varieties of beauty. There is still a delicate bloom in all of these expressions of technical ingenuity and social purpose. Thoreau records his protest, but he records as well his irrepressible satisfaction.

It is scarcely more difficult to document the central role of "life" for Emerson's imagination than it is to establish the importance of "life" in *Walden*. The struggle with his own health in Emerson's early years – the painful imbalance between his ambitions and his vitality that Stephen Whicher describes so memorably – made it perhaps inevitable that once his survival was assured, "the great and constant fact of Life" would take on a critical importance for him precisely because life's constancy was such an exhilarating and unexpected achievement.[22] Accordingly it becomes, in Emerson's view, the poet's central subject.[23] The opening paragraph of *Nature* announces Emerson's grateful loyalty to those "floods of life" in the natural world that "stream around and through us," urging upon "the living generation . . . our own works and laws and worship" (7). Through his thirteen most productive working years, between 1836 and 1849, this vision of the generosity and the urgency of life never ceases to be the central metaphor through which Emerson expresses his understanding of virtually every subject he takes up – a degree of imaginative consistency that Emerson clearly forecasts in his first short book.[24]

But largely as a consequence of the unfocused nature of this key term itself, it is every bit as easy to misconstrue Emerson's own commitment to "life" as it was for Emerson himself to misconstrue Thoreau's. Indeed, it is considerably easier, for Thoreau at least has the advantage – or the disadvantage – of providing a palpable example of what he might mean by life. Thoreau himself felt sufficiently constrained by the romantic appeal of his residence in the woods to insist that *Walden* offered no pattern for others to follow, that his personal retirement had meaning only in the context of a community of less retired lives, including finally his own. But this scrupulous disclaimer has little or no effect on the vividness of the Walden experiment. Thoreau's preaching is so intimately connected with his practice that it has always been easy to mistake the one for the other. There is no opportunity for such confusion in Emerson. The power of example – even of a misunderstood example – is absent. He had a formidable capacity for attracting disciples the most gifted of whom he consistently alienated by his refusal, or his inability, to offer them the sort of model that is the material for discipleship.[25] He lived most of his life in the anomalous position of having no profession but a great necessity to profess, and the result of this predicament is the sense one sometimes gets that an Emerson essay, for all its exhilarating rhetorical movement, stands curiously still. It is a wholly sensational performance in that one "feels" its impact, as Emerson loved to feel it, without quite being able to convert that feeling into some more lasting or more stable form. Emerson himself noted a bit mischievously in his journal that he found Nathaniel Hawthorne's literary reputation to be "a very pleasing fact, because his writing is not good for anything, and this is a tribute to the man."[26] Emerson here is expressing the contemporary disesteem for fiction, but this backhanded compliment applies at least as readily to his own work as it does to Hawthorne's.

What compensates in Emerson for the absence of Thoreau's exemplary concreteness or Hawthorne's historical invention is his remarkable power of reassurance, his conviction of life's adequacy, and his conception of its extraordinary extension. In many respects, in fact, Emerson undertook to recast in his own day and idiom the vision of a unified life that John Winthrop described for his fellow emigrants in 1630. Nature and "A Modell of Christian Charity" share many of the same purposes and means. Many of Winthrop's essential metaphorical tools come genuinely alive in Emerson's hands. Winthrop's sense of his occasion, his audience, and his purpose is, of course, much more clearly defined than is Emerson's. Winthrop's piety is more conventional, and his title alone suggests an attempt at a degree of system building to which Emerson would never have consented and that Emerson's own title characteristically evades. But like Emerson in Nature, Winthrop too is striving to shape the consciousness of his listeners, addressing them on matters that are prior to, and more significant than, any of the specific challenges that they face in Massachusetts Bay. Both Nature and "A Modell of Christian Charity" hope to promote in their audiences the capacity to build more lasting, more meaningful worlds, a common goal to which Emerson's Orphic poet alerts us in Nature's famous closing injunction. Like Winthrop, Emerson too identifies this goal with the central significance of marriage and with the choice of life over death.[27]

This relationship between Emerson's work and the intellectual heritage of Puritanism has been clear to scholars for years. Emerson himself was the first to acknowledge his admiration for the kind of ancestral piety that his Aunt Mary represented. As F. O. Mathiessen and others have suggested, the numbered divisions of Nature are in some measure a survival of the formal rhetoric of Puritan discourse with which Emerson had grown familiar in his own, early sermons. Joel Porte has recently suggested that *Nature* is organized, at least to some degree, as an explication of several key biblical texts, just as standard Puritan rhetorical usage required.[28] But the fundamental similarities to Winthrop's text are imaginative rather than structural. In the first place Emerson improvised in quite surprising ways upon the conceit of bodily members that Winthrop employed as one of his primary illustrations of the selfless bonds of community. In "A Modell of Christian Charity" the conceit is fairly straightforward: Just as the parts of the body are mutually serviceable and mutually dependent, so must men envision themselves as bound to and identified with the welfare of the communal "body." In Emerson this metaphor is released from the stable context of Winthrop's single analogy and applied to a hundred expressive tasks. He comes closest to Winthrop's usage in the opening paragraphs of "The American Scholar," which lament the fragmentation of society and the distortion of human character into single appendages that "have suffered amputation from the trunk, and strut about so many walking monsters, – a good finger, a neck, a stomach, an elbow, but never a man." Even an analogy as brief as this one is unusually elaborate for Emerson. It is far more typical of him to prize the sudden, imaginative thrust that characterizes human power or human weakness in a rapid series of anatomical images: The Understanding is the Hand of the mind (26); the scholar is the world's eye, the world's heart (63); "That which shows God out of me, makes me a wart and a wen" (81); the enraptured soul is a transparent eyeball (10).[29]

This pattern of imagery is critical to the closing passages of *Nature* in which the Orphic poet describes deluded man as " the dwarf of himself," living a shrunken existence inside the vast shell of a universe whose "veins and veinlets" he no longer has the vitality or the vision to fill (46). George Herbert, Winthrop's poetically more distinguished contemporary, is Emerson's immediate source for this traditional correspondence between the bodily microcosm and the macrocosm of nature, but whether or not Winthrop is directly involved in shaping the language of *Nature* is, for the moment, less important than the fact that Emerson is able to elicit new vigor from inherited forms. That is precisely the mode of procedure that he recommended to the graduates of Harvard's Divinity College two years later when he urged them to "let the breath of new life be breathed by you through the forms already existing. For, if once you are alive, you shall find they shall become plastic and new" (91). The newness, in this case, results from the prismatic effect that Emerson is able to obtain by dividing a single, conventional analogy into dozens of metaphorical strands, weaving through his prose in what amounts to a figurative illustration of the higher unity for which Emerson is arguing.

The importance of the body as an emblem for unity is reinforced both in Winthrop and in Emerson by the high value each places upon action, the embodiment of truth in deeds. "Words," Emerson complains, "are finite organs of the infinite mind. They cannot cover the dimensions of what is in truth. They break, chop, and impoverish it. An action is the perfection and publication of thought" (30). The superb passages in "The American Scholar" celebrating action as the mind's resource give classic expression to this preference of Emerson's, which clearly owes a great deal to his lifelong admiration for Plutarchan heroism and the ideal of "manliness" that he found ready-made in the Latin root of "virtue." The allusion to Caesar at the end of *Nature,* in a rather odd conjunction with Adam as exemplary heroes, is a sign of the wedding of Plutarch and piety in Emerson's imagination. But the ideal of action is indigenous in the Puritan tradition as well. In "A Modell of Christian Charity" Winthrop too had revealed his distrust of words detached from deeds. Truths honored only in profession were acceptable, perhaps, to the churches of England, but churches in America (according to Winthrop) must earnestly live their beliefs. And when he prepared to close his discourse, Winthrop did so with a resounding emphasis upon what the emigrants must do, not upon what they must think: "Wee must delight in eache other, make others Condicions our owne rejoyce together, mourne together, labour, and suffer together . . . soe shall wee keepe the unitie of the spirit in the bond of peace."[30]

As we have seen in Chapter 1, the figure whom Winthrop selected as an example of this extraordinary social devotion was the unfallen Eve, greeting her spouse in the Garden of Eden. Perhaps for the same exegetical reasons that influenced Winthrop, Emerson as well chooses this moment of recognition to dramatize his sense of the bodily integration of truth and deed. Eve is not his explicit example, but the echoes of Genesis are unmistakable, and the parallel to Winthrop's use of Eve's monologue is equally marked:

> Words and actions are not the attributes of brute nature. They introduce us to the human form, of which all other organizations appear to be degradations. When this appears among so many that surround it, the spirit prefers it to all others. It says, "From such as this, have I drawn joy and knowledge; in such as this, have I found and beheld myself; I will speak to it; it can speak again; it can yield me thought already formed and alive." In fact, the eye, – the mind – is always accompanied by these forms, male and female; and these are incomparably the richest informations of the power and order that lie at the heart of things. Unfortunately, every one of them bears the marks as of some injury; is marred and superficially defective. Nevertheless, far different from the deaf and dumb nature around them, these all rest like fountain-pipes on the unfathomed sea of thought and

virtue whereto they alone, of all organizations, are the entrances. (30–1)

What distinguishes this passage from Winthrop's use of Genesis in "A Modell of Christian Charity" are the lengths to which Emerson has gone to render a fundamentally intimate moment in distant terms. This is not Eve, the mother and wife, greeting her beloved; it is the sexually neutral "spirit" (or "mind," physically embodied in the equally neutral "eye") observing as if from a dispassionate distance the human form that is in turn described in a conventional, and depersonalized, nineteenth-century metaphor as an "organization." Male and female are present to Emerson's vision, but only as they are present in the first of Genesis's two creation stories: as complementary parts of a single being that the biblical source calls, simply, "man" but that Emerson depersonalizes still further as "informations." This instance of spiritual unity itself, then, is already marred and superficially defective. The recognition it describes is partly a social achievement and partly an acknowledgment of an insurmountable residue of loneliness.

Emerson's treatment of this "marriage" is far more reserved than Winthrop's in his own evocation of marriage and family as the models for the state. But the image of marriage is no less critical to Emerson as an embodiment of the idea of unity. The marriage between the barren facts of nature and human history is the source of the "life" of language upon which Emerson grounds his fundamental article of faith: that nature is the symbol of spirit. Nature, indeed, first presents itself to Emerson as a "great apparition" but the tendency of *Nature* as a whole is to convert this apparition into a loving mother – not unlike Winthrop's Eve – and Emerson himself into her merry and thriving infant. "Infancy is the perpetual Messiah," Emerson proclaims in *Nature*, "which comes into the arms of fallen men, and pleads with them to return to Paradise" (46).

Erik Thurin has anatomized Emerson's lifelong absorption with images of marriage and family so thoroughly as to leave no room for doubt about their pervasive importance, but Thurin's conviction of Emerson's deep "philosophical hostility to marriage" seems unwarranted in part because of the very absorption that Thurin describes.[31] Emerson may proclaim his determination in "Self-Reliance" to "shun father and mother and wife and brother, when my genius calls me," but his genius never really called upon him to do so. Indeed, it requires these same essential elements of household life and affection in order to express its higher aspirations (262). Worldly marriage, like man himself, may be fallen – or "marred and superficially defective," as Emerson put it in his recasting of Genesis in *Nature* – but Emerson's imagination continued to yearn for a marital paradise that the Orphic poet of *Nature* hints at when he describes the baffling alienation between man and woman in the fallen world and characterizes the universe not as man's lost dominion but as his "house" (46).

The closing paragraph of the essay "Compensation" is as perfect an instance as Emerson ever wrote of this balance between the soul alone on the one hand and its household longings on the other. Just as Winthrop recognized the necessity to incorporate mourning and suffering in his vision of communal unity, so Emerson identified both calamity and its remedy with the idea of the state as a kind of perfected household embracing a wider community that proves coextensive with the family:

> And yet the compensations of calamity are made apparent to the understanding also, after long intervals of time. A fever, a mutilation, a cruel disappointment, a loss of wealth, a loss of friends, seems at the moment unpaid loss, and unpayable. But the sure years reveal the deep remedial force that underlies all facts. The death of a dear friend, wife, brother, lover, which seemed nothing but privation, somewhat later assumes the aspect of a guide or genius; for it commonly operates revolutions in our way of life, terminates an epoch of infancy or of youth which was waiting to be closed, breaks up a wonted occupation, or a household, or style of living, and allows the formation of new ones more friendly to the growth of character. It permits or constrains the formation of new acquaintances, and the reception of new influences that prove of the first importance to the next years; and the man or woman who would have remained a sunny garden-flower, with no room for its roots and too much sunshine for its head, by the falling of the walls and the neglect of the gardener, is made the banian of the forest, yielding shade and fruit to wide neighbourhoods of men. (302)[32]

The interplay between loneliness and intimacy characteristic of Thoreau's redemptive household at Walden or of Emerson's earlier uses of the metaphor of marriage is equally marked in this evolution of character from sunny garden flower to "banian of the forest." But Emerson's metaphorical botany here is, once again, an outgrowth of the landscape of Genesis and its domestic myth. The "neglect" that more conventional piety would attach to Adam and Eve, Emerson has adroitly displaced upon the absentee "gardener," whereas the fall of "man or woman" takes the form of the collapse of the constraining walls of an unacceptably limited dwelling. The new "neighbourhoods" to which Emerson looks forward spring out of the same biblical and typological origins from which Winthrop hoped to derive the cohesive bonds of Massachusetts Bay.

Emerson's affirmation in *Nature* of "the power and order that lie at the heart of things" calls attention to one of the most important of his affinities with Winthrop. In Winthrop's words, they share a conviction of the knit-together life. The success of Massachusetts Bay depended, in Winthrop's view, on the ability of the colonists to remain "knitt together in this work as one man" (203). Such closeness was desirable, not only for the sake of practical, cooperative advantage, but because such a tightly unified community would also amount to a worldly image of the perfection of Christ, who knits together with "ligaments" of love all sanctified creation in one "glorious body without spott or wrinckle" (197). This vision of unity accounts for the energy and passion with which Winthrop exhorted his companions to embrace their special marriage bond with God and with one another. Emerson's language is less directly dependent on biblical imagery, but his sense of the interconnectedness of all life is as deep as Winthrop's and far more dramatically expressed.

The drama derives, in part, from indirection, for the first signs of this faith in *Nature* are the bold assertions of his opening paragraphs, which seem to spring from some hidden (and profoundly enviable) vein of confidence: "We must trust the perfection of the creation so far, as to believe that whatever curiosity the order of things has awakened in our minds, the order of things can satisfy; . . . nature is already, in its forms and tendencies, describing its own design; . . . to a sound judgment the most abstract truth is the most practical" (7). Statements like these lead naturally to the half-glorious, half-irritating self-assurance with which Emerson passes off all problems of terminology in his essay by asserting that "no confusion of thought will occur." He is already writing with the full conviction that, regardless of the thread with which he takes up his discussion, it will lead inevitably and securely to the heart of his vision.[33]

When Emerson is finally ready to express that vision openly, he thoroughly subsumes Winthrop's image of the body and reaches out beyond human communities alone to the boundaries of nature:

> All things are moral; and in their boundless changes have an unceasing reference to spiritual nature. Therefore is nature glorious with form, color, and motion, that every globe in the remotest heaven; every chemical change from the rudest crystal up to the laws of life; every change of vegetation from the first principle of growth in the eye of a leaf, to the tropical forest and antediluvian coal-mine; every animal function from the sponge up to Hercules, shall hint or thunder to man the laws of right and wrong, and echo the Ten Commandments. Therefore is nature ever the ally of Religion: lends all her pomp and riches to the religious sentiment. Prophet and priest, David, Isaiah, Jesus,

have drawn deeply from this source. This ethical character so penetrates the bone and marrow of nature, as to seem the end for which it was made. Whatever private purpose is answered by any member or part, this is its public and universal function, and is never omitted. (28)

Winthrop's ligaments of love reemerge in *Nature* as Emerson's pervasive ethical character, but it is still an "embodied" universe that the ethical character pervades, infusing "bone and marrow" with "the end for which it was made." Indeed, even Winthrop's traditional sense of the cohesive role of love – "Love is the bond of perfection" in Winthrop's communal vision – retains its force in Emerson's rejuvenation of the seventeenth-century ideal. In the closing paragraphs of "Prospects," *Nature*'s chapter of incitement for the "torpid spirit," Emerson appropriates the metaphors of marriage and love to describe the unified perception of the world that will follow upon the redemption of man's soul:

> The reason why the world lacks unity, and lies broken and in heaps, is, because man is disunited with himself. He cannot be a naturalist, until he satisfies all the demands of the spirit. Love is as much its demand, as perception. Indeed, neither can be perfect without the other. In the uttermost meaning of the words, thought is devout, and devotion is thought. Deep calls unto deep. But in actual life, the marriage is not celebrated. There are innocent men who worship God after the tradition of their fathers, but their sense of duty has not yet extended to the use of all their faculties. And there are patient naturalists, but they freeze their subject under the wintry light of the understanding. Is not prayer also a study of truth, – a sally of the soul into the unfound infinite? No man ever prayed heartily, without learning something. But when a faithful thinker, resolute to detach every object from personal relations, and see it in the light of thought, shall, at the same time, kindle science with the fire of the holiest affections, then will God go forth anew into the creation. (47)

For Winthrop too the deterioration of human nature was traditionally marked by an act of self-mutilation by Adam, the type of all mankind, who had "rent himself" from his Creator, "rent all his posterity allsoe one from another," and set in motion the events in history that Winthrop understood as culminating in the emergence of the second Adam, Christ.[34] Emerson's language as well honors this typological succession from the divided self to the redemptive "faithful thinker" whose presence marks the reentry of God into Creation, the apocalyptic marriage envisioned in the Puritan lyrics of Bradstreet and Taylor. Out of the "marriage" between love and perception, devotion and thought, springs Emerson's healing conviction that no calamity can befall the faithful thinker that nature cannot repair, that there is "no object so foul that intense light will not make beautiful," that the miraculous inheres in the common. In "The Divinity School Address," Emerson gives these images still greater scope. The Mosaic choice with which Winthrop closed "A Modell of Christian Charity" becomes, in Emerson's hands, the sure equivalence between benevolence and life, between "absolute badness" and "absolute death" (78). "In the sublimest flights of the soul," Emerson affirms, "rectitude is never surmounted, love is never outgrown" (78). The critical elements of Winthrop's conception of community – love, the sacramental body, marriage, and the image of a unified life – pervade Emerson's prose much as the ethical character pervades Emerson's universe.

What appears, at first, to distinguish Emerson from Winthrop is the role of the self. In Emerson's brief reconstruction of the moment of human recognition in Genesis, the selfless devotion of Winthrop's Eve seems transformed into a distinctly self-centered discovery: "From such as this, have I drawn joy and knowledge; in such as this have I found and beheld myself." The sense of a transcendent bond with another seems less important in Emerson's treatment than the self's affirmation of its own considerable powers. Emerson is such a passionate spokesman for the infinitude of the private man that there seems little room in him for the kind of social commitment represented by "A Modell of Christian Charity." The ringing advice of the Orphic poet – "Build, therefore, your own world" – could not be more opposed in spirit to Winthrop's cooperative demands.[35]

The opening pages of *Nature*, however, had promised to explore an experience of the unity of life in which "all mean egotism vanishes" (10). This vanishing of "self" is not simply the isolated achievement of individual devotion and enlightenment. In moments of supreme exaltation, a mystical ecstasy may obliterate personality, but even in Emerson such moments are quite rare. The self is most often absorbed in society, and the central experiences for Emerson, as for Winthrop, are not mystical but communal. Emerson's journal, as a number of readers have pointed out, is more than anything else an engrossing record of Emerson's involvement with his times. The fondness with which he himself recalled the social and intellectual "community" comprising his brothers and his Aunt Mary is an early indication of this dimension to his thought.[36] In *Nature* one of the chief powers of "the advancing spirit," of the perfectly liberated soul, is its capacity to draw about it "beautiful faces, warm hearts, wise discourse, and heroic acts" (49). Emerson is not secretly lamenting his own messianic failures here, so much as he is evoking in a fresh context his own affectionate portrayals of life in the "poor but educated family," and foretelling the nurturing concern for "wide neighborhoods of men" that he will express later in the essay "Compensation."

Only men who are "imbruted" by nature are selfish. The healthy spirit is "not hot and passionate at the appearance of what it calls its own good or bad fortune" (39) – just as in "A Modell of Christian Charity" the ideal citizen regards the affairs of others with more interest and care than she devotes to the affairs of the self. But neither is the healthy spirit detached from the worldly struggle. In a curious but really quite typical sentence from *Nature* Emerson sternly observes that "a man is fed, not that he may be fed, but that he may work" (13). This observation is not the solace to exploitative, capitalistic management that it might seem to be. Emerson is taking pleasure in man as a participant in what he thought of as the social exaltation of labor. Even the speculative and studious American Scholar is a worker and a joiner: "The world, – this shadow of the soul, or *other me,* lies wide around. . . .I run eagerly into this resounding tumult, I grasp the hands of those next to me, and take my place in the ring to suffer and to work, taught by an instinct, that so shall the dumb abyss be vocal with speech" (60). To Winthrop the ring of suffering and of work led to the unity of spirit in the bond of peace. To Emerson it leads, initially at least, in the opposite direction: to the formation of individual character, the cultivation of the great soul. "Character is higher than intellect," he proclaims; "thinking is the function. Living is the functionary. The stream retreats to its source. A great soul will be strong to live, as well as strong to think" (62).

But one dimension of Emerson's faith in the unity of life is his conviction that the great soul is neither singular nor isolated. Such greatness, like genius, is "the sound estate of every man" (57), and great actions have the effect of cementing together the human community by instructing us "that the universe is the property of every individual in it" (16). Even the exhilarating individualism of "Self-Reliance" is finally founded upon selflessness. The attribute of self-reliance is, in fact, the peculiar, paradoxical reward of complete triumph in Winthrop's war with the self:

> For, the sense of being which in calm hours rises we know not how, in the soul, is not diverse from things, from space, from light, from time, from man, but one with them, and proceeds obviously from the same source whence their life and being also proceed. We first share the life by which things exist, and afterwards see them as appearances in nature, and forget that we have shared their cause. Here is the fountain of action and of thought. Here are the lungs of that inspiration which giveth man wisdom, and which cannot be denied without impiety and atheism. We lie in the lap of immense intelligence, which makes us receivers of

its truth and organs of its activity. When we discern justice, when we discern truth, we do nothing of ourselves, but allow a passage to its beams. (269)

The soul at its finest moments, in other words, discerning justice and truth, is cradled in the lap of a suggestively maternal "intelligence"; our independence is the result of a forgetfulness as natural as a child's tendency to forget the degree of dependence that ties it to its parent and at the same time as momentous as the forgetfulness that Winthrop feared might give rise to "impiety and atheism" in Massachusetts Bay. Familial, communal, and theological conditions form a single fabric of meaning for Emerson, as for Winthrop, in which the aspirations of the "self" are both solicited and contained. Emerson continues with typical vigor both to exalt and to discount the powers of individual man. Willful actions and individual opinions, Emerson asserts, are merely notional or "roving." Impersonal perception, however, is "as much a fact as the sun," and though it is "fatal," rather than individual in origin, Emerson insists that it may still be "my perception," that, in time, alters the vision of all mankind.

Like Anne Bradstreet's poetic persona in "The Arthur to Her Book," the self is both powerful and powerless, in Emerson's formulation – both central and peripheral. The last two sentences in "Self-Reliance," heading as they do in different directions, capture this bewildering fusion of attributes so clearly and so gracefully that they seldom cause the kind of confusion in readers that they ought to cause: "Nothing can bring you peace but yourself. Nothing can bring you peace but the triumph of principles" (282). The sentence structure encourages us to accept as nearly equivalent two statements that ascribe the origins of peace to quite different sources: the first, the inherently isolating privacy of the self; the second, the impersonal and integrative sphere of common principle. Emerson is proverbially comfortable with contradiction, however, only because he is convinced that it does not exist. Self and principle, individual and community, are expressions of the same tendency. Their differences "are lost sight of at a little distance, at a little height of thought" (266). There is, indeed, a very great difference between Emerson's Olympian confidence in unity and Winthrop's anxious exhortation to his fellow immigrants, but it derives chiefly from the fact that Winthrop must convince his colleagues to live in hard fact what Emerson is free to celebrate in the insulated world of belief.

4

HAWTHORNE'S MARRIAGES

Nathaniel Hawthorne is the first of the writers we have been examining to have had direct access to John Winthrop's text of "A Modell of Christian Charity." Two years after the appearance of Emerson's *Nature,* in 1838, the Massachusetts Historical Society printed Winthrop's speech in its *Collections* from an eighteenth-century manuscript copy held by the New York Historical Society.[1] It is hardly likely that Hawthorne, with his well-documented commitment to research in colonial history as the groundwork of his writing, would have overlooked the appearance of so pivotal a work by a figure in whom he had displayed his own artistic interest as early as 1830.[2] By 1838, however, Hawthorne had already established the importance he placed upon the domestic images that Winthrop had drawn upon as the model for communal life in 1630. A careful reading of Winthrop's text may well have confirmed that importance and contributed to Hawthorne's decision to place key events in *The Scarlet Letter* on the night of Winthrop's death and to unite in Hester Prynne the distinct dramatic powers that Winthrop found readily available in the typological significance of Eve. But "A Modell of Christian Charity" is clearly more an impetus than an influence on Hawthorne's artistic course. As such it can help clarify both his relations with his contemporaries and the repeated concerns of his fiction.

Hawthorne's exploitation of the themes touched upon in Winthrop's address to the *Arbella* emigrants is far more pervasive and wide-ranging than that of his Concord neighbors. In Emerson the images of gender and marriage are always secondary to the great task of self-culture, and although *Nature* suggestively echoes "A Modell of Christian Charity," it is equally clear that Emerson's most intense interest continues to reside in the figure of the selfless self that takes so many forms in his essays: the poet, the scholar, the preacher, the self-reliant man. Thoreau establishes a model household at Walden, and presents an example of domestic charity there that is sensitive to the extraordinary range that Winthrop had associated with that virtue, but there is no precise equivalent in Thoreau's work for the pivotal emblems of marriage and of the family that shape Winthrop's ideal.

With Hawthorne, the case is quite different. The central subject of his fiction, from the beginning, is an unusually complex treatment of marriage. Marriage is a property of language in Hawthorne, a metaphor for the knitting together of apparently opposed modes of speech and thought as well as a social and romantic vow between characters. It is the guiding image behind the often cryptic ways in which Hawthorne described his artistic process, and its fragility both as an artistic method and as a human bond reflects quite closely Winthrop's understanding of the imperiled life of the founders of Massachusetts Bay.[3]

Hawthorne's marriages are very seldom the stable models of Christian charity that Winthrop sought to invoke, but his stories consistently respond to the appeal of such a model, reaching out from the tainted and sometimes disastrous unions of husband and wife at their centers toward a wider perception of marriage that strives to reconstitute a human family in spite of human failures. The stark competition between life and death that Hawthorne could present with such allegorical clarity often seems fatalistically resolved, in his work, in favor of death. When a sketch like "The Wives of the Dead" or *The House of the Seven Gables* draws toward a sentimentally affirmative conclusion, we have come to see it not simply as an aesthetic lapse but as an uncharacteristic divergence from Hawthorne's otherwise gloomily ironic temper.[4] Such resolutions are, it is true, false notes but only by degree not by nature. Hawthorne's imagination, much like his life, begins in loneliness and moves toward a vision of community that is represented, even in its failures, by the promises of marriage.

The extraordinary series of journal entries in which Hawthorne records the final illness and death of his mother capture this interplay between human loneliness and the human family.[5] Nina Baym and Gloria Erlich have singled these entries out for critical attention both because of their pivotal location in Hawthorne's career – he was on the point of beginning *The Scarlet Letter* – and because of the light that they shed on his character.[6] In his journal Hawthorne describes the contest between "coldness" and "overpowering emotion" that unexpectedly reduces him to tears at his mother's bedside, but he notes as well the contrast between the hushed and somber atmosphere in the curtained sickroom and the "shouts, laughter, and cries" of his children coming up "into the chamber from the open air." Over the duration of his mother's illness, Hawthorne's wife, Sophia, and his sisters were the nurses at Mrs.

Hawthorne's bedside. Hawthorne himself took care of his children, Julian and Una, recording in detail in his journal the games they played and the innocent pleasure they derived from taking turns at pretending to be their dying grandmother. As he watched his daughter at one point from the sickroom window, Hawthorne thought that Una resembled "life itself," while turning to his mother he seemed to see "the whole of human existence at once, standing in the dusty midst of it."

Hawthorne's treatment of his own life in this entry is strikingly in harmony with the treatment he accorded life in his fiction. In one of his earliest major tales, "The May-Pole of Merry Mount," Hawthorne had described the conflict between Merry Mount's revelers and their Puritan neighbors as a war between jollity and gloom that neither side completely wins. The central characters in that tale, a young couple named Edith and Edgar, whose marriage is about to be celebrated, experience at a crucial moment a sudden sense of mystery in the heart, an awareness of "earth's doom of care and sorrow, and troubled joy" that sets them apart from their fellow worshipers of the maypole. Their discovery – analogous to Hawthorne's own, later perception – of "the whole of human existence at once" prepares them to celebrate a truer marriage than they might have been able to attain among their former, pleasure-seeking companions. John Endicott, the stern Puritan who puts an end to the pagan rituals of Merry Mount, recognizes their new spiritual position and sanctifies their union with a wreath of roses lifted "from the ruin of the May-Pole."[7]

Despite their comparative youth, Edith and Edgar's sudden vision of themselves in the context of the whole of life quite closely matches Hawthorne's vision in his mother's sickroom. But there are more important features of the tale that help make it representative of the treatment of domestic experience as a whole in Hawthorne's career. Many readers, for example, have called attention to the highly charged sexual atmosphere about the maypole and related that sense of conflict between repressed and indulged appetites to other notable Hawthorne protagonists – Arthur Dimmesdale, Goodman Brown, the Reverend Hooper, Reuben Bourne, Owen Warland, Giovanni Guasconti, Hester Prynne – as well as to Hawthorne himself. These readings are too well known to require review and too suggestive and well supported to be usefully challenged. But it is critical to keep in mind the deliberateness with which Hawthorne addressed his sexual themes, the care with which he made them both explicit and metaphysically (as well as physically) significant.[8]

This deliberateness has a great deal to do with a property of Hawthorne's style that surfaces repeatedly in his fiction, not always – although most dramatically – in connection with his sexual themes. There often seem to be at least two sorts of discourse in Hawthorne, one furtively revealing and the other genteelly euphemistic, even evasive. In the opening paragraph of "The May-Pole of Merry Mount," for example, Hawthorne describes the seasons in such a way as to suggest that the revelers – predominantly men, celebrating a fantasy of male sexual indulgence – have a hidden fear of fully mature female sexuality: "Midsummer eve had come," Hawthorne innocently observes, "bringing deep verdure to the forest, and roses in her lap, of a more vivid hue than the tender buds of Spring. But May, or her mirthful spirit, dwelt all year round at Merry Mount, sporting with the summer months, and reveling with Autumn, and basking in the glow of Winter's fireside" (360). Nothing is really concealed in such language. Midsummer's luxuriant roses are openly erotic and fruitful, whereas the revelers' "tender-budded" May time is the first sign of their elaborate attempts to deny the wholeness of life that Edith and Edgar ultimately recognize and accept.[9]

The first embodiment of this wholeness in the tale itself, then, is in the kind of reading it requires. The messages in the landscape contain reminders of time and of the progress of sexuality that both of the polarized communities of Hawthorne's story would do well to heed. The revelers' maypole and the Puritan whipping post are alike in their refusal to deal with a complexity that Hawthorne is able to capture in language that both restrains and incites its sexual meaning. We are no more meant to reduce such passages to their sexual content alone (as the revelers themselves might willingly do) than we are encouraged, or allowed, to deny that content in favor of its meticulously polite presentation. "The May-Pole of Merry Mount" requires from the reader a capacity to see sexuality as part of, or as emblematic of, all human growth, including death. This is a kind of imaginative marriage that Hawthorne himself enacts in his suggestive language and that Edith and Edgar commit themselves to at the story's end.

This is, moreover, a vision of marriage that is peculiarly entrusted to women, much as Winthrop entrusted his familial model of community to Eve. Edith is the first to announce to Edgar a sense of the emptiness of Merry Mount's revelry, and it remains largely "Edith's mystery" in the story. Among Hawthorne's fictional marriages this one is (in anticipation at least) singularly successful, but it is so largely because of the degree of mutual authority it assigns to each partner. Edgar's resistance to Endicott's perceived threat is melodramatic and a bit blustery: "Were the means at hand," he grandly asserts to his Puritan antagonist, "I would resist to the death." Hawthorne still identifies Edgar at this moment as the "May Lord" – a title that calls attention to his particular complicity in the revels and to the deficiencies of his chivalric ardor. Edith's resistance to Endicott's question about the couples' fate ("What sayest thou, maid?") is much simpler and, like Eve's reply to her divine inquisitor in

Genesis, more personal: "'Be it death,' said Edith, 'and lay it all on me.'"
In the end they approach their "difficult path" in life "supporting each
other" rather than supplanting one another in endless contests for authority.

No other marriage in Hawthorne's short fiction carries with it quite
the prospective promise of this one. Annie Hovenden and Robert Dan-
forth in "The Artist of the Beautiful" come closest to Edith's and Edgar's
success, but Hawthorne exposes too many of Robert's limitations and too
little of Annie's sensitivity to permit them to match the purer and simpler
balance of "The May-Pole of Merry Mount." Even so, Edith and Edgar
are not so completely "one flesh" as their euphonious names imply.
Their marriage is complicated by differences in character that are reflected in Edgar's initial puzzlement at Edith's sadness and that time is not
likely to eradicate. In this way too they suggest the sense of the wholeness
of human existence that Hawthorne sought to evoke.

Most of his fiction sets out either to assemble or to reassemble marriages and families very few of which arrive at any state of completeness
or stability. The most extreme instance of such failure is perhaps "Ethan
Brand," a story whose subtitle, "An Abortive Romance," calls attention
not so much to its textual condition as to its familial and sexual plight.[10]
Though the story itself does take place in a family circle of sorts, the only
female presence at the grotesque "hearth" of Bartram the lime burner is
"the tender light of the half-full moon" that tries to compete with the
fierce glow of the kiln. Ethan Brand himself made a victim out of his
only potential partner in life, Esther, the daughter of old Humphrey,
whom Brand "had made the subject of a psychological experiment,
and . . . perhaps annihilated her soul, in the process" (1060). Like Edith
and Edgar in "The May-Pole," Ethan and Esther are named in such a way
as to imply a bond between them that precedes the traditional joint
surname of marriage and that aggravates the calculated, inhumane intimacy that Brand established between them. Their relationship suggests
the same sort of abuse of science and marriage that serves as the basis of
"The Birth-mark," but with an intensified destructive power that hints at
the fundamental prohibition that Brand may have transgressed. His relationship with Esther was not, Hawthorne suggests, purely experimental
or simply sexual but – as its drastic repercussions imply – potentially
incestuous, and the only sort of intimacy of which he remains capable
now is the equally incestuous intimacy of sins that circulate between him
and the people he meets as if the sins themselves "were all of one family . . . and carried dark greetings from one to the other."[11]

Grim as these hints are, Ethan Brand has not dehumanized himself so
much as he has aborted his sexual and nuptial powers. He is still very
much a candidate for pity, as Joe, the lime burner's son, clearly demon-

strates and as Hawthorne himself indicates in his employment of the sentimental convention of the heart's "temple" to describe Brand's psychic state. But Ethan Brand represents so disturbing a challenge to the familial basis of Hawthorne's art – as Jaffrey Pyncheon, perhaps, does only a year or two later in Hawthorne's career – that even the formidable powers of sentimental piety cannot completely rescue him from his lost condition. Brand's midnight recollections before his suicide introduce the redemptive image of the heart's temple and provide Hawthorne with the opportunity to pronounce his judgment on Brand's character.

During that midnight vigil the narrator examines Brand's terrible history. At first his investigations into sin had been motivated by "tenderness," "love and sympathy," and "pity for human guilt and woe." The heart of man had seemed to him a "temple originally divine, and, however desecrated, still to be held sacred by a brother" (1064). But with his great intellectual development, Brand's heart "had withered, – had contracted, – had hardened, – had perished! It had ceased to partake of the universal throb. . . . He was no longer a brother-man, opening the chambers or the dungeons of our common nature by the key of holy sympathy, which gave him a right to share in all its secrets" (1064). The narrator's dramatic urgency in this retelling underscores the fact that it is really two kinds of desecration that are at issue in Brand's past: the violation of "our common nature" by a dispassionate investigator, and the violation of the role of a "brother-man," a peculiar coinage that unites familial and sexual status in a way that is both appealingly idealistic and disturbing.

Such a brother man would have "rights" of intimacy that seem consistent only with those of a spouse or a parent, and it is Brand's failure to achieve this extraordinary familial ideal that prompts both the narrator's anguish and his horror at the travesty of familial closeness that has taken its place. The materials of a genuine intimacy were present in Brand at the beginning of his quest and to some degree are present until his death. All around Bartram's lime kiln are the fragments of marble that serve both as food for the kiln and as reminders of the shattered domestic temple that is Hawthorne's subject. But such fragments are the materials of a temple as well as its remains, and Brand's heart, corrupted though it is, proves nevertheless to have been made of marble and reduces in Bartram's kiln to what the gruffly colloquial lime burner acknowledges as "special good lime."

One has to reason backward from Brand's destruction to recover this full sense of his promise, but the effect of such a recovery is to cast some doubt upon the status of the "Unpardonable Sin" in Hawthorne's story. The narrator of "Ethan Brand" indicates rather equivocally that Brand himself had "produced" the Unpardonable Sin, but producing it is quite different from "discovering" it, as Brand had originally set out to do. If the subtext of the story hints at the genuinely repellent crime of incest, its overt dramatic structure suggests that one can produce such a monstrosity as the Unpardonable Sin only by believing in it and by sacrificing all of the domestic instincts of sympathy and pity that are the foundations of the act of pardon. The context in which Ethan Brand's suicide is set indicates that the forces of pardoning are largely undisturbed by his Promethean rhetoric and his horrible death. He seems even to have underestimated the state of his own heart when he proclaims bitterly, "What more have I to seek? what more to achieve? . . . My task is done and well done!" Brand has been resoundingly unsuccessful at the central domestic task of Hawthorne's art, but he does not fall outside of its borders.

Indeed, Hawthorne may well intend his readers to detect in "Ethan Brand" an indirect allusion to the same circumstances in Deuteronomy from which Winthrop drew his closing quotation in "A Modell of Christian Charity." The mysterious figure of the wandering Jew with whom Brand shares some dark knowledge is, in part, an element of Gothic atmosphere in the story, but the Jew's presence among the marble fragments scattered about the limekiln suggests at the same time a reference to the shattered tables of the Law, which Moses broke upon discovering that the Jews had reverted to idolatry during his absence on Mt. Sinai (Exodus 32). The festive atmosphere among Brand's former neighbors gathered about the kiln underscores the parallel – the idolatrous children of Israel ate, drank, and played about their golden calf – and the angry words of the Lord to Moses anticipate Brand's actual fate at the end of Hawthorne's story: "I have seen this people, and behold, it is a stiff-necked people; now therefore let me alone, that my wrath may burn hot against them and I may consume them" (Exodus 32:9). Brand's own appetite for isolation and for fire echoes this language; he is more nearly a grim parody of Jehovah than of Prometheus.

What Hawthorne's "abortive" romance in fact aborts, however, is Moses' first intercession with God on behalf of Israel, which follows immediately upon the judgment of the Lord quoted above and which induces the Lord to repent of his fiery anger. This pattern of intercession and pardon is what Deuteronomy as a whole enacts when Moses restores the broken tables, in effect reconstructing the shattered temple that Hawthorne's story allows to remain in fragments. In this sense "Ethan Brand" recapitulates only half of its source – the judgmental rather than the pardoning half – and it is this truncation that leaves Brand in the midst of a spiritual gloom from which the reader is free to appeal. Hawthorne's strategy is not to obliterate his literary debts but to revivify them.

The instinct to pardon – the durability of charity even in the face of

formidable odds – is closely interwoven with marriage and family in
Hawthorne's work, just as it is in Winthrop's "A Modell of Christian
Charity." "The May-Pole of Merry Mount" once again is paradigmatic in
Hawthorne's career in the way that it unites both a marriage ceremony
and an act of judgment that is conditioned by charity. After Edith and
Edgar, the third critical figure in the story is John Endicott, "the Puritan
of Puritans," who makes such an unpromising entry into the tale with his
grim frowns and his harsh sentences. Prompted by his enthusiastic "Ancient" Peter Palfrey, Endicott seems to relish the prospect of many whip-
pings, much branding, and cropping of ears as penalties for the maypole
revelers. He even outdoes Palfrey in his disposition of the revelers' dancing bear, which Palfrey (rather oddly) seems prepared to whip until
Endicott orders a swifter, more brutal punishment: "'Shoot him through
the head!' said the energetic Puritan. 'I suspect witchcraft in the beast'"
(369).

In such a context an adjective like "energetic" in itself represents a
marriage of irony and bemusement. "The May-Pole of Merry Mount" as
a whole is conditioned not by the desperate jollity of the revelers or the
gloom of the Puritans but by the much gentler sense of humor in the
narrator, who mocks his own much too simple (and inaccurate) account
of "these authentic passages from history" and playfully chides his own
paragon of authority, Endicott, for mistaking the identity of the revelers'
priestly leader. These features of the tale are, of course, clues that might
send us off into a study of Hawthorne's sources, but they are also signs of
a temperament that is more sensibly balanced between the extremes of
debauched frivolity and unrelieved seriousness than either Endicott or his
antagonists at the maypole. The narrator's tone, in other words, is something like an equivalent for Edith and Edgar's position between communities and represents a marriage of its own between the elements of joy
and sorrow in life.

Hawthorne is even able to derive a measure of amusement from the
apparently righteous violence of Endicott.[12] The punishments that Endicott envisions and pronounces are not only caricatures of casual brutality, they are also distinctly out of harmony with the only sentence that
he executes "forthwith": the cutting of Edgar's hair. It is not Endicott
who is being lighthearted here. Seventeenth-century punishments were,
by modern standards, brutal, and all the extreme penalties that Endicott
seems to envision for the chastened revelers were inflicted in colonial
Massachusetts, though not with the offhanded regularity that Hawthorne's zealot suggests. The bemused, parental charity reflected in the
"sentence" to have one's hair cut is Hawthorne's proposed basis of reconciliation between sternness and levity, a basis that Hawthorne himself had
already explored in his account of the revelers' history and motives. As

Michael Colacurcio quite rightly reminds us, these mummers, rope dancers, and mountebanks are self-deceived, in Hawthorne's view, and ultimately self-destructive.[13] Endicott's prophetic fervor is not necessary for a proper assessment of their behavior and for a fitting punishment. But more important still is Hawthorne's own ability to pity. In the process of exposing the revelers' shallowness, he does not neglect their humanity:

> The men of whom we speak, after losing the heart's fresh gaiety, imagined a wild philosophy of pleasure, and came hither to act out their latest day-dream. . . . Light had their footsteps been on land, and as lightly they came across the sea. Many had been maddened by their previous troubles into a gay despair; others were as madly gay in the flush of youth, like the May Lord and his Lady; but whatever might be the quality of their mirth, old and young were gay at Merry Mount. The young deemed themselves happy. The elder spirits, if they knew that mirth was but the counterfeit of happiness, yet followed the false shadow wilfully, because at least her garments glittered brightest. Sworn triflers of a lifetime, they would not venture among the sober truths of life, not even to be truly blest. (364)

On strictly moral grounds it would seem that Hawthorne and Endicott have a good deal in common. But Hawthorne's moral vision clearly expresses itself in terms that John Winthrop rather than John Endicott would recognize.

A measure of Hawthorne's power of pardoning, in other words, is historical as well as moral. From the point of view of Hawthorne and his contemporaries, only one of the communities represented in "The May-Pole of Merry Mount" really mattered. The Puritans were the founders of New England and were in many respects the shapers of culture still in nineteenth-century America. Thomas Morton's revelers were more or less incidental to New England's history. To some degree, then, Hawthorne is choosing not between jollity and gloom in his text but between two versions of Puritanism: one Winthrop's and one Endicott's, the pitying father or the punishing zealot. This aspect of choice accounts for the story's two Endicotts – the executioner and the parent – and may also have something to do with Hawthorne's decision to modify history by placing Endicott in a role that Miles Standish (Morton's less than formidable "Captain Shrimp") had actually filled with much less militancy than Hawthorne's Endicott initially seems capable of.[14]

In "The Custom-House" Hawthorne playfully (and a bit ruefully) imagines the Past, in the form of his dignified ancestors, sitting in judgment upon him and pronouncing him a trifler for choosing to devote his life to writing fiction. But the characteristic form of Hawthorne's work involved the Present sitting in judgment on the Past and bringing in a surprisingly forgiving verdict much as Hawthorne's narrator does in "The May-Pole of Merry Mount." It is not difficult to think of exceptions to this exercise of historical charity in Hawthorne; Judge Pyncheon and his forebears in *The House of the Seven Gables* or the caricature of Cotton Mather in "Alice Doane's Appeal" seem prominently unpardonable ancestors. But these are exceptions to the ordinary operation of Hawthorne's understanding, and the figure of Cotton Mather, of course, is a deliberate distortion of history in an attempt on the part of a boyishly vain narrator to awaken the historical sympathies of his attractive listeners: "But here my companions seized an arm on each side; their nerves were trembling; and sweeter victory still, I had reached the seldom trodden places of their hearts, and found the well-spring of their tears. And now the past had done all it could" (216). The past serves, in Hawthorne, to awaken present humanity as well as to burden it. That, in fact, is the case in "The Custom-House" itself, and such a pattern of forgiveness – or, if that is too strong a word, of sympathy – is responsible for much of Hawthorne's power.

"The Birth-mark" draws together many of these threads in a particularly helpful way. Like "The May-Pole of Merry Mount" it too revolves around a marriage that is inextricably bound up with acts of judgment and charity. Aylmer's displacement of his sexual longings and responsibilities – his retreat into a grotesquely testicular laboratory full of tubes, retorts, and crucibles where he can distill his precious fluids – would seem a classic instance of the marriage of two discourses in Hawthorne that we noted earlier.[15] The body and spirit are bound up together in Hawthorne's prose but not so tightly that one cannot discern the presence of both in an uneasy alliance that is the mark of what Hawthorne calls "the composite man." Rather than dwell on Aylmer's marital failures, however, or on Georgiana's equally irritating pliability, it is important to recognize the point in the story where both Aylmer's "science" and Georgiana's powers of sympathy express themselves most constructively. This moment occurs when Georgiana is reading in Aylmer's scientific journal what is, in effect, the record of his past and discovering his limitations:

> But, to Georgiana, the most engrossing volume was a large folio from her husband's own hand, in which he had recorded every experiment of his scientific career, with its original aim, the methods adopted for its development, and its final success or failure, with the circumstances to which either event was attributable. The book, in truth, was both the history and emblem

of his ardent, ambitious, imaginative, yet practical and la-
borious, life. He handled physical details, as if there were nothing beyond them; yet spiritualized them all, and redeemed himself from materialism, by this strong and eager aspiration
towards the infinite. In his grasp, the veriest clod of earth assumed a soul. Georgiana, as she read, reverenced Aylmer, and
loved him more profoundly than ever, but with a less entire
dependence on his judgment than heretofore. Much as he had
accomplished, she could not but observe that his most splendid
successes were almost invariably failures, if compared with the
ideal at which he aimed. His brightest diamonds were the merest
pebbles, and felt to be so by himself, in comparison with the
inestimable gems which lay hidden beyond his reach. The volume, rich with achievements that had won renown for its author,
was yet as melancholy a record as ever mortal hand had penned.
It was the sad confession, and continual exemplification, of the
short-comings of the composite man – the spirit burthened with
clay and working in matter – and of the despair that assails the
higher nature, at finding itself so miserably thwarted by the
earthly part. Perhaps every man of genius, in whatever sphere,
might recognize the image of his own experience in Aylmer's
journal.

So deeply did these reflections affect Georgiana, that she laid
her face upon the open volume, and burst into tears. (775)

This passage is a good example of what Edgar Dryden has called the
motif of the sphere in Hawthorne's fiction, a means that Hawthorne
consistently employs to emphasize the intermingling of human privacy
with human susceptibility to the presence and experience of others.
Georgiana's response to these intimate records of the "sphere" in which
Aylmer moves reflects the poise between enchantment and disillusion
that Dryden identifies as critical to Hawthorne's art.[16] But this depiction
of reading also represents an extension of Hawthorne's historical sympathies into a domestic setting. Georgiana's act of research is as much a filial
gesture as it is connubial. With very little adjustment her posture of pity,
mixed with reverence and distrust, could stand for Hawthorne's own
posture as he "reads" the history of his Puritan predecessors whose aspirations toward the infinite had also been eager, and had also fallen short.
Hawthorne's fiction quite often "ends" in the middle – that is, his imagination delves most deeply into character and finds the most effective
means of recording its insights in the middle of his tales rather than at
their conclusions, where his morals can often seem, as Frederick Crews
has memorably put it, impertinent.[17] At this middle point in "The Birth-

mark" Georgiana has an intelligence and authority that her pious, death-bed pronouncement lacks, while Aylmer's recorded experiments seem much grander than do his pathetic efforts, through "penetrating" fra-grances and crystal goblets of "colorless" liquor, to remove his wife's birthmark.

The story, of course, goes on to describe Georgiana's lofty submission to Aylmer's experiments and her equally lofty death, but the failure and forgiveness of the conclusion are melodramatically heightened to the point where neither main character seems wholly sympathetic. The story had reached its moment of balance as Georgiana studied Aylmer's jour-nal. Missing that moment produces an aesthetic as well as a marital collapse. This view of the formal meaning of "The Birth-mark" may be giving Hawthorne too much credit for duplicating in his prose the mar-ried poise that his characters first approach and then fail to achieve, but it does suggest the extent to which marriage is both a subject and a method in his tales. Joel Porte has observed that one of the distinguishing marks of the genre of the "romance" in America is the degree to which it makes its form its subject.[18] Porte's observation applies especially well to Hawthorne precisely because in the latter's eyes "form" was never pri-marily a technical issue so much as a psychological or a moral one. In Hawthorne both the subject and the method involve a wedding of ex-tremes, a vision of the compositeness of life that art shares because it is a product of life.[19] Characters (or stories) can fail to attain this vision and still leave the vision itself intact. In the most dramatic, and problematic, of Hawthorne's failed marriages, that is precisely what occurs.

"Roger Malvin's Burial," though among the earliest of Hawthorne's surviving stories, is one of his most disturbing and most complicated. The rich critical literature it has generated is evidence of this complexity, and I will not pretend to solve, or even to address, all the story's prob-lems here.[20] To some degree, however, placing "Roger Malvin's Burial" in the context of Hawthorne's marriages, and in the context of Win-throp's tradition of the communal marriage, helps to illuminate the sto-ry's meaning. The central marriage around which the tale is built, of course, is that of Reuben Bourne and Dorcas Malvin, but there are at least two additional "marriages" that add to the familial richness knitting the events together. At the outset, as most readers have observed, Roger Malvin and Reuben Bourne most closely resemble a father and a son. The debate in which they almost immediately engage one another, however, involves what is, in effect, both a violation of a familiar portion of the marriage vows ("Until death do us part") and a kind of courtship. Hawthorne calls attention to this range of comparisons when he ac-knowledges that Reuben "might worthily demand the hand of the fair maiden, to whose father he had been 'faithful unto death'" (97). In the

aftermath of "Lovell's Fight" Roger Malvin tries through a series of
fictions and tactics to convince Reuben to leave him behind in the forest
to die of his wounds alone rather than wait with him and perhaps imperil
his own chances for life. Reuben's resistance to this proposal is as complete as anyone could wish, but in the end he yields to Roger Malvin's
"generous art" and agrees to go.

At this point in the characters' mutual predicament not even self-
deception seems necessary. Malvin abandons the hunter's and warrior's
posture of romantic indifference to burial that he had adopted earlier – he
is not a "hunter" in any case, but an unusually prosperous farmer – and
Reuben abandons the belief that he might meet a rescue party in time to
save Malvin. Neither the older nor the younger man has any illusions
about the starkness of their circumstances, but it has required some
exertion of the imagination to be able to bear that starkness. In the end
Malvin requires one illusion more, however: that Reuben will "return to
this wild rock, and lay my bones in the grave, and say a prayer over
them" (94). After the required vow, Malvin says, perhaps significantly,
"It is enough," and the story's events are effectively set in motion.

It seems at least a possibility that Malvin's last words to Reuben (with
all their biblical finality) are meant to characterize the "vow" as only a
further tactic, a way of reassuring both parties rather than of binding one
of them. The making of the vow alone may be "enough"; now each man
can face his future. Even if that is not the case, Hawthorne clearly means
us to see in both Reuben and Roger a contest, and a marriage, between
the instincts of "generous art" and the "weakness of mortality" (94).
Roger Malvin is not so free of fear and superstition as his representations
to Reuben would lead one to believe, and Reuben's willingness to ac-
quiesce in Malvin's fictions is aided "by the hidden strength of many
another motive" besides hope or common sense (93). Neither man can
completely sacrifice or completely indulge the demands of the self, and
this shared nature unites them even more firmly than Reuben's vow.

The strength and complexity of this first union in the story have a
direct effect on the human bonds that spring from it, each one characterized by the same mixture of generosity and weakness, selflessness and
the self. Reuben's own marriage to Dorcas becomes all the more assured
by Dorcas's imaginative generosity in retelling the tale of Reuben's loyalty to her father. When Dorcas in turn is supplanted in her husband's
affections by Cyrus, it is a sign both of the "deep and silent strength" of
the father's love and of the father's paradoxical selfishness: "He could no
longer love deeply, except where he saw, or imagined, some reflection or
likeness of his own mind. In Cyrus he recognized what he had himself
been in other days; and at intervals he seemed to partake of the boy's
spirit, and to be revived with a fresh and happy life" (100). Indeed, in

Cyrus's presence alone, Reuben is able to spend two autumn months in the wilderness, clearing land for their new homestead, apparently without feeling any of the mysterious magnetism that later draws him to the site of Malvin's body.

When the three critical marriages of the story begin to converge, Hawthorne suddenly enlarges the scope of his tale by invoking a fourth, wholly fictive marriage that fuses personal and national destinies, presenting itself partly as a celebration and partly as a lament that seems to spring both out of the consciousness of Cyrus and out of the narrator:

> Reuben, a moody man, and misanthropic because unhappy, strode onward, with his usual stern brow and downcast eye, feeling few regrets, and disdaining to acknowledge any. Dorcas, while she wept abundantly over the broken ties by which her simple and affectionate nature had bound itself to everything, felt that the inhabitants of her inmost heart moved on with her, and that all else would be supplied wherever she might go. And the boy dashed one tear-drop from his eye, and thought of the adventurous pleasures of the untrodden forest. Oh! who, in the enthusiasm of a day-dream, has not wished that he were a wanderer in a world of summer wilderness, with one fair and gentle being hanging lightly on his arm? In youth, his free and exulting step would know no barrier but the rolling ocean or the snow-topt mountains; calmer manhood would choose a home, where Nature had strewn a double wealth, in the vale of some transparent stream; and when hoary age, after long, long years of that pure life, stole on and found him there, it would find him the father of a race, the patriarch of a people, the founder of a mighty nation yet to be. When death, like the sweet sleep which we welcome after a day of happiness, came over him, his far descendants would mourn over the venerated dust. Enveloped by tradition in mysterious attributes, the men of future generations would call him godlike; and remote posterity would see him standing dimly glorious, far up the valley of a hundred centuries!
> (100)

This is a biblically grandiose version of the fiction of domestic tranquility with which Roger Malvin had sought to entice Reuben into life at the beginning of the story, and its reappearance at this crucial moment underscores how unsatisfactory a vision it is. Nothing about the circumstances of Reuben Bourne and his actual family corresponds to this dream of frontier life. Cyrus, the only "youth" left in the tale, has no "gentle being" hanging lightly on his arm, and the "adventurous pleasures" of the wilderness to which he actually looks forward seem less noble and more self-centered than the vision of free, exulting promise that the narrator celebrates. Reuben's actual manhood is moody and downcast rather than "calmer," and Dorcas's steady and appealing mixture of regret and faith is completely unaccounted for in the patriarchal future that the narrator envisions, in which women are reduced first to the status of a genteel euphemism ("fair and gentle being") and finally obliterated by generations of men venerating the dust of their fathers.[21]

Imperfect as they are the Bournes are preferable to this platitudinous future, much as the mortal weakness of Roger Malvin and Reuben Bourne at the beginning of the story proved to be the humanizing ingredient that gave Malvin's equally implausible fictions their generosity. A marriage between mortal weakness and generous art is what the story itself strives to preside over, and to this end Hawthorne arranges the fateful repetitions of his conclusion. The patterns of the tale circle around on one another, as many readers have observed, with a menacing regularity: Once more it is a day in early May, Reuben Bourne is once more "waking" from a dream of battle, once more an older man (consciously or unconsciously) is about to exact some comfort from a younger one, while a younger man seems again to have "crept back impelled by a wild and painful curiosity" to gaze earnestly at a "desolate" parent (95). Cyrus's fatal concealment at the story's end echoes Reuben's earlier concealment as he watched Roger Malvin's "fervent prayer," just as the words of that earlier prayer seem to prefigure Reuben's fatal marksmanship as they steal "through the stillness of the woods" from Malvin's lips and penetrate Reuben's heart, "torturing it with an unutterable pang." Reuben's own prayer over his son's body will, in turn, echo Malvin's.

These details underscore the story's horrible fatality, but there is a kind of generosity to them as well, not only in their artful completeness but in their moral purpose. Reuben Bourne's heart is stricken, like the "untrodden places" in the hearts of Hawthorne's listeners in "Alice Doane's Appeal," and his tears gush "like water from a rock" (107). Cyrus and Dorcas maintain a strange complicity in this emotional climax that has the effect of making the three of them seem a harmonious unit for the first time. Dorcas's startling pun ("How is this, Reuben? Have you slain the deer, and fallen asleep over him?") underscores Cyrus's own contented (though subdued) submission to the "mystery" of his father's wayward journey and Dorcas's equally marked contentment in their perplexing turns of fortune. Dorcas's short journey to the place where her son, her husband, and her father are waiting is "charmed" in much the way that Reuben's steps had been guided by memory and by things "long-past" to this portion of wilderness:

> "Cyrus! Cyrus!"
> His coming was still delayed, and she determined, as the re-

port had apparently been very near, to seek for him in person. Her assistance, also, might be necessary in bringing home the venison, which she flattered herself he had obtained. She therefore set forward, directing her steps by the long-past sound, and singing as she went, in order that the boy might be aware of her approach, and run to meet her. From behind the trunk of every tree, and from every hiding place in the thick foliage of the undergrowth, she hoped to discover the countenance of her son, laughing with the sportive mischief that is born of affection. The sun was now beneath the horizon, and the light that came down among the trees was sufficiently dim to create many illusions in her expecting fancy. Several times she seemed indistinctly to see his face gazing out from among the leaves; and once she imagined that he stood beckoning to her, at the base of a craggy rock. Keeping her eyes on this object, however, it proved to be no more than the trunk of an oak, fringed to the very ground with little branches, one of which, thrust out farther than the rest, was shaken by the breeze. Making her way round the foot of the rock, she suddenly found herself close to her husband, who had approached in another direction. Leaning upon the butt of his gun, the muzzle of which rested upon the withered leaves, he was apparently absorbed in the contemplation of some object at his feet. (106)

Hawthorne has gone to great lengths to establish the mixture of forces at work in these closing passages. Perhaps a selfish compulsion is one of those forces, but so are affection, memory, trust, loyalty – the love of Heaven, as Dorcas suggests in her appeal to her absorbed and speechless husband, as well as its judgment. Dorcas and Cyrus have, in some measure, made Reuben's condition their own, and the story's atmosphere of stern isolation – represented in the opening pages by the lonely figure of Roger Malvin, watching death steal "gradually towards him through the forest . . . . from behind a nearer, and yet a nearer tree" – is drawing to a close. "Roger Malvin's Burial" provides a conclusion that is among the more demanding marriages of Hawthorne's fiction precisely because it brings into such sudden and surprising union the forces of life and death.

The troubled marriages of *The Scarlet Letter* are nearly so numerous as to defy description. They appear in the half-reserved, half-intimate posture of Hawthorne himself as he begins "The Custom-House," and scarcely a page or a character thereafter is unmarked by some echo of this central body of familial images: the truculent American eagle with her fierce maternity, the familial kinship of dust with dust that binds Hawthorne to Salem, the extraordinary blend of filial sympathy and contempt

that shapes the portraits of his customhouse colleagues, the paternal influences of Surveyor Pue, the mixture of masculine and feminine traits in
the stout matrons who view Hester's disgrace, the resemblance between
the opening scaffold scene itself – "a separate and insulated event,"
Hawthorne calls it, "to occur but once" in Hester's lifetime – and the
ceremony of marriage.[22]

Hawthorne's celebrated attempt in "The Custom-House" to describe
the conditions necessary for the writing of romance is heavily indebted to
familial imagery. The marriage of the actual and the imaginary that
Hawthorne tries to promote there must take place in a familiar room
filled with "little domestic scenery," objects that reflect a day's activities
and that lend themselves after hours to the spiritualizing light of art:
chairs, a workbasket, the sofa, a child's shoe, a doll "seated in her little
wicker carriage," a hobbyhorse. This atmosphere suggests a close relationship between the apparently disengaged artistry of writing and the
deeply engaged activities of marriage. According to Hawthorne, moon-
beams mingle with the "faint ruddiness" of a coal fire to produce fictive
men and women out of lifeless snow images – that, at least, is the ideal
outcome for the writer of romance. And it resembles quite closely the
sexual mingling that produces actual men and women out of the inti-
macies of human marriage. Hawthorne emphasizes that the task of writing is lonely, but it has as well affinities with conception and birth that are
as conventional as Anne Bradstreet's conceits in "The Author to Her
Book" and, in Hawthorne's treatment, strikingly literal. In this sense, the
sexual act that Hawthorne is sometimes chided for having excluded from
The Scarlet Letter is present in displaced but vivid form in "The Custom-
House."

The customhouse itself has a complex sexual identity both as a spouse
upon whose "mighty arm" the trusting public servant might lean and as
a type of womb that, from time to time "ejects" an officer with an
"unkindly shove . . . to totter along the difficult footpath of life as he
best may" (39). The consequence of this kind of perverse marriage and
reluctant birth is, according to Hawthorne, a loss of all the "manly"
powers of both the retained and ejected officer, but for Hawthorne those
manly powers are motherly powers too. The customhouse gives him
economic security, but he forfeits by working there the ability to preside
at the creative marriage and birth that produce his fiction. These same
sexually entangled images apply as well to Hester's residence in the
Boston jail. That period was a term of "confinement" in several senses,
not simply as a punishment and as the time of Pearl's birth, but also as the
prelude to Hester's rebirth. Like Hawthorne she also had formerly been
able to lean for support upon the "iron arm" of the law "through the
terrible ordeal of her ignominy" (76). Once she is released Hester too

confronts the anxiety of her "first unattended footsteps" into a world in which she too has been curiously desexualized.

The first sign of Winthrop's presence, then, in the events of Hawthorne's novel is not the prophetic meteor that illuminates the sky on the night of his death but Hawthorne's systematic application of the binding imagery of the family throughout his own text. John Wilson is notable in the story, not only for his historic associations with the founding of Massachusetts Bay – he accompanied Winthrop on the *Arbella* – and with the Antinomian controversy, but for the beautiful reply he gives to Roger Chillingworth's leering speculations about Pearl's nature and parentage:

> "A strange child!" remarked old Roger Chillingworth. "It is easy to see the mother's part in her. Would it be beyond a philosopher's research, think ye, gentlemen, to analyze that child's nature, and, from its make and mould, to give a shrewd guess at the father?"
>
> "Nay; it would be sinful, in such a question, to follow the clew of profane philosophy," said Mr. Wilson. "Better to fast and pray upon it; and still better, it may be, to leave the mystery as we find it, unless Providence reveal it of its own accord. Thereby, every good Christian man hath a title to show a father's kindness towards the poor, deserted babe." (112)

Chillingworth's hint is not so improbable as it seems. Hester later suggests Pearl's resemblance to her father when she comments fondly to Dimmesdale during their forest meeting, "But I know whose brow she has!" (195). This sort of speculative study, of course, is far more tender than the scrutiny that Chillingworth implies, which Wilson quickly recognizes as both sinful and inhumane. Wilson, himself like the figure of Endicott in "The May-Pole of Merry Mount," is an embodiment of the two Puritanisms that Hawthorne recognized and contrasted with one another. He willingly steps in for Dimmesdale and harangues Hester with "a discourse on sin, in all its branches" for more than an hour during her exposure on the scaffold. But he is capable as well of this genuinely charitable admonition on Pearl's behalf.

It would be misleading to imply, however, that directness of any sort is a decisive feature of Hawthorne's imagination. Ornamental needlework appeals to him as an emblem of creativity, both in Hester Prynne's case and in his own, precisely because of its capacity to link elements of his art by indirections that are too well hidden to be traced by anyone uninitiated in the mysteries of "sewing." When Hawthorne gives his celebrated account of the difference between the romance and the novel in the preface to *The House of the Seven Gables,* he appeals on romance's behalf to just these domestic mysteries of "fashion and material" in dress, of subtly mingled flavors in accomplished cooking, of literary effects "fairly, finely, and skilfully wrought out," like good embroidery. The image of the labyrinth surfaces repeatedly in *The Scarlet Letter* partly as a means of giving physical scope to this sense of baffling intricacy and partly as a way of multiplying still further the implications of the image of marriage in his text.

On several occasions in *The Scarlet Letter* Hawthorne alludes to the fable of the Minotaur – a story that had intrigued him throughout his career and that he retells, at some length, with great charm, three years after the publication of *The Scarlet Letter* in *The Tanglewood Tales*. The allusions are chiefly to the labyrinthine doubts that beset Hester with regard to Pearl's nature or to the "dark labyrinth" of Hester's own mind as she contemplates suicide (158). Once Hawthorne mentions in passing the Reverend Mr. Blackstone, "that half mythological personage who rides through our early annals, seated on the back of a bull," like the Athenian bull riders whom Theseus eventually rescues from sacrifice to the Minotaur (102).[23] The Minotaur itself is related to the book's pattern of troubled marriages – a deeply troubled human marriage, after all, is the origin of the Minotaur's existence – and to the phenomenon of human degeneracy that Hawthorne depicts so vividly in the deterioration of Roger Chillingworth. But its imaginative presence in *The Scarlet Letter* has less to do with Chillingworth's demoniacal uniqueness and more to do with the distortion and pain experienced, to some extent, by all human beings, as well as with the pity that such pain evokes. Hawthorne suggests these meanings most openly in *The Tanglewood Tales* when (with Ariadne's help) Theseus finally penetrates the labyrinth and confronts the emblematic creature itself:

> And there he was, the wretched thing, with no society, no companion, no kind of a mate, living only to do mischief, and incapable of knowing what affection means! Theseus hated him and shuddered at him, and yet could not but be sensible of some sort of pity, and all the more, the uglier and more detestable the creature was. For he kept striding to-and-fro, in a solitary frenzy of rage, continually emitting a hoarse roar, which was oddly mixed up with half-shaped words; and, after listening a while, Theseus understood that the Minotaur was saying to himself how miserable he was, and how hungry, and how he hated everybody, and how he longed to eat up the human race alive!
>
> Ah, the bull-headed villain! And, Oh, my good little people, you will perhaps see, one of these days, as I do now, that every human being, who suffers anything evil to get into his nature, or to remain there, is a kind of Minotaur, an enemy of his fellow-creatures, and separated from all good companionship, as this poor monster was! (1333)

The Minotaur's unbearable loneliness and Theseus's convulsive shudder suggest perhaps most clearly the relationship between Chillingworth and Dimmesdale, but Hawthorne in fact explored several versions of this fable during his writing life. The revelers at Merry Mount, like Comus's crew, had been willfully descending into bestial status like a community of self-made Minotaurs. Ethan Brand rebuked his former neighbors with a similar sort of epithet: "'Leave me,' he said bitterly, 'ye brute beasts, that have made yourselves so, shrivelling up your souls with fiery liquors!'" (1059). Somewhat later, in *The Blithedale Romance* Hawthorne would evoke the figure of the Minotaur again in the mixture of womanly gentleness and "shaggy" animality that comprise the character of Hollingsworth.

The image haunted Hawthorne, as he suggests in *The Tanglewood Tales,* because of its ability to sum up in the most vivid terms the idea of compositeness that comprises his understanding of adult life. Moreover, Theseus's pity and commiseration with the loneliness of this marred and defective creature suggest the central, moral posture of *The Scarlet Letter,* a vision of the predicament of human life that (as the narrator of *The Tanglewood Tales* suggests) embraces children as well as guilty lovers and wronged husbands. Even Pearl is a kind of Minotaur in Hawthorne's story, given over from time to time to solitary frenzies of rage, living (it would seem) only to do mischief, "and incapable of knowing what affection means." That, at any rate, is how Hester perceives her – as "a kind of Minotaur," a "poor Monster" whose nature is imperfectly "married" both to its fellow creatures in the social world and within itself.

The Minotaur's despair is in fact the same that afflicts Aylmer in "The Birth-mark," a condition that "assails the higher nature, at finding itself so miserably thwarted by the earthly part." Hawthorne suggests that every "man of genius" might well find that Aylmer's condition mirrors his own, but it is not really to "men of genius" that Hawthorne directs our attention. Georgiana's act of recognition while reading Aylmer's journal is the key to Hawthorne's meaning in "The Birth-mark." Pearl's intelligence – along with Chillingworth's pertinacity and Dimmesdale's acute sense of guilt – is the irreducible obstacle to Hester and Dimmesdale's attempt to evade the consequences of their natures. And it is Hester who detects the same double message that Theseus hears in the cry of the Minotaur in the complex, powerful tones of Dimmesdale's election sermon:

> Muffled as the sound was by its passage through the church-walls, Hester Prynne listened with such intentness, and sympathized so intimately, that the sermon had throughout a meaning for her, entirely apart from its indistinguishable words.

These, perhaps, if more distinctly heard, might have been only a grosser medium, and have clogged the spiritual sense. Now she caught the low undertone, as of the wind sinking down to repose itself; then ascended with it, as it rose through progressive gradations of sweetness and power, until its volume seemed to envelope her with an atmosphere of awe and solemn grandeur. And yet, majestic as the voice sometimes became, there was for ever in it an essential character of plaintiveness. A loud or low expression of anguish, – the whisper, or the shriek, as it might be conceived, of suffering humanity, that touched a sensibility in every bosom! At times this deep strain of pathos was all that could be heard, and scarcely heard, sighing amid a desolate silence. But even when the minister's voice grew high and commanding, – when it gushed irrepressibly upward, – when it assumed its utmost breadth and power, so overfilling the church as to burst its way through the solid walls, and diffuse itself in the open air, – still if the auditor listened intently, and for the purpose, he could detect the same cry of pain. What was it? The complaint of a human heart, sorrow-laden, perchance guilty, telling its secret, whether of guilt or sorrow, to the great heart of mankind; beseeching its sympathy or forgiveness, – at every moment, – in each accent, – and never in vain! (229–30)

This is a justly celebrated passage that does not need an awareness of *The Tanglewood Tales* to register its meaning, but Dimmesdale's power also, like that of the Minotaur, springs from a despair within him that, nevertheless, makes him eligible for Hawthorne's triumphant charity.

Hester is the character who sets in motion these climactic events when she recognizes, on the night of John Winthrop's death, the obligations that bind her to Dimmesdale and that her vow of silence to Chillingworth had led her to neglect. Much earlier in the book Hawthorne suggests this pivotal relation between Hester and Winthrop when Hester makes her superb defense of her maternal rights in Governor Bellingham's house:

"God gave me the child!" cried she. "He gave her, in requital of all things else, which ye had taken from me. She is my happiness! – she is my torture, none the less! Pearl keeps me here in life! Pearl punishes me too! See ye not, she is the scarlet letter, only capable of being loved, and so endowed with a million-fold the power of retribution for my sin? Ye shall not take her! I will die first!"

"My poor woman," said the not unkind old minister, "the child shall be well cared for! – far better than thou canst do it."

"God gave her into my keeping," repeated Hester Prynne,

raising her voice almost to a shriek. "I will not give her up!" –
And here, by a sudden impulse, she turned to the young cler-
gyman, Mr. Dimmesdale, at whom, up to this moment, she had
seemed hardly so much as once to direct her eyes. – "Speak thou
for me!" cried she. "Thou wast my pastor, and hadst charge of
my soul, and knowest me better than these men can. I will not
lose the child! Speak for me! Thou knowest, – for thou hast
sympathies which these men lack! – thou knowest what is in my
heart, and what are a mother's rights, and how much the strong-
er they are, when that mother has but her child and the scarlet
letter! Look thou to it! I will not lose the child! Look to it!"
(108–9)

In its urgent use of dashes and in the pitch of a "shriek" to which Hester's
voice almost rises, this passage is a precursor both of Dimmesdale's
election sermon, in which a plea for sympathy is also buried, and of the
"solitary frenzy" of the Minotaur in *The Tanglewood Tales* that provokes
Theseus to a shudder of recognition just as Hester provokes Dimmesdale
with her mixture of plea and threat. In "A Modell of Christian Charity"
John Winthrop gives more than a hint of this formidable mixture of love
and desperation in Eve's determination not to "endure" the want of any
good her child might enjoy:

> If by occasion shee be withdrawne from the company of it, shee
> is still looking towards the place where shee left her beloved. If
> shee hear it groane, shee is with it presently. If shee finde it sadd
> and disconsolate, shee sighes and moanes with it. Shee hath noe
> such joy as to see her beloved merry and thriving. If shee see it
> wronged, shee cannot bear it without passion.[24]

Hawthorne might have found instances of the power of maternal love in
many sources other than Winthrop's text, of course, but few other
sources would have combined as Winthrop does the typological tempt-
ress and the redeeming mother that Hawthorne also captures in the figure
of Hester. If it would be going too far to suggest "antitype" as yet
another gloss for the symbolic letter, it is at least clear that, just as Pearl
represents both sin and retribution in her mother's life, so Hester represents both fall and redemption in Hawthorne's story, a double function
that is bound up with her maternal status.

When she finds Dimmesdale on the scaffold on the night of Winthrop's
death, Hester recognizes that her responsibilities to him combine those of
a parent and a spouse.[25] Dimmesdale's moral force has lapsed into "more
than childish weakness," a condition that in itself has a claim on her
sympathies. But like Adam and Eve, the two of them are also bound by

"the iron link of mutual crime. . . . Like all other ties, it brought along with it its obligations" (152). Hester's recognition of these personal obligations of charity – shaped both by mutual crime and by maternity – coincides with Hawthorne's characterization of the Puritan community's new relations with its most celebrated sinner. Those changed relations are already implicit in the narrative from the story's beginning. Hawthorne makes it clear that he is retelling what amounts to a proverbial tale in which certain details are "said" to have taken place, as Pearl is said to have been greeted by wolves in the untrodden forest or as some especially noteworthy rosebushes are "kept alive" in history and tradition for their singularly human meanings. The facts of *The Scarlet Letter* are preserved in the dustbin of the customhouse, but they are also registered in the communal memory upon which the author draws. The reason for this durability lies in the nature of the central figure of the drama. Hester's own natural sympathies – "a wellspring of human tenderness," Hawthorne calls her in language that evokes the Mariolatry of mid-nineteenth-century culture, "unfailing to every real demand, and inexhaustible by the largest" (154) – had bred in turn a sympathy for her in the hearts of her sternest judges, a sympathy that Hawthorne describes once more in the striking sexual metaphors that characterize so much of his work:

> The rulers, and the wise and learned men of the community, were longer in acknowledging the influence of Hester's good qualities than the people. The prejudices which they shared in common with the latter were fortified in themselves by an iron framework of reasoning, that made it a far tougher labor to expel them. Day by day, nevertheless, their sour and rigid wrinkles were relaxing into something which, in the due course of years, might grow to be an expression of almost benevolence. (154)

The "wise and learned men" may still be in "labor" with their ancient prejudices and with the new birth of benevolence, but the people have long since recovered the familial powers of Winthrop's vision and reasserted his ligaments of love as replacements for the iron framework of reasoning. Hester is the midwife of that birth, much as she is the seamstress of Winthrop's funeral robe.[26]

Her own mind, however, is less at ease than these images of reconciliation might suggest. Dark questions still trouble her about the meaning of Pearl, about the fate of women, about the restrictive, and restrictively masculine, laws of the world. Hester comes very close indeed to drawing the wrong conclusions from the rebirth of charity with which she is surrounded: "At times, a fearful doubt strove to possess her soul, whether it were not better to send Pearl at once to heaven, and go herself to such futurity as Eternal Justice should provide" (158). The plight of Dimmesdale rescues her from these self-centered reflections and turns her energies outward in the chain of events that bring the story to its close:

> Hester could not but ask herself, whether there had not original-ly been a defect of truth, courage, and loyalty, on her own part, in allowing the minister to be thrown into a position where so much evil was to be foreboded, and nothing auspicious to be hoped. Her only justification lay in the fact, that she had been able to discern no method of rescuing him from a blacker ruin than had overwhelmed herself, except by acquiescing in Roger Chillingworth's scheme of disguise. Under that impulse, she had made her choice and had chosen, as it now appeared, the more wretched alternative of the two. She determined to redeem her error, so far as it might yet be possible. (159)

This second choice that Hester makes, reversing her acquiescence in Chillingworth's plan, is the choice of life, the identification of Hester herself with an act of redemption that, imitating Mary's relationship to Eve, compensates for the serious "defect of truth, courage, and loyalty" that had come after her publicly exposed but ultimately less consequential sin. Unlike his practice with the act of adultery, Hawthorne does indeed dramatize this sin of silence, committed under the influence of a serpen-tine intelligence. But by keeping the sexual circumstances of Hester's maternity hidden – by keeping her child "unfathered" – he is true both to the requirements of secrecy in his plot and to the requirements of ty-pological identity that underlie his extraordinary heroine.

5

MELVILLE, WHITMAN, AND THE PREDICAMENT OF INTIMACY

Hawthorne's conscious exploitation of the Puritan background is unmatched in the writing of his contemporaries. For this reason the pertinence of Winthrop's example is much clearer in Hawthorne's work than it is in that of Melville and Whitman, each of whom participates only indirectly in the New England literary tradition. To a surprising extent, however, both Melville and Whitman adopt forms of the jeremiad as literary models that effectively bind their most distinctive work to the imaginative universe within which Winthrop lived and wrote.[1] Michael Gilmore suggests, in fact, that Melville's most elaborate statement of his own artistic values and aspirations – in "Hawthorne and His Mosses" – takes the form of a secular jeremiad, a public chastisement of American readers for neglecting the nation's true literary prophets and saviors.[2] Moreover Gilmore pursues this grim prophetic thread by demonstrating the extent to which *Moby-Dick* and "Benito Cereno" in particular draw upon the Books of Revelation and Daniel, as well as on Milton and Spenser, to dramatize the terrible collapse of America's millennial hopes.[3]

This view of the extent of Melville's commitment to a Hawthornean "power of blackness" is persuasive in part because of the emphasis it places upon the most dramatic elements of Melville's conception of the artist's mission: his apparent devotion to subjects drawn from "the dark half of the physical sphere," his celebrations of prophetic madness, and his glorification of "the great Art of Telling the Truth" – usually truth that shatters rather than truth that nourishes.[4] It is important to keep in mind, however, that just as Hawthorne responded to two competing Puritanisms in his background, so Melville responded to two competing Hawthornes in his famous review. The apostle of blackness is one of these, but the other is (as Jane Tompkins reminds us) quite a different figure: a writer marked by his capacity for tenderness and sympathy, by "the mild moonlight of contemplative humor" in his work, by the experience of "omnipresent love" that he conveys. Melville saw (as he said) the thunderclouds in Hawthorne's imagination, but he saw just as clearly the "ever-moving dawn" that "circumnavigates his world."[5]

In an examination of Melville's relationship to his own Calvinist heritage, T. Walter Herbert notes this mixture of attributes in Melville's portrait of Hawthorne and traces them to "logical discontinuities" in Melville's own religious background that ultimately produce the serious spiritual crises in his work.[6] But it seems equally likely that for Melville the discontinuities were not disabling but invigorating. What appealed to him in Hawthorne and what he sought to capture in his own fiction were not powers of logical resolution but powers of fusion that would permit him to unite the apparently irreconcilable extremes of imaginative appeal that he found in the older writer's work.[7] At the close of "Hawthorne and his Mosses," Melville described this fusion in domestic terms by endorsing Hawthorne's own words from the sketch "A Select Party" as a summation and a self-portrait: "Nathaniel Hawthorne, a man, who already in some few minds, has shed 'such a light, as never illuminates the earth, save when a great heart burns as the household fire of a grand intellect.'"

This image is not a simple one, but its complexity is the basis of its appeal for Melville. It is a composite of domestic peace and uncompromising isolation, of omnipresent love and the blackness of darkness. Great literary achievement, in Melville's view, grows out of these contrary forces, out of the writer's capacity to join them together in a single body. The most lasting models of such achievement, in Melville's experience, were the plays of Shakespeare and the Bible, and in his own books he consistently strove to match the exemplary power those models displayed of uttering "the sane madness of vital truth." The intimate fusion of such "antagonistic influences" – madness and truth, love and the blackness of darkness – is the structural principle of Melville's own most ambitious work, uniting scene and character in the balance of life and death:

> Walking the deck with quick, side-lunging strides, Ahab commanded the t'gallant sails and royals to be set, and every stunsail spread. The best man in the ship must take the helm. Then, with every mast-head manned, the piled-up craft rolled down before the wind. The strange, upheaving, lifting tendency of the taffrail breeze filling the hollows of so many sails, made the buoyant, hovering deck to feel like air beneath the feet; while still she rushed along, as if two antagonistic influences were struggling in her – one to mount direct to heaven, the other to drive yawingly

to some horizontal goal. And had you watched Ahab's face that night, you would have thought that in him also two different things were warring. While his one live leg made lively echoes along the deck, every stroke of his dead limb sounded like a coffin-tap. On life and death this old man walked.[8]

Melville's fiction too – like the jeremiads upon which it draws – walks on life and death, not grimly as Ahab does but with the *Pequod*'s strangely resilient buoyancy, a quality that Melville derives in part from his immersion in the biblical books that figured prominently in the jeremiad tradition itself and in part from his own personal energies.[9] The surrogate for the author's imagination in the passage above is not the haunted captain but the "piled up craft" of Melville's art, explicitly designed as a hybrid vehicle to catch the winds of heaven and harness them to serve a horizontal goal. Against this background Melville's own scrutiny of the war with the self and his own celebration of the human household take on their characteristic scope. He is seldom as completely domesticated in his sympathies as Hawthorne, but he is never as far from the central values and images of Winthrop's model as his worldwide voyages might appear to take him. In his work, and in Whitman's as well, great geographic and rhetorical range become in effect the means of a new, rejuvenated intimacy that follows quite closely Winthrop's call for a rejuvenated household at the outset of American life. Just as the Puritan jeremiad sees its community's peculiar status as both an opportunity and a predicament, so Melville and Whitman perfect their arts of intimacy in the face of great antagonists.

The primary antagonist for Melville, as for his Puritan predecessors, was the resistant self. His most memorable characters are singular egotists, and his model of human identity, drawn as always from nautical life, is the island rather than the integrating and uniting continent. "Isolato" is the term that Ishmael coins to describe the crew members of the *Pequod* – island dwellers of the spirit, "not acknowledging the common continent of men" (123). In an important sense, Melville insists that this inhospitable solitariness is the common plight of all, but it is also true that a ship's crew was his most frequent metaphor for humanity at large. These bodies of men are often bound together by force and directed toward ambiguous ends in Melville's work, but they are at the same time a potent source of communal feeling as well as the setting and occasion for the comradely marriages that so abound in Melville's fiction.[10] When Mrs. Hussey is trying to make sense of Ishmael's hysteria during Queequeg's "Ramadan" at the Try-Pots, she seizes him by the arm and uses the form of address that, in Melville, most often replaces individual singularity with a common identity: "What's the matter with you? What's the matter with you, shipmate?" (87). The round robin petition by which the crew members of the *Julia* in *Omoo* seek a redress of their grievances is signed in a circle, all the sailors inscribing their forecastle names around a central wheel labeled "All Hands" so that no one man might be singled out as the ringleader of their mutiny.[11]

In the exuberant, early chapters of *Mardi,* Melville expands on this sense of general equality and unity. Common sailors and other "Helots" of the world should hold up their heads, he claims, "blood potential flows through your veins":

> All of us have monarchs and sages for kinsmen; nay, angels and archangels for cousins; since in antediluvian days, the sons of God did verily wed with our mothers, the irresistible daughters of Eve. Thus all generations are blended; and heaven and earth of one kin: the hierarchies of seraphs in the uttermost skies; the thrones and principalities in the zodiac; the shades that roam throughout space; the nations and families, flocks and folds of the earth; one and all, brothers in essence – oh, be we then brothers indeed! All things form but one whole; the universe a Judea, and God Jehovah its head.[12]

This great erasing of all distinctions in a universal household is embodied in the compacted pluralism of the community of sailors. "Your aboriginal tar," Melville goes on to observe, is a man without individual idiom: "Long companionship with seamen of all tribes: Manilla-men, Anglo-saxons, Cholos, Lascars, and Danes, wear away in good time all mother-tongue stammerings. You sink your clan; down goes your nation; you speak a world's language, jovially jabbering in the Lingua-Franca of the forecastle" (673). Ishmael's philosophical acceptance of the "universal thump" of sailor life is a sign of his personal resignation of the self to the common conditions of nautical humanity.

In a number of ways, then, a ship's crew at sea served the same purposes for Melville that the unifying conceit of the body or the image of a city on a hill served for Winthrop. Moreover, just as Winthrop recognized the persistent vulnerability of his communal ideal to the formidable forces of self-interest, so the community of the crew in Melville is always uneasy and incomplete. In *Typee* Tommo and Toby keep their plans to jump ship a secret, for fear that their shipmates might betray them. In *Mardi,* Jarl and Taji abandon the "good old *Arcturion*" in the open sea, stealing a whaleboat and isolating themselves in a "watery world" a thousand miles from land. The mutual hostilities of the *Pequod*'s crew are barely contained by the common perils of nature or by the force of Ahab's will. The *Pequod,* of course, is manned at times not so much by a body of men as by a collective instrument of its captain's revenge – a fact in which Ahab himself exults. When Ishmael surrenders his "self" to the power of Ahab's obsession, the act has very little in common with the life-giving triumph over selfishness that Winthrop strove to promote in "A Modell of Christian Charity."

Indeed, even at moments when Ishmael is expressing his contentment with the common life of the forecastle, the reader is most acutely aware not of Ishmael's representative status but of his uncommon qualities: his wit, his charm, his garrulity, the odd pleasure he takes in seizing a subject and worrying it, his sense of mystery. You may sink your clan and your nation at sea, and hide behind an enigmatic alias, but the essential self is irrepressibly alive, even in the act of surrender.

Melville's war with the self, in other words, is painfully unresolved, a condition that can take very different forms in the course of Melville's fiction. The moral absolutism of Ahab or of Pierre Glendinning is the most extreme instance of unshackled and destructive egotism in his work. The self-serving philosophy of Mark Winsome in *The Confidence-Man* is a much meaner, much less dramatically engaging kind of self-ishness. Against such failures Melville pits the impressively appealing force of a series of countercharacters – one dimension of the "elaborate pattern of countercommentaries" that R. W. B. Lewis suggested as the formal structure of *Moby-Dick*.[13] The genial temperament of Tommo, in those chapters from *Typee* devoted to a generously sympathetic portrait of Polynesian life, is an example of one such figure. During much of the book, Tommo is able to shed his civilized self and become an advocate for cannibals much as Ishmael becomes an advocate for whalemen in *Moby-Dick*. In a similar fashion, of course, Ishmael is the great counter-weight to Ahab. Melville hints at this view of compensating character himself in the punning title of one of the early chapters in *Moby-Dick*, "The Counterpane," in which the familiar name for a quilt describes with surprising economy the healing effect of Queequeg upon Ishmael. The "counterpain" for the self is selfless generosity and good humor, the qualities that finally combine to heal Ishmael's splintered heart and make his verbal presence so much more satisfying than the Promethean displays of Ahab.[14] Unlike Ishmael, Ahab remains quite explicitly a divid-ed, a splintered, self. The "eternal, living principle or soul" within him is engaged in a fruitless struggle with the "characterizing mind" that has given itself over to the insane project of vengeance:

> But as the mind does not exist unless leagued with the soul, therefore it must have been that, in Ahab's case, yielding up all his thoughts and fancies to his one supreme purpose; that purpose, by its own sheer inveteracy of will, forced itself against gods and devils into a kind of self-assumed, independent being of its own. Nay, could grimly live and burn, while the common

> vitality to which it was conjoined, fled horror-stricken from the unbidden and unfathered birth. Therefore, the tormented spirit that glared out of bodily eyes, when what seemed Ahab rushed from his room, was for the time but a vacated thing, a formless somnambulistic being, a ray of living light, to be sure, but without an object to color, and therefore a blankness in itself. (205)

Behind Ishmael's complex and vivid psychological vocabulary lies a richly sexual understanding of Ahab's plight that suggests an extended dimension of Melville's familiar absorption with the idiom of the seventeenth century.[15] Ahab's divided self is, figuratively, a shattered household, a sexual union broken apart by a horribly unnatural birth that Melville's language invites us to compare to the corrupted sexuality of *Paradise Lost*. Milton's account of the creation of Death involves Satan's incestuous union with his daughter, Sin, and her own horror-stricken flight from the grim child of that partnership, Death, who incarnates the "inveterate will" of his father and rapes his mother. The correspondence between Milton's hellish genealogy of "gods and devils" and the sexual entanglements of Ahab's being is close enough to suggest that Ishmael is borrowing the images directly, if haphazardly, and applying them to Ahab's inner torment. The passionate marriage between soul and soul that forms the basis of Winthrop's vision of communal health is wrenched violently out of shape in Ishmael's description, and the stark biblical alternatives of life and death engage in a frightening struggle for the "vacated thing" that Ahab has become.[16] The struggle has a special, internal fury in this passage, but it is by no means confined to Ahab alone.

The religious text of Father Mapple's sermon in *Moby-Dick* is that obedience to God is disobedience to self, but Mapple too holds fast to this truth only at the cost of an inner struggle intensified by physical and social isolation. The warmth of his priestly address is characterized by the same note of familiar feeling as Mrs. Hussey's anxious inquiry in the Try-Pots – "Beloved shipmates, clinch the last verse of the first chapter of Jonah" – but at the close of the sermon he covers his face and silently waves the congregation away. If we put aside for the moment the message that he preaches, it is very difficult to distinguish the final posture of Father Mapple from the inaccessible egotism of Ahab. The sharpest antagonists in Melville's fictional world often hauntingly resemble one another, as Ishmael's restless probing after the secret of whiteness or the hidden lure of the sea resembles Ahab's relentless pursuit of "the little lower layer" of meaning in Moby Dick.

In *Typee*, sympathetic advocacy alternates in Tommo's narrative with a deep sense of alienation from the life of the islanders around him, just as the living principle and the obsessed mind compete in Ahab. Only the threat of being tatooed – of having his self irrevocably erased – galvanizes all of Tommo's old fears of his Typee hosts and leads quickly to his escape. The war with, and within, the self in *Typee* is typified by the awkward device of Tommo's puzzling leg injury and the alternating atmospheres of adoption (complete with baptism) and imprisonment, or abandonment, that the cyclical revival of the injury reflects.[17] This pattern of a sinking and a rising "self" – an adopted and an orphaned narrator, as Samuel Kimball has suggested – becomes gradually incorporated into the imaginative fabric of Melville's work.[18] In *Moby-Dick* in particular this phenomenon is both explicit in Ishmael's personal admission of his oneness with the crew and implicit in the narrative process. The early chapters slip back and forth between recollection and immediate experience ("Heavens! look at that tomahawk") as if Ishmael's control over his material possessed both the poise of memory and the exhilaration of immediate surprise. His character fuses the roles of participant and observer in such an unsettling and invigorating way that, when he finally emerges out of the maelstrom of the climactic chase, it is as if he has suddenly recollected as well as rescued himself. Much like the whale that he helps to pursue, Ishmael composes in an alternating rhythm, now moving silently and invisibly beneath the narrative surface, now openly displaying his presence and going through his sequence of spoutings before diving again. He is the quintessential example of Melville's overwhelmed and overwhelming narrators. When Melville himself observed to Hawthorne that he "had pretty much made up his mind to be annihilated," he expressed perfectly this fusion in his imagination between a self of dramatic ambitions and the idea of contented self-surrender. The antagonistic influences that shape the *Pequod*'s course shape every bit as decisively Melville's account of the self.

For Melville as for Winthrop, however, the most generous attribute of human nature remained the capacity to make others' conditions one's own, as Ishmael and Queequeg do in the early chapters of *Moby-Dick*:

> After supper, and another social chat and smoke, we went to our room together. He made me a present of his embalmed head; took out his enormous tobacco wallet, and groping under the tobacco, drew out some thirty dollars in silver; then spreading them on the table, and mechanically dividing them into two equal portions, pushed one of them towards me, and said it was mine. I was going to remonstrate; but he silenced me by pouring them into my trowsers' pockets. I let them stay. He then went about his evening prayers, took out his idol, and removed the paper fireboard. By certain signs and symptoms, I thought he seemed anxious for me to join him; but well knowing what was

to follow, I deliberated a moment whether, in case he invited me, I would comply or otherwise.

I was a good Christian; born and bred in the bosom of the infallible Presbyterian Church. How then could I unite with this wild idolator in worshipping his piece of wood? But what is worship? thought I. Do you suppose now, Ishmael, that the magnanimous God of heaven and earth – pagans and all included – can possibly be jealous of an insignificant bit of black wood? Impossible! But what is worship? – to do the will of God – *that* is worship. And what is the will of God? – to do to my fellow man what I would have my fellow man to do to me – *that* is the will of God. Now, Queequeg is my fellow man. And what do I wish that this Queequeg would do to me? Why, unite with me in my particular Presbyterian form of worship. Consequently I must then unite with him in his; ergo, I must turn idolator. So I kindled the shavings; helped prop up the innocent little idol; offered him burnt biscuit with Queequeg; salamed before him twice or thrice; kissed his nose; and that done, we undressed and went to bed, at peace with our own consciences and all the world. (54)

Ishmael's cheerful exercise of his reasoning powers owes something to the portrait of Launcelot Gobbo's struggles with his conscience in *The Merchant of Venice,* as well as to the pattern of a parodic catechism that T. W. Herbert detects.[19] It is, at the same time, a more complex domestic affirmation than we sometimes give it credit for being. Ishmael and Queequeg are sympathetically and comically married, but the division of possessions, in some sense, makes them brothers as well as spouses, whereas the affectionate, bedtime ritual with Yojo suggests that they are also parents – a kind of precursor couple to Ahab's adoption of Pip in the book's final chapters. Queequeg's thirty dollars in silver seem calculated to awaken in Melville's infallibly minded Christian readers an image of Christ's betrayal just sufficiently vivid to make Ishmael's triumph over religious formulas all the more unexpected and gratifying. This is an act of cultural adoption less physically demanding and invasive than the ominous tatoos and cannibalistic rituals in *Typee,* and its very moderation suggests the extent to which the scene is indebted as well to the example of Benjamin Franklin in the *Autobiography,* particularly to Franklin's successful attempt to convince himself to resume the eating of fish. Franklin was important to Ishmael as an instance of the lofty pedigree of whaling, for Franklin's mother came from good Nantucket whaling stock. Moreover, it is Franklin's example of commonsensical piety that strongly influences Ishmael's attitude toward the excesses of Queequeg's "Ramadan." But, more importantly, the figure of Franklin captured for Melville a range of ambiguities and complexity in the war with the self.

The celebrated portrait of Franklin in *Israel Potter* pokes fun at the "sage's" reputation as a niggling, self-centered economist, but Melville is careful to observe at the same time that such passages depict Franklin only "in his far lesser lights" (479). Franklin's chief attributes, in Melville's eyes, were his "philosophical levity of tranquillity" – a phrase that is surprisingly applicable to Ishmael as well – and the "Plato-like graciousness of good-humor" that contributed to making him a "pocket congress of all humanity."[20] Franklin is an instance of the colorful self whose intelligence has probed beyond selfishness much as Ishmael does in his cheerful submission to Queequeg's pagan ritual, and this special status Franklin held in Melville's view is an important ingredient in what many readers regard as the bleakest of his books, *The Confidence-Man*.[21]

The presence of Franklin is very much evident on the *Fidele*. The gullible "good merchant" Mr. Roberts repeats Franklin's experience of being conned by the persuasive powers of George Whitefield into ransacking his pockets for the collection plate.[22] The agent for the Seminole Widows and Orphans Asylum sketches out a plan for a World's Charity that has all the scope and naive grandeur of Franklin's Society of the Free and Easy. The impractical hanging beds in the immigrants' section of the boat are disposed with a "Philadelphian regularity" that pokes fun at Franklin's fondness for inventions that may or may not prove to be ingenious blessings. But the most elaborate of Melville's allusions to Franklin is contained in the story of China Aster, a fable of economic disaster that Egbert uses to defend the universal distrust of Mark Winsome. Like Franklin, China Aster was trained as a tallow chandler and, like Franklin too, China Aster accepted a friendly loan to help him make a start in his business. But unlike Franklin's fortunate experience with Samuel Vernon, China Aster's life is a series of failures and unmet payments that drive him to poverty, disease, and finally death – a remorseless progress downward to an epitaph that parodies the optimistic epitaphs that Franklin wrote for himself and for his own parents.

The piecing together of these references into a consistent pattern is in some respects as futile a task as that of imposing a degree of symbolic consistency upon the Confidence Man himself. When Melville worked from a source he was seldom systematic. Moreover he has built his masquerade around a central figure – the Confidence Man – who incorporates in a particularly unsettling way both positive and negative traits, who is devious and grasping but who has none of the miser's greed and none of the repellent cleverness that permits Mark Winsome to justify selfishness and exalt death in language that reverses the moral and spiritual emphases of Winthrop's Mosaic allusion in "A Modell of Christian

Charity": "For death," as Winsome puts it, "though in a worm, is majestic; while life, though in a king, is contemptible" (1049). The Confidence Man's message is precisely the opposite of this cynical pronouncement, just as Franklin's life is the counterfable to the bleak experience of China Aster. The debate about human nature that provides the ongoing subject of *The Confidence-Man* develops into a war with the self that pits the philosophical levity of Benjamin Franklin and the Confidence Man against the sterile doctrines of Egbert and his lifeless master. Egbert, of course, is one of the passengers whom the Confidence Man cannot dupe, but Melville leaves little doubt about which of the two antagonists he prefers. The Confidence Man too is a kind of pocket congress of all humanity, a self who is at the same time a community.[23]

The bond of comradeship exemplified in the marriage of Ishmael and Queequeg is definitive, in Melville's work, both in the capacity of that union to heal the social and psychic rifts to which *The Confidence-Man* gives expression and in the limitations to those same healing powers. Even in his most enthusiastic celebrations of universal brotherhood – in the sentimental "insanity" of "A Squeeze of the Hand" – Ishmael acknowledges that "attainable felicity" on earth can never equal our ecstatic visions of human intimacy and community. The phrase "all hands" symbolizes the common interests and enterprises of a ship's crew in Melville's world, but those hands themselves never really join. The "clinch" in which Father Mapple invites his congregation to engage embraces a biblical text rather than a living companion, and the most noteworthy instance of a genuine handclasp in all of *Moby-Dick* is not an occasion for joy in Ishmael but a nightmarish memory from his boyhood that he is incapable of properly interpreting even years afterwards.

When Ishmael awakens in Queequeg's inadvertently loving embrace in "The Counterpane" he strives to describe his peculiar feelings to the reader by alluding to an experience he had as a child when he was punished for some misbehavior by being sent to bed early in the afternoon of the longest day of the year. In a dream or a half-conscious doze the young Ishmael imagines that a ghostly hand has taken hold of his own hand as it hangs over his counterpane. The phantom to whom the hand belonged seemed seated by his bedside, and the sensation of its presence held Ishmael "frozen with the most awful fears, not daring to drag away my hand; yet ever thinking that if I could but stir it one single inch, the horrid spell would be broken" (28). The mystery of the hand remains only a fearful puzzle to Ishmael, but Melville gives his reader enough clues to suggest that the phantom visitor is the same "most conscientious of stepmothers" who had punished Ishmael in the first place and now, responding to his boyishly theatrical plea for clemency, has come to his bedside to commiserate – the first, and in some ways the most misunderstood, of this chapter's counterpains.[24] Ishmael is indeed close to breaking the horrid spell and recognizing as a moment of silent sympathy what his own youth or his drowsiness in the darkened bedroom had mistaken for a moment of fear, but Melville prefers to keep the antagonistic influences in a painful, unfulfilled suspension. Loneliness is the dark half of the sphere in Melville's comradely world, but it is seldom total, seldom without the poignancy of memory or of some wider knowledge to sharpen as well as to soothe it.

Even Ahab's loneliness is not completely unapproachable. Peleg's sympathy for the grand, ungodly, God-like man is the forerunner of Ishmael's extraordinary chapters of sympathetic explanation in which the progress and nature of Ahab's madness are presented both with great vividness and great tenderness. It is important for Ishmael's purposes that the reader of his story appreciate the depth and seriousness of Ahab's wounds, but Ishmael is equally adamant that Ahab remain a mighty pageant creature and not degenerate into a spectacle or a clinical specimen. Accordingly he chooses to describe the worst of those wounds in a baroque, architectural vision that preserves Ahab's grandeur and dignity while conveying unmistakably the maimed sexuality that is Ahab's deepest scar:

> This is much; yet Ahab's larger, darker, deeper part remains unhinted. But vain to popularize profundities, and all truth is profound. Winding far down from within the very heart of this spiked Hotel de Cluny where we here stand – however grand and wonderful, now quit it; – and take your way, ye nobler, sadder souls, to those vast Roman halls of Thermes; where far beneath the fantastic towers of man's upper earth, his root of grandeur, his whole awful essence sits in bearded state; an antique buried beneath antiquities, and throned on torsoes! So with a broken throne, the great gods mock that captive king; so like a Caryatid, he patient sits, upholding on his frozen brow the piled entablatures of ages. Wind ye down there, ye prouder, sadder souls! question that proud, sad king! A family likeness! aye, he did beget ye, ye young exiled royalties; and from your grim sire only will the old State-secret come. (187–8)

The progression of this intentionally difficult imaginative journey is not impossible to follow, but it has to be followed (as Ishmael elsewhere suggests) by sympathy and not by logic, down into the Roman baths where Ahab's bearded "root of grandeur" blends into the image of a "broken throne" and of a grand patriarch emasculated into the figure of a Caryatid.[25] In Paul Brodtkorb's beautiful phrase, this is indeed an instance of the "dance of estrangement" that comprises so much of *Moby-*

Dick, but the effect of this language is not to limit our sense of intimacy with Ahab but to make that intimacy possible on the only terms acceptable to Ishmael's charity. The interplay between disclosure and concealment here is an outgrowth of human delicacy, gentleness, and pity – the "costliest robes" that Ishmael would willingly throw over all evidence of human weakness and failure (118). The mixture of intimacy and distance that results is the characteristic feature of all of the human bonds of *Moby-Dick,* from the sailor couples who dance on the *Pequod's* deck in "Midnight – Forecastle" to the more conventional couples whose presence is evoked throughout the text.

The women who sit in the isolation of their grief in the Whaleman's Chapel in New Bedford, for example, are perfect counterparts of the "isolatoes" who sail under Ahab's command. But the tablets in the chapel walls and the mourners who read them, women and men alike, are evidence not of the absence of human bonds but of their importance and of the lonely loyalty they inspire. Widows mourn their husbands, sisters remember their brothers, shipmates memorialize the crew of a lost boat towed out of sight by a stricken whale. Like comradely love, the bonds of marriage and family are both experienced and mourned in *Moby-Dick.* There are no women aboard the *Pequod,* of course, but images of the union with women haunt its crew, from the motherly solicitude of Aunt Charity at the outset of the voyage through the peaceful procreation of the Grand Armada of whales, and the tender domestic memories of Starbuck and Ahab that precede the final chase. Few nineteenth-century books are more explicit about the range of feeling that comprises the complex bond between men and women, and in fewer still is that feeling attenuated over greater distance or more profound separation.

The most profoundly redemptive form of comradeship in Melville is the relationship between narrator and reader, between speaker and audience, that seems to have been indispensable to his work long after he realized that he had little hope of reaching a significant reading public.[26] Ishmael is the most fully developed and most appealing of these convivial narrators, but his expansive geniality is fully present in Melville's prose from the opening sentences of *Typee.* Even the apparently impoverished social atmosphere of the *Fidele* in *The Confidence-Man* is charged with exceptional talk, with fascinating stories told and retold, with contests between generously well matched verbal antagonists whose vitality sometimes recalls the wild energy of the *Pequod's* crew.[27] Melville's arch-deceiver seldom selects his "victims" for their wealth only and indulges in a range and cleverness of physical disguise and verbal display that are frequently more playful than genuinely calculating. The *Fidele* contains many emissaries of death, of whom Mark Winsome is merely the last and most open, but it contains as well a fair proportion of travelers who struggle vocally if more or less ineffectually with "the old Adam." And this complexity to life on board the *Fidele* is reflected in the complexities of the Confidence Man himself, who can seem both a harbinger of the apocalypse of the Civil War, as Carolyn Karcher has recently suggested, and at the same time a redeemer who is reduced to diddling what is in truth a group of very minor sinners into expressing both the best and the worst of themselves.[28] The most fundamental of the Confidence Man's many ambiguities is that in opposition to all of the *Fidele*'s emissaries of death he is the advocate of life, and it is a life for the most part captured in the full indulgence of speech.

The constituent antagonisms of Melville's imagination, however, establish critical limits to the ability of his narrators to "domesticate" the experiences they confront. Ishmael may be cheerfully willing to be sociable with a horror, but the horrors of life do not invariably reciprocate that willingness or accommodate themselves as readily as Queequeg does to a civilized companionship. The contest between the social fluency of Melville's prose and a resistant "darkness" at its heart suggests the extent to which the polarities of "Hawthorne and His Mosses" are fundamental to Melville's form. He explored those polarities perhaps most deliberately in the most problematic of his convivial "narrators," Amasa Delano, the central consciousness of "Benito Cereno." From a formal standpoint this is clearly one of Melville's most ambitious tales. Its nonfictional elements are much less completely assimilated by the imagination, and its actual narrator subordinates himself so completely to Delano's perception that Delano occupies the place in the reader's interest that Melville typically reserves for Ishmael, or Redburn, or even for the elderly lawyer of "Bartleby."

From the outset of the story Delano's "undistrustful good nature" seems more of a crippling liability than a virtue. Cut off as he is from making a direct appeal to the reader's sympathies, he resembles in some respects the enigmatic Don Benito, who is similarly cut off from making a direct appeal to the sympathies of Delano himself. The only hints that Melville gives of Delano's actual voice suggest that he has some of the natural effervescence of Ishmael:

> "What, I, Amasa Delano – Jack of the Beach, as they called me when a lad – I, Amasa; the same that, duck-satchel in hand, used to paddle along the waterside to the school-house made from the old hulk; – I, little Jack of the Beach, that used to go berrying with cousin Nat and the rest; I to be murdered here at the ends of the earth, on board a haunted pirate-ship by a horrible Spaniard? – Too nonsensical to think of! Who would murder Amasa Delano? Fie, fie, Jack of the beach! you are a child indeed; a child of the second childhood, old boy; you are beginning to dote and drule, I'm afraid."[29]

But for the most part Melville strips this jovial figure of the advantages of his conviviality and takes the risk that the reader of "Benito Cereno" will come to see Delano only as spectacularly naive, or as so blinded by his stereotypical bigotry as to be unable to recognize Babo's plot.

That plot – the disguise of the slave mutiny in an attempt to seize Delano's ship along with Cereno's – is carried out so clumsily and with so many flagrant hints to Delano about the irregularity of affairs aboard the *San Dominick* that only by great effort is Delano able to chide himself out of his suspicions. It is, in fact, his extraordinary capacity to impose charitable interpretations upon his circumstances that saves Delano from detecting the mutiny and in turn being murdered by the mutineers. His charity and natural good humor are, of course, materially assisted by his racism. Delano is unable to think of the slaves on board the *San Dominick* as anything more than "indisputable inferiors," docile, cheerful, gifted barbers or valets, loyal as dogs (716). He even tries to buy Babo for fifty doubloons. Delano's prejudice, however, is far less deep-seated than the metaphysical horror of "the negro" is in Cereno himself. The discovery of Babo's capacity for imaginatively executed evil drives the Spanish captain into a kind of abstract racism that contributes to his own apparently irreversible decline. By contrast, Delano's characteristically forthright attitude toward the experience of the story is often represented as being more simplistic than it really is. Addressing himself to Cereno's settled gloom, he appears to dismiss the vision of evil upon which it is based, but that dismissal is also an acknowledgment and an acceptance: "You generalize, Don Benito; and mournfully enough. But the past is passed; why moralize upon it? See, yon bright sun has forgotten it all, and the blue sea, and the blue sky; these have turned over new leaves" (754). The sun's memory may be obligingly (and troublingly) short, but Nature does not really disguise its blackness here; it contains it, as a book contains many leaves or as the shroud of the ocean contains the experience of *Moby-Dick* in Ishmael's epilogue. Delano's recognition of that process is a more complex achievement than denial and a more life-sustaining posture than despair. He has clearly passed beyond the cognitive position from which slaves can be comfortably viewed as ideal valets into a more complex, and mysterious, future – the new leaf upon which a new history of the racial antagonists will be written. The subject under discussion between Cereno and Delano is not whether blacks are human but whether Nature is. Delano's universe is not the unhurt organism that Emerson describes in "Spiritual Laws." But neither is it the living tomb of Cereno's fatal melancholy.[30] Indeed, Melville's object in the story seems less to target the limitations of an individual (or a national) consciousness than gradually to reveal the full dimensions of an experience the richness of which tends to expose the inadequacies of judgment.

The *Sam Dominick* becomes, in fact, a man-made Moby Dick, with much of the extraordinary complexity of meaning that gradually gathers about the white whale. When Delano's sailors retake Cereno's ship, they pursue it as if it were indeed a whale, chasing it in a whaleboat and a yawl rather than in the more heavily armed *Bachelor's Delight,* until they can draw near, fire a few rounds at the mutineers, and then fall back, repeating the rhythmic process of assault and retreat until the final bloody climax of the boarding. During that contest the slaves defend their liberty with a mixture of ferocity and poignancy that substantially enriches the portrait of their community as Amasa Delano had first perceived it. Even the women whom Delano had thought of as instances of maternal nature's "pure tenderness and love" prove to be not only vindictive warriors but elegiac bards, possessed of a haunting gift both for inflaming their comrades and for mourning their defeat almost simultaneously. Only in the ritualistic clauses of the closing deposition does this earlier, deeper sort of ritual become apparent:

> That the negresses, of age, were knowing to the revolt, and testified themselves satisfied at the death of their master, Don Alexandro; that, had the negroes not restrained them, they would have tortured to death, instead of simply killing, the Spaniards slain by command of the negro Babo; that the negresses used their utmost influence to have the deponent made away with; that, in the various acts of murder, they sang songs and danced – not gaily, but solemnly; and before the engagement with the boats, as well as during the action, they sang melancholy songs to the negroes, and that this melancholy tone was more inflaming than a different one would have been, and was so intended; that all this is believed, because the negroes have said it. (750)

The tendency of Melville's imagination to prize the fusion of antagonistic influences is responsible for the impact of this passage, as it is for his conception of the character of Amasa Delano and for the perplexing mixture of skilled deceit and awkward self-exposure that mark Babo's management of the mutiny. Indeed, it seems at moments as if Babo's larger purpose is perfectly congruent with Melville's: not to escape at all but to be caught, to be recorded in the story's peculiarly fused text, on his own terms. His stubborn silence after his capture and at the trial seems less a reflection of his Shakespearean despair than of this sense that his work is finished. The richness of the deposition itself is a consequence not of Cereno's testimony but of the testimony of the slaves. They disclose so willingly so much more of their intention and of their dignity than the legal necessities require, and they are so implicitly believed: "because the negroes have said it." What gives this tale its mesmeric power is the tendency nearly all of its participants feel to permit what Melville early in the story refers to as the "living spectacle" to fulfill itself.

The example of the *San Dominick* is a particularly concise instance of Melville's determination in his fiction to follow what the narrator of *Pierre* calls "the most mighty of Nature's laws . . . . that out of death she brings Life." One of the central themes underlying Newton Arvin's impressive discussion of Melville's work as a whole and especially of *Moby-Dick* is that much of Melville's imaginative output reflects "a will to life triumphing over the will to die."[31] A critical touchstone of Arvin's perception is the passage from *White Jacket* in which the narrator, after falling from a mast, is suspended "in the mid-deep," listening to the competing appeals of life and death "as he who stands upon the Corinthian shore hears both the Ionian and the Aegaen waves." Such a clear, iconographic resemblance to the predicament in which Winthrop cast the *Arbella* emigrants – like the echoes of Ahab's dead and living limbs on the *Pequod*'s deck – suggests that life and death are seldom far from Melville's thoughts not simply as indices to his artistic temperament but as abstract embodiments of the plight of human beings. Ishmael allegorizes the whale line and the monkey rope into specific emblems of the interplay of life and death. Queequeg's coffin is every bit as emblematic in its dual import. Even the blustery Captain Peleg is in sympathy with the grand dualism that Melville establishes as the groundwork of his finest book:

> "Hear him, hear him now," cried Peleg, marching across the cabin, and thrusting his hands far down into his pockets, – "hear him, all of ye. Think of that! When every moment we thought the ship would sink! Death and the Judgment then? What? With all three masts making such an everlasting thundering against the side; and every sea breaking over us, fore and aft. Think of Death and the Judgment then? No! no time to think about Death then. Life was what Captain Ahab and I was thinking of; and how to save all hands – how to rig jury-masts – how to get into the nearest port; that was what I was thinking of." (95)

In the simplest terms that is what Melville is thinking of too – not death and judgment, for as Sacvan Bercovitch has pointed out, those are only a preliminary part of the jeremiad's rhetorical design, as death and evil are only a part of the hopeful design that Winthrop offers at the close of "A Modell of Christian Charity." To the bluff imagination of Peleg, of course, the choice his passage describes presents itself with a reassuring clarity that little else in Ishmael's experience reflects, but the fact that the great antagonists are often bewilderingly intertwined does not make it impossible to identify their presence. Indeed, their very confusion constitutes the imaginative consensus of *Moby-Dick,* as the jeremiad constitutes the cultural consensus of American writing.[32] To sense the intimacy with which life and death sustain and involve one another is to break through the mask of Moby Dick, as Ishmael does quite literally in the Arsacidean bower, when he recognizes in the work of its unseen weaver an analogue to the wonderful complexities of his art: "Life folded Death; Death trellised Life; the grim god wived with youthful Life and begot him curly-headed glories" (460).

Perhaps the most important of the critical similarities in vision that unite the work of Melville and Whitman is the interplay between loneliness and comradeship characteristic of the experience of Melville's narrators and of the lonely omnipresence of Whitman's "I." The central poems in *Drum Taps* and the most memorable passages of *Specimen Days* are built upon the competing powers of death and comradely love, just as Melville's sensibility responded powerfully to the interplay between death and life in his own comradely marriages. Moreover, the extraordinary loneliness of Whitman's speaker, combined with his extraordinary range of sympathy and superhuman attentiveness, has the effect of combining within a single consciousness both the isolation and the intimacy that form the poles of Melville's experience as well.[33]

"Intimately impersonal" is the oxymoron that Jerome Loving coins to describe this paradoxical fusion of qualities in the work of both Emerson and Whitman.[34] *Leaves of Grass* is, finally, a marriage that fails because of Whitman's inability to locate a lover, outside himself, who could sustain the immense weight of significance and expectation that Whitman attached to "adhesiveness." There is, in other words, no "counterpain" for the loneliness of Whitman's self, and so his verse is trapped in an auto-erotic isolation that belies the romantic or marital promise that the poems often appear to celebrate.[35] The famous opening lines of the 1855 edition are, in fact, a version of the marriage ceremony carried out with Whitman's peculiar and striking ability both to surrender and to assert the primacy of the self simultaneously: "I celebrate myself, / And what I assume you shall assume / For every atom belonging to me as good belongs to you."[36] These lines affirm the ceremonial identity of flesh with flesh – of atom with atom, as Whitman puts it, in a characteristic escalation of closeness – the result, however, is anything but a partnership.[37]

As Kerry Larson has suggested, these Whitmanian marriages, and the assertions of representative speech that they entail, are invariably "transgressive acts" rather than genuinely inclusive ones.[38] They implicate Whitman's speaker in a network of paradoxical relationships with the reader that cripple his ability to embody a democratic consensus in his verse but which reflect at the same time the urgency of Whitman's communal purposes. What Larson recognizes as the "prolific barrenness" or the "impotent potency" of Whitman's rhetorical embraces testifies to the intensity with which Whitman addressed himself to political predicaments through the medium of sexual metaphor that had offered itself in 1630 to John Winthrop.[39] Whitman clearly viewed *Leaves of Grass* as in some degree a social and political document, a *Democratica Commedia* James Miller has called it, in which the poet undertakes not to argue with his times so much as to redeem them.[40] Both Melville and Whitman grasped and exploited this antiargumentative basis of the jeremiad tradition. It is not possible to argue a community into works of mercy, as Winthrop initially recognized, just as it is not finally possible to argue with Ahab or with his diametrical opposite, Whitman's multimaniacal speaker. Life and good, death and evil, simply present themselves to the instructed eye, and even the smallest acts of the most insignificant lives are a constant exercise of choice between them.

Whitman's strident advocacy for America and his relentless poetic optimism would seem to suggest that he is singularly free of the burdens of choice that face the *Arbella* emigrants or the challenge of death that confronts Ishmael wherever he turns aboard the skeletal *Pequod*. But the concerns and the language of the 1855 preface to *Leaves of Grass* are provocatively close to those of "A Modell of Christian Charity," and the plight of Whitman's speaker in the poem that became "Song of Myself" is a direct reflection of the urgency of the preface. Whitman's abiding sense of mission sprang from a conviction that America might give birth to a poet of Christ-like omnipresence and affirmation precisely because it was in a Job-like predicament of great virtue poised upon the brink of momentous choices.

Whitman in fact exploited just this typological pairing in the voice of the opening poem of *Leaves of Grass*, a speaker who is alternately besieged by doubt and filled with a sense of assurance that celebrates a complete triumph over death and suffering. If the transgressive "marriages" and triumphant mothers of Whitman's preface and of "Song of Myself" recall the typological union of Eve and Mary to which Winthrop had turned, Whitman's revolutionary speaker in his longest poem unites the figures of Job and Christ in a similar poetic appropriation of typology. None of the secular heroes whom Whitman once considered in an early notebook entry entirely pleased him, "after none of them . . . does my stomach say enough and satisfied. – Except Christ; he alone brings the perfumed bread, ever vivifying to me, ever fresh and plenty, ever welcome and to spare."[41] The sacramental vivification in question, however, is less a matter of personal salvation than of poetic fertility. Such an act of dramatic, typological appropriation influences the conception of the speaker in Anne Bradstreet's lyrics and, as we shall see, finds its most ambitious expression in the multiple appropriations of Emily Dickinson's poems. In

Whitman's work, however, it is not the compressive but the expansive potential of a typological "voice" that he seizes upon.

"Song of Myself" is marked by moments of great lyric intensity, but its most memorable features are the richly extended catalogues that challenge and reward the reader's associative ingenuity at the same time that they put "hierarchy to sleep," in Lewis Hyde's memorable phrase.[42] As no other element of the verse itself does, the catalogues constitute the "new life of the new forms" that Whitman had foretold in the preface, and in doing so they disclose more vividly than any other feature of Whitman's work his insistent and exhilarating identification of himself with the forces of "life." The opening scene of the 1855 preface in fact describes the approach of the "stalwart wellshaped heir" who represents the "new life of the new forms" as if he were at once poet, heir, and spouse – a new bridegroom for the widowed America that watches the corpse of her former partner borne from the household with such marvelous complacency. This vision at the outset would seem to be a typological moment in Whitman's book – an older Adamic lover that was "fittest for its days" yielding to the new Adam, whose peculiar fitness will consist in the dissolution of all distinctions, including the fundamental distinction between life and death.

As the preface proceeds it becomes still more clear how intimately Whitman has fused his prophetic and redemptive identities. He is the poet of life, "the caresser of life wherever moving . . . less the reminder of property or qualities, and more the reminder of life" (49). This sense of his role is responsible for the inclusive spirit of the catalogues themselves and for the boldness with which he claims to be able to absorb death, to "pass death with the dying, and birth with the new-washed babe" and to pronounce these epochal human events equally "lucky" (32). Whitman "breathes" into even the smallest subject some of his own inspiriting vigor, and "it dilates with the grandeur and life of the universe" (10).

This candid devotion to a prophetic and redemptive self promotes an equal candor in Whitman's evocation of creative models. No reader in his own day could miss the biblical scope of his claims.[43] The breath of life, which Whitman appears to appropriate as his own, is the divine metaphor of creation in Genesis. Whitman too is the poet who goes before us and who is always with us, like the visionary Jesus who addresses his disciples at the end of Matthew. And he is the apocalyptic lover, the bridegroom, who returns to claim his bride:

> Smile O voluptuous coolbreathed earth!
> Earth of the slumbering and liquid trees!
> Earth of the departed sunset! Earth of the mountains misty-
>   topt!

> Earth of the vitreous pour of the full moon just tinged with
> blue!
> Earth of shine and dark mottling the tide of the river!
> Earth of the limpid gray of clouds brighter and clearer for my
> sake!
> Far-swooping elbowed earth! Rich apple-blossomed earth!
> Smile, for your lover comes! (47)

The ongoing paradox even of Whitman's most extravagant sensualism is
that it always evokes its roots in biblical metaphor, in the visionary
eroticism of Canticles, and reaches out from individual indulgence and
pleasure to sacramental status. A description of his own genitals can, in
the context of the poet's unlimited powers of identification and incarnation, seem at once coyly euphemistic and genuinely mythic. One never
quite knows whether God or man is speaking, even when Whitman
appears most humanly contemptuous of "churches or bibles or creeds"
and turns to what seems like a wholly narcissistic absorption in his own
"firm masculine coulter," his "Root of washed sweet-flag, timorous
pond-snipe, nest of guarded duplicate eggs" (51). Whitman may indeed
take a kind of aggressive pleasure in subordinating all spiritual humility
to the "scent of these arm pits . . . aroma finer than prayer," but from
the calculated (and juvenile) vulgarity of that claim his lines open out into
a nearly bewildering interplay between the body and nature that succeeds
in restoring much of the mystery that such a brash assertion had apparently denied.

That opening out, in fact, is the consistent, rhetorical pattern of Whitman's verse: the movement from formulaic assertion into mystery, a
movement that he achieves not through the power of argument but by
plunging into sequences of concrete images. When these sequences work
they transform the rather commonplace romantic arrogance of his time
("This head is more than churches or bibles or creeds") by dissolving
what had seemed to be an unusually assertive "self" into the rich texture
of what Emerson would call the Not-me:

> Sun so generous it shall be you,
> Vapors lighting and shading my face it shall be you,
> You sweaty brooks and dews it shall be you,
> Winds whose soft-tickling genitals rub against me it shall be
> you,
> Broad muscular fields, branches of liveoak, loving lounger in
> my winding paths, it shall be you,
> Hands I have taken, face I have kissed, mortal I have ever
> touched, it shall be you. (51)

A bold physicality governs such lines, but there is a tremendous gain in
poetic power when we move from the speaker who exalts his own earthy

aroma to the speaker who feels the "Winds . . . soft-tickling genitals" or who can describe his own "Root of washed sweet-flag" with a gentle, furtive tenderness, much as Ishmael approaches Ahab's "root of grandeur" and "broken throne" only with the utmost delicacy and sadness.

Whitman frankly had embarked upon the task of assembling what he thought of as the new Bible and recorded in his notes to himself that he expected it to be ready by 1859. But *Leaves of Grass* was never really a "new" Bible at all. In its key features it was the old one rearranged, with all the essential elements intact — creator, savior, incarnation, intercession, sin, redemption, apocalypse — a framework of familiar, inherited concepts reemployed as elements of a single speaker, reexperienced and transmitted through a compound identity that, quite literally, left Whitman with too much to say. The recourse to catalogues is both exultant and desperate in Whitman's verse, for given the claims of his persona, the catalogues themselves can never be full enough to embody the vision they embrace.[44] Like Milton, Whitman would risk retelling the complete history of creation — not in the secondhand language of an emissary angel, however, but from the point of view of an unborn member of the Trinity:

> I am an acme of things accomplished, and I an encloser of
>   things to be.
>
> My feet strike an apex of the apices of the stairs,
> On every step bunches of ages, and larger bunches between
>   the steps,
> All below duly traveled — and still I mount and mount.
>
> Rise after rise bow the phantoms behind me,
> Afar down I see the huge first Nothing, the vapor from the
>   nostrils of death,
> I know I was even there . . . . I waited unseen and always,
> And slept while God carried me through the lethargic mist,
> And took my time . . . . and took no hurt from the foetid
>   carbon.

"Immense have been the preparations for me," Whitman concludes, "Faithful and friendly the arms that have helped me / . . . Now I stand on this spot with my soul" (79–80). Like much of the first poem in the 1855 *Leaves of Grass,* this passage is a skillful fusion of the self-exaltation of democratic and scientific man with the characteristic act of divine condescension that is the crux of Christian myth.[45] Whitman's speaker is simultaneously rising out of geological time and descending from Heaven, evolved and incarnated, human and divine. It is precisely this fluid movement between states of being that gives his poem its special power of fascination and that is reflected in the drift that characterizes it from a preparative self-absorption to a redemptive selflessness.

The identity of the beleaguered prophet is only one among these multiple states of Whitmanian being, but it is a vital state, and Whitman clearly grasped its typological capacity to unite his other identities, just as the traditional typological reading of Job treated that persecuted servant as a forerunner of the persecuted Christ. Indeed, Whitman's exploitation of the persona of Job is among the most decisive of several signs of the relationship between the structure of the jeremiad as John Winthrop practiced it and the first edition of *Leaves of Grass*. Throughout most of "Song of Myself" Whitman's speaker may represent himself as the indiscriminate absorber of all life – the universal lover – but at the same time he is surrounded by doubters, by "talkers" who "were talking . . . . the talk of the beginning and the end," by "trippers and askers," by snivelers who snivel "That life is a suck and a sell," by whimpering, by truckling, by a vexatious "blurt" about virtue and vice, by mockers and insults. In his preface, Whitman celebrates the stability of the American Union, but that stability too, though always "calm and impregnable," is always "surrounded by blatherers." The speaker of "Song of Myself" and the nation that he addresses share the traditional plight of the virtuous man, the besieged predicament of the unhonored prophet.

At the same time Whitman's poet is never given over to lamentation in anything like the degree to which the Book of Job is. Indeed, Whitman's indifference to lamentation is so firm and explicit that it cannot help but suggest his awareness of the pertinence of the biblical model and his desire to evoke it as part of the poem's necessary background: "I do not snivel that snivel the world over," Whitman proclaims, "I keep no account with lamentation; /What have I to do with lamentation?" (79). Whitman's proverbially vigorous speaker combines the condition of beleaguered humanity with the superhuman range of sympathy reflected in God's speech from the whirlwind with which the Book of Job closes and from which Whitman himself derived much of his characteristic idiom. That speech, of course, is a catalogue – and rather a bragging one – in which God asserts both his power and his solicitude for life by confronting Job with a barrage of questions, many of which Whitman undertakes to answer directly or indirectly in the course of his own song: "Where were you when I laid the foundation of the earth?" "Have the gates of death been revealed to you or have you seen the gates of deep darkness?" "Can you send forth lightnings, that they may go and say to you, 'Here we are'?" "Do you give the horse his might? Do you clothe his neck with strength?" "Is it at your command that the eagle mounts up and makes his nest on high?"

> Deck thyself now with majesty and excellency; and array
> thyself with glory and beauty.

Cast abroad the rage of thy wrath: and behold every one that
    is proud, and abase him.
Look on every one that is proud, and bring him low; and
    tread down the wicked in their place.
Hide them in the dust together; and bind their faces in secret.
Then will I also confess unto thee that thine own right hand
    can save thee. (Job 40:10–14)

Whitman's response to this cumulative assault – at once similar and
dissimilar to those of both Ahab and Ishmael – is to participate in it. He
does not engage in monomaniacal contests with God so much as he
reimagines these extraordinary lines as a kind of human experience, to be
relished by a human figure at play amidst a nature that is, paradoxically,
his own handiwork:

A gigantic beauty of a stallion, fresh and responsive to my
    caresses,
Head high in the forehead and wide between the ears,
Limbs glossy and supple, tail dusting the ground,
Eyes well apart and full of sparkling wickedness. . . . ears
    finely cut and flexibly moving.

His nostrils dilate . . . . my heels embrace him . . . . his well
    built limbs tremble with pleasure . . . . we speed around
    and return.
I but use you a moment and then I resign you
    stallion . . . . and do not need your paces, and outgallop
    them,
And myself as I stand or sit pass faster than you. (58–9)

Whitman's speaker takes both human and divine pleasure in a stallion
every bit as imposing as the majestic creature in Job that "paws in the
valley and exults in his strength . . . laughs at fear and is not dismayed."
Whitman does not explicitly claim the power of command over all the
beasts of field and air, as God clearly does in his reply to Job, but like the
triumphant God in Job, Whitman can indeed mount up with them to
their inaccessible nests:

In vain the speeding or shyness,
In vain the plutonic rocks send their old heat against my
    approach,
In vain the mastadon retreats beneath its own powdered
    bones,
In vain objects stand leagues off and assume manifold shapes,
In vain the ocean settling in hollows and the great monsters
    lying low,

> In vain the buzzard houses herself with the sky,
> In vain the snake slides through the creepers and logs,
> In vain the elk takes to the inner passes of the woods,
> In vain the razorbilled auk sails far north to Labrador,
> I follow quickly . . . . I ascend to the nest in the fissure of the
>   cliff. (57–8)

And in his prose portrait of the poet, which occupies the bulk of the 1855 preface, Whitman exults in a vision of artistic potency, abasing tyrants and exalting the common, through the power of his own right hand, in a direct reply to the challenge of his biblical precursor. The poet in peace is the "equalizer of his age and land," a builder "of vast and populous cities." In war he is "the most deadly force . . . he can make every word he speaks draw blood," just as Winthrop envisioned the spiritual purity of the community at Massachusetts Bay as an augmentation of military potency. "Obedience does not master [the poet]," Whitman claims, "he masters it" (9).

This evocation of the beauty and amplitude of life, in the tradition of the powerfully antagonistic forces of the Puritan jeremiad, is deeply conditioned by the pressure of death, a pressure that is reinforced in Whitman's case by an acute sense of national circumstances. Within the first poem of *Leaves of Grass,* death seems scarcely the menace that it is in *Moby-Dick.* The poet not only asserts his power over it; he imagines it in detail, as a part of his own experience. He becomes "the mashed fireman with breastbone broken" lying in a circle of "white and beautiful faces," enjoying the "pervading hush . . . exhausted but not so unhappy" (65). In his descriptions of a massacre and of a sea battle, Whitman contains the horror and the struggle of events within a formal and natural calm. Even the account of the deaths of the captured Texas Rangers is curiously free of the outrage one might have expected from such an experienced editorialist. But within a few lines of the passage describing the rangers' execution, and its companion piece on the battle between the *Serapis* and the *Bonhomme Richard,* Whitman experiences the most serious crisis of "Song of Myself." His "fit" masters him and the burden of identification with all human pain drives him to what he calls "a verge of the usual mistake":

> That I could forget the mockers and insults!
> That I could forget the trickling tears and the blows of the
>   bludgeons and hammers!
> That I could look with a separate look on my own crucifixion
>   and bloody crowning! (70–1)

Whitman regains his poise, of course, but it is clear from the beginning of *Leaves of Grass* that he writes out of a sense of impending, catastrophic failure that is much more far-reaching than his considerable powers of recovery might at first suggest. All literary manifestos are, by definition, self-assured, but few can match the air of serene confidence that Whitman appears to exude in the 1855 preface. America, he announces, is content to wait while the corpse of the past makes its ceremonial departure. The "new life of the new forms" has great patience, but the disturbing dimension to Whitman's stately transition is that the new life and the new forms themselves are yet to be established. Whitman himself is a sort of hybrid between the voice of John crying in the wilderness and the master spirit whom that prophet foretells. He is both certain and uncertain of his status, sometimes within the space of three or four lines. "I ascend from the moon," he proclaims near the end of his first great poem, "I ascend from the night," but two lines later that smooth ascension seems baffled: "There is that in me . . . . I do not know what it is . . . . but I know it is in me" (86). Whitman has no doubt that the forms of the future will prove "solid and beautiful," but at the same instant he recognizes that "there are now no solid forms" (8).

The America that inspires Whitman's faith is in an extremely equivocal position, so equivocal that many of Whitman's sentences in his preface acquire a peculiar capacity to seem both brash and ominous: "The largeness of nature or the nation were monstrous without a corresponding largeness and generosity of the spirit of the citizen." Whitman for the most part is sure that this corresponding largeness of spirit is present, but it is no accident that he has cast this memorable sentence as a warning. The significance of American elections is "terrible" in Whitman's eyes because of the stark choice each contest represented between candidates committed to slavery and those committed to freedom. The United States, as Whitman puts it, most "need" poets both as a confirmation of the rich "poetical stuff" that Whitman finds so abundant in them and as a reminder of their great potential for life or death. The poet, in fact, is the giver of commandments that, like all commandments, are in some measure an inverse portrait of the community to which they are given:

> This is what you shall do: Love the earth and sun and the animals, despise riches, give alms to every one that asks, stand up for the stupid and crazy, devote your income and labor to others, hate tyrants, argue not concerning God, have patience and indulgence toward the people, take off your hat to nothing known or unknown or to any man or number of men, go freely with powerful uneducated persons and with the young and with the mothers of families, read these leaves in the open air every season of every year of your life, re-examine all you have been told at school or church or in any book, dismiss whatever insults your

own soul, and your very flesh shall be a great poem and have the richest fluency not only in its words but in the silent lines of its lips and face and between the lashes of your eyes and in every motion and joint of your body. (11)

The great confidence with which Whitman opens his preface resembles, in its scope, the confidence with which Winthrop began his discourse on Christian charity by announcing his intention to disclose the reasons behind all human social division. Whitman shares with Winthrop as well the conviction that a community's vigor and durability do not descend from its leaders but ascend from its most ordinary members. And these extraordinary "commandments" are strikingly similar to the exhortations to mutual love and selflessness with which Winthrop brought his own American preface to a close. These words too are an extended call to live in fact what others only profess.

More importantly, perhaps, Winthrop's sense of urgency is the forebear of the atmosphere of contest that pervades this critical passage from Whitman's initial address to his reader. A firm adherence to these commandments involves resistance: against the "arguers" concerning God whom Whitman in fact resists in the course of his poem ("I have no mockings or arguments . . . . I witness and wait"), against those who persecute the stupid and crazy, against tyrants, against the voices of church, school, or book that may tempt you to abandon your convictions, against the rich and the selfish. The result of this resistance is a strikingly purified life and, finally, a kind of power that Whitman, like Winthrop, derives from the "familial" commitments of his poetry. It is in some respects paradoxical to insist that Whitman – a great poet of the exultant self – should have any sympathy with the tradition of selflessness that Winthrop describes. But perhaps the most distinctive trait of Whitman's poet and of Whitman's poetics is that he is the enemy of exclusiveness, even of the exclusiveness of his own vision. His constant contention is that his experience and expression are precisely those of his reader, and as Kerry Larson has perceptively observed, the only exclusion Whitman is forced to accept is that the proof for such an extraordinary claim must of necessity fall outside the borders of the poem.[46] Whitman may indeed seem ahead of us, but he is always solicitously looking backward, waiting, and at the same time almost oppressively close by. One of the organizing assertions of "Song of Myself" is that its speaker is "around, tenacious, acquisitive, tireless . . . . and can never be shaken away" (33). The next several pages of verse following this claim are devoted to giving it the greatest possible particular weight in the first of the formative catalogues of "Song of Myself."

In the opening lines of the poem, Whitman seems almost completely submerged in the private intensity of himself:

> The smoke of my own breath,
> Echos, ripples, and buzzed whispers . . . . loveroot,
>   silkthread, crotch and vine,
> My respiration and inspiration . . . . (27)

But with a suddenness that retains its power of surprise regardless of how many times one has read the poem, one discovers this self-absorbed speaker quite close by, catching at the reader's own, private complacency:

> Have you reckoned a thousand acres much? Have you
>   reckoned the earth much?
> Have you practiced so long to learn to read?
> Have you felt so proud to get at the meaning of poems?

"Song of Myself" is an intimate poem not only in the sense of personal disclosure but in the personal bond with his reader that Whitman succeeds in establishing. His voice is always distinct and individual, but it is not separatism that he celebrates. He called attention to this paradox in a few lines from the earliest part of the poem, representing Whitman's version of the marriage of Genesis that is such a ubiquitous presence in the American imagination:

> Urge and urge and urge,
> Always the procreant urge of the world.
>
> Out of the dimness opposite equals advance . . . . Always
>   substance and increase,
> Always a knit of identity . . . . always distinction . . . . always
>   a breed of life. (28)

For Winthrop the union of Adam and Eve, "opposite equals" emerging out of the dimness of Creation, had great representative value as the model for the "knit" of community that he sought to establish among his fellow emigrants. For Whitman that value is diffused across every time and place, and throughout his greatest poem. It is a "knit of identity" that is always occurring and represents, as far as Whitman is concerned, the central message of his art. "To elaborate is no avail," Whitman asserts just after the passage quoted above, "Learned and unlearned feel that it is so." And in spite of the apparently endless extension of which *Leaves of Grass* was capable, Whitman never did elaborate on this central mystery. He simply repeated his fears and his confidence, in the guise of a thousand particular images, through all the richest catalogues of his imagination.

6

LITERARY ARCHAEOLOGY AND THE PORTRAIT OF A LADY

In the remaining two chapters the imaginative models of John Winthrop and the American jeremiad will prove much less central to an examination of the creative enterprises of Henry James and Emily Dickinson than they were to those of Melville and Whitman. In each instance more traditionally literary precursors are at work: Hawthorne and Shakespeare, in James's first major novel; Milton, in a surprising number of Dickinson's most challenging poems. But the assumptions to which "A Modell of Christian Charity" gives expression remain critical to the performance of each writer. Both Dickinson and James in some measure appear to fall outside of the struggle of what Quentin Anderson has called "associated life."[1] In distinct ways each writer seems an example of the American "imperial self," working "by incorporation" to absorb the world into consciousness and its aesthetic products. But each is equally committed to the war with the self that Winthrop proclaimed and to the establishment of charity in the human community. In James that commitment is experienced in stages through a complex imaginative inheritance. In Dickinson the process is more sudden, accomplished in a striking series of dialogues with her most influential male forebear. An act of creative recovery is involved in each case, a recovery that James in particular associates both with the formal disciplines devoted to recovering and preserving culture and with Shakespeare's great romance, *The Tempest*. Daniel Mark Fogel has treated the influence that key images from Shakespeare's late romance exert upon the moral transformations of Milly Theale and Merton Densher in *The Wings of the Dove*.[2] In strikingly similar fashion James employs Shakespeare's characters as shadow identities for the central characters of *The Portrait of a Lady*, most importantly for Isabel Archer, whose dual nature both as Miranda and as Prospero is a critical index to the redemptive strategy of James's book.

Although *The Portrait of a Lady* is, in many respects, further removed from the Puritan tradition than the biblically informed work of Melville and Whitman, the sensibility that shapes its characters and events is nevertheless that of a moral and imaginative historian. The authorial pose of the historian of life and manners, of course, is an old one in the novel. James's version of this "historicism," however, involves much more than simply the convention of the omnipresent narrative voice. Richard Brodhead has described the importance of *The Portrait of a Lady* in James's career; it marked, for him, his first full-scale attempt to write realistic fiction along the lines laid down by the Continental practitioners whom he most admired: Balzac, Turgenieff, Flaubert. It would signify (James thought) his maturity as a "modern" novelist.[3] But the book's modernity from the beginning is characterized by a sensitivity to the past at least as acute as its interest in the present or the future.

This chronological double focus is reflected in the complex narrative pathways that James takes. The trajectory of *The Portrait of a Lady* is, at first, geographical, from the American provinces toward older and richer centers of culture, but it is also backward in time to a past that is increasingly dependent upon sheltered enclosures – Gardencourt, Lockleigh, Palazzo Roccanera – for protection from a future that is partly comic (Henrietta Stackpole) and partly menacing. A vague but militant Germanic presence troubles the horizon of *The Portrait of a Lady* much as the patriotic fervor of the Mexican War vaguely "itched" at the horizon of Walden Pond. Isabel waits for the future in her empty Albany house, reading a history of German thought, through which she had been driving her restless mind with a "military step."[4] Madame Merle seems to her at first French, but James eventually concludes (with a telling verb) that "extended observation might have ranked her as a German" (228). It is at the German Ball that Isabel decisively fends off Lord Warburton's courtship of Pansy Osmond, and where Pansy herself suffers much damage to her dress from the spurs of all of the men in uniform.

The issues of the American Civil War are clearly on James's mind in a book in which the marketing of women has displaced – or has come to express – the marketing of human beings in the recent past. Caspar Goodwood grapples both with the challenges of courting Isabel and with the difficulty of living in the second of America's postheroic phases: He has missed opportunities for a traditional, chivalric heroism in the war "that had overdarkened . . . his ripening youth" (170). James centers the events of his book on the centennial year of 1876 and reaches still deeper into the militant past at a Gardencourt "bruised and defaced in Cromwell's wars," but his Germanic allusions suggest that under the stimulus of the Franco-Prussian War or the Russo-Turkish War of 1877–8, James is also groping his way forward toward 1914.[5]

Caspar Goodwood is the human dynamo with whom James identifies the future, whereas Isabel is his virgin, married yet essentially unmarried, a mother rather than a spouse, whose moral authority for James, as well as for his characters, is vastly out of proportion to her intellect, her accomplishments, or her experience. James foretells, in other words, in remarkably compressed and complex forms the dualistic opposition between past and future that Henry Adams explores in the stark images of *The Education*. But the past that counts in *The Portrait of a Lady* is American rather than European, Puritan rather than Catholic, and proves capable of confronting the future on equal terms. The scope and importance of James's novel derive to a significant degree from its ability to recast in its own vocabulary the Puritan war with selfishness, the Puritan pursuit of insecurity and value for charity, not in the context of a traditional marriage but in an untraditional one that echoes the central family from Hawthorne's Puritan novel of thirty years earlier. "The Old Protestant tradition had never faded from Isabel's imagination," James notes, referring most directly to Isabel's dread of convents and the authority of the church (578). In even more fundamental ways, however, the old Protestant tradition had never faded for James himself.

When Laurence Holland first traced the relationship between *The Scarlet Letter* and *The Portrait of a Lady,* his interest lay in emphasizing how the forces of marital and family responsibility united the two.[6] James placed marriage much more firmly in the foreground of his book, but the result was, according to Holland, "a response to Hawthorne's novel so profound as to constitute a reworking of the earlier work's materials."[7] That reworking, as Holland has described it, consists of an attempt on Isabel's part to recover some genuinely "magnificent form" of marriage out of what Caspar Goodwood rightly identifies as the "ghastly form" that her actual union with Osmond has taken. The new magnificence springs from the discovery of what Holland characterizes as "the role of parenthood as a mission."[8] That role, Holland argues, is the straight and purposeful road that Isabel sees guiding her from Gardencourt back to Rome at the novel's end.

The main outlines of Holland's discussion offer a convincing case for James's sensitivity to Hawthorne's example, but the conclusive orientation that Holland discovers in James's novel is toward the future. In the combination of qualities that James attributes to Isabel, Holland contends, "the *Portrait* prefigures some of the conspicuous features of marriage in modern America."[9] What Isabel's experience and choices in fact resemble, however, are the circumstances of the national marriage that John Winthrop had first described in 1630.

It may be useful to remind ourselves of the main features of that earlier marriage. Winthrop contended in "A Modell of Christian Charity" that the new American community demanded a selfless commitment to the well-being of others that resembled most closely the selfless bonds of marriage. He found an example of these bonds – the model for his "modell" – in the devotion of Eve, to whom Winthrop assigned a significant measure of Adam's role as the paradigmatic founder. It is Eve, in Winthrop's formulation, who addresses Adam as "fleshe of my fleshe" and whose example of spousal and parental love inspires Winthrop's own exhortation to his fellow emigrants on board the *Arbella:* "Wee must delight in eache other, make others Condicions our owne rejoyce together, mourne together, labour, and suffer together . . . soe shall wee keepe the unitie of the spirit in the bond of peace."[10] These key aspects of the commitment to the emigrant errand Winthrop summed up as a choice between life and death, quoting Moses from the last chapters of Deuteronomy and identifying life with the selfless marriage of community, death with that marriage's failure.

Like Winthrop, James begins his exploration of marriage not with a story, or with some template for action, but with a "model." In James's painterly case, as in Winthrop's conceptual one, it is the figure of a woman, but where Winthrop can draw upon Genesis and upon typological traditions for the immediate means of setting his human model in motion, James faces all the kinetic problems of "genesis," of providing the impetus to action, alone.[11]

Part of the reason for the steady, motionless presence of Isabel, as James initially invokes her in his preface to the New York edition, has to do first of all with the inheritance from Hawthorne. What we are most acutely aware of at the beginning of *The Scarlet Letter* is the figure of a woman alone in her architectural context, on a scaffold by a church in a public square. The square is full of people who have come to witness her shame, some of whom have already commented privately on her plight, but until John Wilson speaks to open the public ceremony of judgment and punishment, even the citizens of Boston have a kind of architectural identity, "levelling their stern regards at Hester Prynne" with a nearly intolerable uniformity and silence. A single life in the midst of the architecture that both sustains and imprisons it is precisely how James tells us he first envisioned Isabel Archer. Even the term with which James rather self-consciously labels her – his *disponible,* his "available" one – suggests the letter that Hester wears and, indirectly, evokes the sexual tensions of Hawthorne's superb opening scene. A woman who seems "available" in precisely this way has already been categorized by her observers as, at best, sexually ambiguous. Turgenieff's methodological term is the first of countless instances in *The Portrait of a Lady* in which apparently mannered language conceals only in part a subtext of sexual aggression. It is simply a remarkable intensification of that atmosphere of aggression that the author, as well as his characters, should be implicated in it. Manners, quite literally, are violence in Henry James, as the example of the perfectly mannered Madame Merle makes clear.

More importantly, Isabel's stillness in James's preface is the earliest indication of the novel's meaning. It is a thematic pose as well as a description of method, for Isabel's characteristic posture in the book – echoing, again, the paradigm of Winthrop's emigrants – is that of hesitation at the point of choice. She does make choices, of course – most notably rejecting two suitors while accepting one – and lays claim to a relish for movement that even the peripatetic Henrietta Stackpole cannot quite share. But this decisiveness and movement are finally misleading. She is, for the most part, engaged in fending off futures that others would like to impose upon her, hoping in the meanwhile to get a clearer grasp of her own, dimly sensed vocation. Her ultimate decision to accept Osmond, like the birth and death of her nameless infant son, occurs in a scene that James chooses not to write. Instead he emphasizes the stillness of choice into which Isabel falls just after Osmond has declared his love and left her hotel room in Rome:

> When he had gone she stood a moment looking about her and seated herself slowly and with an air of deliberation. She sat there till her companions came back, with folded hands, gazing at the ugly carpet. Her agitation – for it had not diminished – was very still, very deep. What had happened was something that for a week past her imagination had been going forward to meet; but here, when it came, she stopped – that sublime principle somehow broke down. The working of this young lady's spirit was strange, and I can only give it to you as I see it, not hoping to make it seem altogether natural. Her imagination, as I say, now hung back; there was a last vague space it couldn't cross – a dusky, uncertain tract which looked ambiguous and even slightly treacherous, like a moorland seen in the winter twilight. But she was to cross it yet. (362)

The decisive instance of such an imaginative breakdown of motion into the posture of choice is the long, reflective chapter late in the book in which Isabel assesses her marriage and first begins puzzling over the mysterious connection between Osmond and Madame Merle, but that long evening and morning of focused thought also stops short before a last vague space, the image of "her husband and Madame Merle unconsciously and familiarly associated" (484).

When Henrietta Stackpole irritably asks Isabel whether she knows where she is drifting, Isabel's answer seems a spirited endorsement of all the energy that we sense within her: "No, I haven't the least idea, and I find it very pleasant not to know. A swift carriage, of a dark night, rattling with four horses over roads that one can't see – that's my idea of happiness" (219). Such a vision seems at least romantically purposeful, and (as Henrietta quickly observes) it is exactly the sort of reply to "sensible" advice that a Victorian heroine ought to make, not in the context of the "immoral novel" that Henrietta in fact scorns, but at some stage on that heroine's predestined path to a redemptive marriage.[12] Isabel, however, is not on that path – she has, indeed, lost all her formidable powers as a "reader" for either moral or immoral purposes – and under these circumstances it is easier to see once again that space is only vaguely defined in Isabel's murky vision, while the passenger in her carriage is simultaneously going forward (as her own imagination went forward to Osmond's proposal) and hanging back.

In this sense the "model" of Isabel Archer is the opposite of Winthrop's figure of Eve, who (as we have seen) is associated not with Adam's definitive mastery of her being but with her own decisive, and familial, passions. In Eve's typologically expanded role she has an immediate grasp of the straight path uniting passion and vocation; James's novel, in the very simplest sense, is an effort to recover that purposefulness in the clear course that Isabel suddenly sees after her escape from Caspar Goodwood at Gardencourt, when she too assumes the second half of a "typic" identity as the Madonna whose portrait Henrietta Stackpole so admires in the Uffizi. But this attainment of a certain measure of control over the future is the result of a newly awakened sympathy with and understanding of the past. James suggests this transformation when he describes the spiritual and psychological comfort that Isabel is able to take in her discovery of the antiquity of Rome, her conversion of antiquity from a collectible commodity – as it exists for Osmond, for Madame Merle, or Edward Rosier – into an extended and healing vision. But Roman objects and the Roman landscape are in many ways the least personal elements of the past with which James surrounds his central character. More critical still to her recovery of power are the elements of the literary past that shape her story. Like the ruined condition of Rome, these literary inheritances come down to Isabel in garbled form, but if the monetary inheritance from Daniel Touchett is the means of putting wind in Isabel's sails, this literary inheritance is the means of charting her course.[13]

The architectural similarities between James's treatment of Isabel in his preface and the opening exposure of Hester Prynne on the scaffold, for example, are at once a form of this inheritance and the keys to a profound difference between the predicaments of the two women. Hester is by no means "available" to anyone, in any sense, at the beginning of The Scarlet Letter. Her single violation of a sexual taboo suggests to no one in Hawthorne's world that she is predisposed to violate it again. The casual and cheerful availability of a figure like the Countess Gemini is the precise spiritual and sexual opposite to Hester's untouchable status. She presents herself to the reader (or rather Hawthorne presents her) with an iconographical completeness, holding the child who, as she herself passionately affirms, will be the means of saving her soul. By contrast, James presents Isabel as a sexual target who must work her way back through the bonds that Hester has already experienced in order to have some hope for a livable future.[14] The intimate sequences of *The Scarlet Letter* – the encounters that free Hester from her suicidal labyrinth of doubt – begin with her bond with Pearl and move first through a discharging of her responsibilities to Roger Chillingworth toward a recovered sense of obligation to the by now dying Arthur Dimmesdale. Isabel, on the other hand, precisely reverses this sequence of affective bonds, first establishing her fondness for the doomed Ralph Touchett, then perversely marrying her Chillingworth, and discovering only at last in Pansy the obligation that restores her humanity. If the whole relationship that James establishes to Hawthorne's novel is indeed analogous to the archaeological presence of Rome in *The Portrait of a Lady,* then Isabel's progress backward through *The Scarlet Letter* is an excavation within an excavation.

A concise measure of the distance between the two books is the contrast between John Winthrop himself and Daniel Touchett. The deaths of these two patriarchal figures transmit inheritances to Hester and to Isabel that shape decisively the experience of each character. Winthrop's bequest, however, is exclusively spiritual and, in the central scaffold scene of *The Scarlet Letter,* marks the beginning of Hester's psychological redemption and her resumption of authority over the novel's events. Daniel Touchett, under the coaxing of his son, leaves Isabel the money that he quite accurately foresees will be the means of Isabel's psychological imprisonment and the end of her independence. Underscoring this paradoxical contrast, of course, is the disparity between the presences of these "fathers." Winthrop appears in Hawthorne's novel only as a celestial phenomenon – a meteor in the night that marks the departure of his soul for Heaven. James, however, has envisioned his own departing patriarch in precisely opposite terms as the invalided, and infantile, master of Gardencourt, his poor old legs wrapped in a blanket, holding a child's teacup.[15]

James's relationship to the example of his predecessor, then, is suggestively like a reclamation, a digging out or a digging down through the imaginative strata to bring to light the "relics" of Hawthorne's art, not as the menacingly "urgent ancestry" that Richard Brodhead describes but as a source of reassurance and direction.[16] The anxiety at work, in other words, involves not an attempt to avoid or to deny artistic influence but an attempt to recover precisely the kind of influence that distinguishes

healthy human dependence from the sort of false independence that
Gilbert Osmond, for example, represents.[17] These concepts of dependence and independence, in fact, are restlessly unstable and ubiquitous in
The Portrait of a Lady itself, as we might expect from James's personal
struggle at once to please and to distance himself from his demanding and
gifted family. Isabel's pursuit of independence is only the most memorable and explicit instance of this concern in the book. James carefully
places every character that he creates somewhere on the complex continuum between absolute self-sufficiency and absolute helplessness.

Mrs. Touchett, for example, has many of the trappings of complete
independence. She comes and goes at her pleasure, manages her invest-
ments, dictates social custom or compels others to observe propriety,
speaks her mind or refuses to speak it as the whim seizes her ("Clearness
is too expensive," she once observes to Ralph). Only at the moment of
Ralph's death, in her admonition to Isabel, does this radical independence
reveal itself as an equally radical, and fearfully expensive, privation: "'Go
and thank God you've no child,' said Mrs. Touchett, disengaging herself" (625). The poignancy of this advice is considerably intensified both
by its inadvertent cruelty – Isabel too has lost a child – and by its own
paradoxical powers of engagement. Mrs. Touchett has finally fulfilled the
promise of her name (and the conditions of her marriage) by proving
susceptible to the touch of sorrow and by eliciting from the reader, for
the first time, pity rather than bemusement. At precisely this moment
she reenacts what she has always been, a disengaged self, but the price
and the status of this disengagement are clearer now than at any other
point in the book. It is not Mrs. Touchett's nature that is at issue here,
however, so much as the subjects of human relatedness and the possibility
of independence. Even the most carefully maintained and reinforced self-
sufficiency breaks down in *The Portrait of a Lady* into what Whitman had
called the inescapable knit of identity, just as this curt command from
Mrs. Touchett at Ralph's deathbed is knit into the fabric of the book and
the lives of its characters, joining and separating in a single instant.

James is equally skeptical about radical dependence. Pansy Osmond
seems at first to be a definitive illustration of this opposite, absolute
condition, but at the end of the novel Pansy's fate is every bit the open
question that Isabel's is. Isabel herself appears to foresee Pansy's complete
submission to her father's will ("She had no vocation for struggling with
combinations"), but the collapse of Pansy's modest resistance is at least
partly traceable to her inability to find any significant support. Struggling with combinations, as Isabel has good reason to know, requires
combinations of one's own. That is the need that Isabel's final promise to
Pansy recognizes and that her return to Rome is intended to meet. But
even Pansy's first, characteristically dutiful and subservient moments in

the book hint at powers of artifice that are, at least for a time, equal to the strategies of her father:

> "Well, my dear, what do you think of it," he asked of the young girl. He used the Italian tongue, and used it with perfect ease; but this would not have convinced you he was Italian.
>
> The child turned her head earnestly to one side and the other. "It's very pretty, papa. Did you make it yourself?"
>
> "Certainly I made it. Don't you think I'm clever?"
>
> "Yes, papa, very clever; I also have learned to make pictures." And she turned round and showed a small, fair face painted with a fixed and intensely sweet smile. (280–1)

The knit of identity at work in Pansy unites her both with Isabel, in her vulnerability to combinations, and with her father, in her capacity to present highly accomplished and quite deceptive appearances.

Many readers of *The Portrait of a Lady* have noted what Annette Niemtzow described some years ago as the tendency of the book's major characters to "mirror" one another, but under the influence of James's own characterization of his methods and goals, this mirroring, or knit of identity, seems credited as an exclusively aesthetic accomplishment. It is equally important to recognize its moral origins in the magnetic chain of humanity to which Hawthorne had attached supreme importance. The mirroring of her own character and experience in those of other people is what Hester Prynne senses as she walks the streets of Boston. Pearl's behavior mirrors her mother's passionate spirit, and Dimmesdale's flesh may come to mirror the letter on Hester's breast. The forces that keep a community together in one body may be temporarily mistaken for supernatural or Gothic mechanisms of punishment in *The Scarlet Letter,* but they are always at work even under conditions of the greatest stress. In just this way they are always at work in *The Portrait of a Lady* even when, as with Pansy and her father in the passage above, they seem to isolate rather than unite.

The concern with dependence and independence, then, is a small but significant part of the inheritance that James is engaged in excavating. Moreover, what that concern makes clear is that the impetus of *The Portrait of a Lady* is not forward toward modern marriage, as Laurence Holland suggests, but backward toward Puritan marriage, toward its aspirations for shaping public as well as private life, and toward the Puritan war with the self. Paul John Eakin touches on this feature of the book when he treats Isabel's experience as a "tragedy of self-culture," but he bases his sense of tragedy on a simplified version of the contrast between "the glowing creed of Emersonian individualism" that Isabel embodies as the book begins and the "Hawthornian world of shadows"

that engulfs Isabel as the circumstances of her marriage become clear to
her.[18] James in fact seems to invite Eakin's comparison of Isabel to Margaret Fuller. The names Osmond and Ossoli are suggestively close, and
Fuller's fate too involves a lost child, Nino, who is swept to his death a
few hours before his mother also drowns in a shipwreck off Fire Island.[19]
But neither fate, Isabel's or Margaret Fuller's, is precisely tragic. Both
women, finally, choose lives that are more selfless than self-cultivating,
and neither one does so out of an absence of alternatives. The war with
the self is James's primary subject in his book, and that fact, in turn, is the
reason why his controversial ending is the proper conclusion of what we
might call a Puritan novel and not the postponed or truncated climax of a
Victorian or a modern one.[20]

Isabel persistently characterizes her pursuit of independence as a pursuit of "life," a word to which James returns repeatedly in his fiction not
as a way of summing up a particular group of goals or values so much as
a way of capturing an urgently felt dualism in human experience. Isabel is
not especially articulate about what the vocation of life means to her, but
from the beginning of the book she understands all of the choices that
face her as choices between life and its opposites. The first form which
that "opposite" takes is not death but, from a Puritan point of view, its
synonym: security. Caspar Goodwood and, still more dramatically, Lord
Warburton offer Isabel security. Warburton is even able to offer in his
sisters an image of what that security might mean, and in her last meeting
with the older Miss Molyneux, Isabel quite explicitly rejects it:

> "I'm afraid we have some people to tea," said Miss Molyneux,
> looking at her brother.
> "Very good, my dear. We'll go."
> "I hoped you would resist!" Henrietta exclaimed. "I wanted to
> see what Miss Molyneux would do."
> "I never do anything," said this young lady.
> "I suppose in your position it's sufficient for you to exist!" Miss
> Stackpole returned. "I should like very much to see you at home."
> "You must come to Lockleigh again," said Miss Molyneux
> very sweetly to Isabel, ignoring this remark of Isabel's friend.
> Isabel looked into her quiet eyes a moment, and for that mo-
> ment seemed to see in their grey depths the reflexion of every-
> thing she had rejected in rejecting Lord Warburton – the peace,
> the kindness, the honour, the possessions, a deep security and a
> great exclusion. She kissed Miss Molyneux and then she said:
> "I'm afraid I can never come again." (188)

Only much later in the novel, after Isabel has awakened to the true nature
of her actual marriage, does life's opposite become death, and the op-

posed choices of John Winthrop's speech take up prominent roles in Isabel's imagination. Choosing Osmond amounted to choosing death, as the vivid images of marital imprisonment, which Isabel herself evokes, unmistakably convey: "the house of darkness, the house of dumbness, the house of suffocation." Nina Baym has pointed out that, in his revisions for the New York edition of *The Portrait of a Lady,* James "hardened" the characters of Madame Merle and Osmond in ways that, in her view, impoverish the novel by making Isabel's predicament less understandable as an exploration of the plight of women in nineteenth-century culture.[21] But what those revisions make more visible is James's deepening interest in categorical modes of dramatizing human life to which typology and allegory are closely allied.

In this context the choice of a spouse for Isabel is even less important to James's "conservative" sensibility than it is to a feminist one. Choosing among husbands is at best a surrogate choice, or a kind of training ground, for the great choice that follows as relentlessly as Isabel seems to imply when she notes, during her nightlong revery in Palazzo Roccanera, the striking of the small hours followed by the striking of the great ones (484). Like Huck Finn a few years later, Isabel recognized that she "would have to decide" at some point between the loyalty she owed to Ralph and the loyalty that considered she owed to her husband. What this choice involves, however, is not a contest between individuals for Isabel's soul but a contest between the conditions of death and life that Isabel first clearly recognized on her journey from Rome to Gardencourt. This return journey initially seems to her to signify personal defeat. Reflecting on the whole of her experience in Europe, Isabel concludes that on first leaving Gardencourt she "had gone forth in her strength; she would come back in her weakness" (607). At the lowest ebb of her spirits she "envied Ralph his dying," but from this closest approach to despair Isabel, like Hester, turns away:

> She had moments indeed in her journey from Rome which were almost as good as being dead. She sat in her corner, so motionless, so passive, simply with the sense of being carried, so detached from hope and regret, that she recalled to herself one of those Etruscan figures couched upon the receptacle of their ashes. There was nothing to regret now – that was all over. Not only the time of her folly, but the time of her repentance was far. . . . This impression carried her into the future, of which from time to time she had a mutilated glimpse. She saw herself, in the distant years, still in the attitude of a woman who had her life to live, and these intimations contradicted the spirit of the present hour. It might be desirable to get quite away, really away,

> further away than little grey-green England, but this privilege
> was evidently to be denied her. Deep in her soul – deeper than
> any appetite for renunciation – was the sense that life would be
> her business for a long time to come. (607)

Isabel's earlier vision of happiness as a swift carriage ride on a dark night
reappears here stripped of its superficial exhilaration in movement and
exposed once more as a moment of choice between dramatically opposed
alternatives.

This rejection of a self-absorbed despair is consistent with the criticism
that James levels at all manifestations of selfishness in the book, from
Osmond's malignant egotism to the self-centered interest Ralph Touchett displays in his desire to convert Isabel's experience abroad into the
entertainment of his dying days. James repeatedly has his characters speak
of one another as specimens or conveniences. That is Isabel's last word on
Madame Merle, for example, "She made a convenience of me" (618), but
Madame Merle shares this propensity with virtually every character in
the book. The dense atmosphere of sexual innuendo in *The Portrait of a
Lady* is less a subject in itself than an instance of this larger phenomenon
of reducing the human world to the status of collectible objects or more
or less desirable services. No one in the book quite matches Gilbert
Osmond's unusual capacity for such dehumanizing reduction, but no one
in the book is entirely free of this quality. Even Isabel's invigorating quest
for independence reduces in some measure to what she herself acknowledges as a "scheme of the agreeable for oneself" to which the misery of
the world is a more or less unwelcome distraction (107). Charity is, in the
highest degree, inconvenient, but James is unmistakably clear in his insistence upon it.

Isabel too, James assures us, will appeal to the reader's charity before
his novel is finished (157). More importantly, she will practice it herself
upon characters who may seem to the reader to be unworthy of it. "Be a
little easy and natural and nasty," the Countess Gemini cheerfully advises
her as she reveals to Isabel the nature of the relationship between Osmond
and Madame Merle: "Feel a little wicked, for the comfort of it, once in
your life" (593). But pity is the emotion to which Isabel is most easily
stirred, for Madame Merle's thwarted maternity and even for her husband's exquisite sensitivity to appearances. The insistent emphasis on
"touching" in the book is not, as at least one reader has argued, a sign of
James's conviction that human relationships are an unwelcome en-
cumbrance upon human freedom.[22] The capacity to touch and to be
touched is the human power that redeems all faults, the counterweight to
the imperious demands of the self. In what amounts to a rather grim
parody of Winthrop's language from "A Modell of Christian Charity"

the Countess Gemini makes clear just how far short of genuine community the union of Osmond and Madame Merle has fallen and, in her
curiously inverted way, pays homage to the ideal against which such a
failure is measured:

> They've always been bound to each other; they remained so even
> after she broke off – or *he* did. But he has always been more for
> her than she has been for him. When their little carnival was over
> they made a bargain that each should give the other complete
> liberty, but that each should also do everything possible to help
> the other on. You may ask me how I know such a thing as that. I
> know it by the way they've behaved. Now see how much better
> women are than men! She has found a wife for Osmond, but
> Osmond has never lifted a little finger for *her*. She has worked
> for him, plotted for him, suffered for him; she has even more
> than once found money for him; and the end of it is that he's
> tired of her. She's an old habit; there are moments when he needs
> her, but on the whole he wouldn't miss her if she were removed.
> And what's more, to-day she knows it. (594)

Caspar Goodwood is puzzled and angered at Gilbert Osmond's portrayal
of his marriage as a "sweet community," but Osmond's alertness to the
language of such idealism, like the acquisitive instincts of a born collec-
tor, only certifies its beauty (554).

The true sweet community of human relations in *The Portrait of a Lady*
is the deepening bond that unites Ralph and Isabel. In these two James has
purified the relationship between Dimmesdale and Hester, freeing it from
the stigma of adultery, but filling it with enough sexual intensity to
distinguish it from the love of a brother and a sister. At least in narrative
terms James has "married" these two characters in the sense that he has
tried to unite in them, almost exclusively, the complex of bonds that
ideally comprises marriage: lover, sibling, spouse, and friend. No other
relationship in the book encompasses more than one of these categories,
and that fact accounts for the conceptual marriage that we feel to exist
between these two figures.[23] But it is also important that this marriage
be, in fact, only conceptual. In symbolic terms Ralph is that "certain
light" whose dawning marks Isabel's triumph in the war with the self
(107). His visit to Rome is, for Isabel, "a lamp in the darkness," something like the faint beacon of light that Winthrop had in mind when he
alluded to the Sermon on the Mount in his own definitive statement of
how we should live: "You are the light of the world. A city set on a hill
cannot be hid. Nor do men light a lamp and put it under a bushel, but on
a stand, and it gives light to all the house. Let your light so shine before
men, that they may see your good works and give glory to your Father

who is in heaven" (Matthew 5:14). James's use of light in *The Portrait of a Lady*, like his exploitation of the motifs of the physician and of disease from Luke in *The Wings of the Dove*, is directly indebted to the Bible as well as to Hawthorne. Under such circumstances Ralph is disqualified from consideration as an earthly spouse both by his health and by his symbolic investment.

An additional source from which James imbibed the ideals of marriage and community that Winthrop endorsed is the series of essays on marriage that Henry James, Sr. published in the *Atlantic Monthly* ten years before James began writing *The Portrait of a Lady*.[24] In particular his father's essay, "The Woman Thou Gavest With Me," draws with striking directness not only upon Winthrop's marriage model but quite explicitly (as its title suggests) upon Winthrop's use of Genesis as a vehicle for placing extraordinary emphasis upon the status of women. The lesson of Genesis for Henry James, Sr. (as in some degree for Winthrop) was not the "generic subserviency" of woman to man but her remarkable acquisition of control over history. Once the transaction of the Fall is complete, man – "the poor, naked, shivering creature," as James rather dramatically calls him – "disappears at once from history, leaving to the woman and *her* seed its exclusive future responsibility."[25] The woman's seed becomes "the pivot upon which the redemption of the race from hardships imposed upon it by [man's] credulity of unbelief is appointed to turn."

As the *Atlantic* essay progresses, James exalts women in particular and marriage in general to quite remarkable heights:

> For woman means not human nature, but human culture. She means human nature no longer outwardly finited by its own necessities, or its own animal, vegetable, and mineral instincts, but inwardly freed from this bondage, or infinited, by God's own indwelling. In short, woman in my opinion symbolizes humanity no longer in its merely created or physical and moral aspect, in which it feels itself under law to God, or to a nature infinitely incommensurate with itself; but in its regenerate, or social and aesthetic, aspect, in which it feels itself divorced from any legal vassalage to God, and becomes, on the contrary, freely and frankly at one with him.[26]

What this symbolic glorification means for James is, in part, the familiar, Victorian association of women with those high spiritual forces that chasten and civilize the sensual rapacity of men: "The ladies will save us," as Daniel Touchett innocently and conventionally remarks (66). But it suggests as well the central social and metaphysical importance of marriage, which the elder James describes in language the allegorical resonance of which would have appealed to Hawthorne:

On the whole and to conclude: – There is vastly more in the woman's movement, so called, than meets the eye of sense, which yet is the eye of the mind with all those who obstinately regard woman as the mere sexual counterpart and diminutive of man. A whole library, full of reconciling significance to the controversy, still remains unpublished and eke unwritten, without which nevertheless the controversy will not have reached its due intellectual dimensions, nor consequently allow itself to be permanently settled. In fact, I am persuaded that we shall never do ripe justice even to the material aspects of the problem, until we come to look upon man and woman as two contrasted terms of a great creative allegory, in which Man stands for what we call the World, meaning thereby human nature in moral or voluntary revolt from God; and Woman for what we call the Church, meaning thereby human nature in spiritual or spontaneous accord with its divine source: the actual point of unity or fusion between the two being furnished by the final *social* evolution of humanity.[27]

This "great creative allegory" is the bridge between Winthrop's typologically conditioned marriage in "A Modell of Christian Charity" and the younger James's application of the meaning of marriage in *The Portrait of a Lady*. Gilbert Osmond's name seems clearly to identify him with man standing for the world, and Isabel Archer's most distinctive characteristic might fairly be described as a spontaneous accord with some principle of divinity that is coming to consciousness within her.

The literary archaeology of *The Portrait of a Lady*, then, leads downward into the reclaimed past and outward to social purposes that echo the communal idealism of John Winthrop. These social purposes are less clearly marked in James's novel than in his father's essay or in Winthrop's speech, but their presence is dramatically underscored by the use that James makes of the pattern of redemptive marriage in *The Tempest*, the play that James was engaged in rereading and introducing for an edition of Shakespeare's *Works*, edited by his friend Sidney Lee, at the same time that he was preparing the New York edition of *The Portrait of a Lady*.[28] Ralph Touchett signals this use when he offers to assist Caspar Goodwood's courtship of Isabel by playing Caliban to Henrietta Stackpole's Ariel, but like the influence of *The Scarlet Letter*, the influence of *The Tempest* on *The Portrait of a Lady* is both pervasive and strangely garbled. Marriage and political life are linked much more directly in Shakespeare than in James, for whom the explicit linkage of Winthrop's vision has broken down. But the relationship between the works is so close as to suggest a possibility of recovering from the events in James's text the communal peace of Shakespeare's final romance. Shakespeare's characters correspond in a dozen unsystematic ways to the characters in *The Portrait of a Lady*. Osmond and Pansy, of course, suggest an inverted portrait of Prospero and Miranda, particularly in the supreme naiveté of the daughters. But Isabel, too, shares some of Miranda's guilelessness as well as the newly "orphaned" status of Ferdinand, commemorated in Ariel's song:

> Full fathom five thy father lies;
> Of his bones are coral made;
> Those are pearls that were his eyes;
> Nothing of him that doth fade
> But doth suffer a sea-change
> Into something rich and strange.
> Sea nymphs hourly ring his knell:
> Ding-dong.
> Hark! now I hear them – Ding-dong bell.   (I.ii.397–405)

Isabel's euphonious name and the sea change that she too experiences may well reflect an imaginative transmutation of Ariel's words. Much closer in their pertinence to the action of the novel, however, are Miranda's confident lines upon first seeing Ferdinand: "There's nothing ill can dwell in such a temple. / If the ill spirit have so fair a house, / Good things will strive to dwell with't" (I.ii.459). Osmond is Isabel's third suitor, as Ferdinand is the third man whom Miranda has ever seen, and the analogy between a spirit and its house that Miranda draws is exactly the analogy that first entices Isabel into Osmond's influence. Isabel quite literally becomes the good thing that strives to dwell in the house of the ill spirit.

In his introduction to *The Tempest* for Sidney Lee's edition, James applies to Shakespeare himself language that is clearly indebted to his description of Isabel in *The Portrait of a Lady*. In that introduction James envisioned Shakespeare as an embodiment of "the spirit in hungry quest of every possible experience and adventure of the spirit, and which, betimes, with the boldest of all intellectual movements, was to leap from the window into the street."[29] Isabel is on precisely this sort of hungry quest as *The Portrait of a Lady* begins, and James had introduced her restless spirit too as "by habit ridiculously active; when the door was not open it jumped out of the window" (86). Daniel Touchett is still another sort of Prospero in James's novel, at least if we apply the implications of Prospero's name literally to the economic status of James's characters. And if there is a Caliban, it is certainly not Ralph but the perennially (and quite comically) "erect" Caspar Goodwood. Ralph in fact is the only candidate for Ariel's magical role. He, much more than his father, is the true agent of Isabel's transformation into an heiress, much as Ariel is the genuinely active element in Prospero's magic; as with Ariel, too, music is Ralph's special medium. He tells Isabel that he keeps a band playing in the anteroom of his spirit to disguise the somber life that he actually lives, and when he has his fateful meeting in Florence with his newly engaged cousin, he is sitting in his mother's courtyard beneath a statue of Terpsichore, the muse of dancing and choral song.

More important than the correspondences among characters, though, is the relationship that James maintains between the meaningful design of *The Portrait of a Lady* and that of *The Tempest*. Both stories revolve around a single character whose final status is that of a wise and forgiving parent. *The Tempest* is a play without the sort of resourceful heroine who figures in so much of Shakespeare's most memorable comic work. In a similar way *The Portrait of a Lady* is a novel without any male counterpart to Isabel. Isabel and Prospero are the dominant figures from each cast of characters, and just as Prospero's magic seems uncontested in *The Tempest*, so by the end of the book is Isabel's in *The Portrait of a Lady*. Osmond and Madame Merle, skilled plotters though they have proved themselves to be, concede that it is Isabel alone who can produce the marriage of Pansy and Warburton by an exercise of "charms" every bit as potent as those that Prospero employs in the courtship of Ferdinand and Miranda.

The marriage that Isabel in fact favors, however, is far closer to the actual marriage of *The Tempest* than the one that Osmond and Merle covet. Pansy and Edward Rosier resemble Miranda and Ferdinand, not only in the chasteness and innocence of their affection, but in their acute need of parental assistance and magical blessing. Like Prospero, Isabel presides over their growing acquaintance and for a time appears to look on their affection with disfavor, even anger, much as Prospero feigns anger at the growing affection between his daughter and the son of one of his enemies. But after coming to a full understanding of the nature of her relationship to Osmond, Isabel looks upon the predicament of the lovers much more gently. Indeed, she comes to resemble the goddess Ceres from Prospero's wedding masque, another "most bounteous lady" who dwells by her "sea-marge, sterile and rocky-head" (Palazzo Roccanera) and whose blessing confers fruitfulness on Miranda and Ferdinand (Iv.i.60–75). James alludes to the story of Ceres, Proserpina, and "dusky Dis" on at least two occasions in *The Portrait of a Lady* as a means of suggesting the parallel between Isabel's marriage and the abduction of Proserpina by Pluto, in conspiracy with Venus, Madame Merle's mythological precursor. But it is far from impossible that he could be thinking as well of the dream visions with which Prospero instructs his daughter and her lover in the responsibilities of marriage. Isabel in this formulation is the mother rather than the bride – a status that is consistent with her final position in James's text.

This structural similarity to *The Tempest* is reinforced by the emphasis placed both by Shakespeare and by James upon the binding nature of love. The relationship between Prospero and Ariel throughout the play, for example, is a continuing mixture of affectionate play and promises of freedom with reminders of duty and bondage. When Prospero first blesses the affection between Miranda and Ferdinand, he does so in a way that constrains as well as liberates them, and in language that is disturbingly reductive even as it purports to be generous:

> Then, as my gift, and thine own acquisition
> Worthily purchased, take my daughter. But
> If thou dost break her virgin-knot before
> All sanctimonious ceremonies may
> With full and holy rite be minist'red,
> No sweet aspersion shall the heavens let fall
> To make this contract grow; but barren hate,
> Sour-eyed disdain, and discord shall bestrew
> The union of your bed with weeds so loathly
> That you shall hate it both. Therefore take heed,
> As Hymen's lamp shall light you.   (IV.i.13–23)

The themes and images of The Portrait of a Lady resonate through this speech: the promising "lamp" of Ralph Touchett's presence in Rome, the reduction of women to commodities, the intense awareness of sexuality, the prospect of a marriage reduced to barren hate, disdain, and discord. As important as these resonances are, however, they are less critical than the shared sense in both The Tempest and The Portrait of a Lady that love entails two sets of possibilities – for death as well as for life – and that the dangerous blend of these possibilities is reflected in the mixture of bondage and freedom that love represents.

Prospero accepts that mixture himself when he acknowledges Caliban as his own and when he begs the audience at the end of the play to release him from his own set of constricting "bands." This epilogue too is part of James's literary archaeology. Like Prospero, Isabel also assumes an indirect sovereignty in Naples, for that is where Osmond lived with his first wife and where Pansy was conceived. Like Prospero, Isabel also has pardoned her deceiver and in some sense – by returning dramatically to Gardencourt – recovered her dukedom. Prospero's closing words recall the metaphor that Ralph Touchett applied to Isabel when he asked his father to split his own inheritance with her – to put some wind in her sails – and Prospero's plea as a whole is so pertinent to Isabel's circumstances that it might readily be her epilogue as well:

> Now my charms are all o'erthrown,
> And what strength I have's mine own,

Which is most faint. Now 'tis true
I must be here confined by you,
Or sent to Naples. Let me not,
Since I have my dukedom got
And pardoned the deceiver, dwell
In this bare island by your spell;
But release me from my bands
With the help of your good hands.
Gentle breath of yours my sails
Must fill, or else my project fails,
Which was to please. Now I want
Spirits to enforce, art to enchant;
And my ending is despair
Unless I be relieved by prayer,
Which pierces so that it assaults
Mercy itself and frees all faults.
As you from crimes would pardoned be,
Let your indulgence set me free.

Isabel too is reduced very much to her own strength at the end of *The Portrait of a Lady,* seeking an escape from a newly barren island as well as some release from the bands that both Osmond and Goodwood are striving to impose upon her. But freedom alone is not the object of her final, precipitate journey in the book. Echoing Prospero, Henrietta Stackpole had accused Isabel of an unrealistic desire to "live by pleasing yourself and pleasing others" (268). It is not the pursuit of pleasure, however, but the recovery of charity that marks the climax of each writer's vision.

7

EMILY DICKINSON'S ADEQUATE EVE

The interplay between security and insecurity is never quite resolved in *The Portrait of a Lady,* a fact that James strives to emphasize by opening up both his heroine and his conclusion to competing visions of failure and success. Such a competition had been a fundamental ingredient of imaginative life in America since John Winthrop's closing evocation of Moses in "A Modell of Christian Charity," and no writer in the nineteenth century carried out the implications of the competition more thoroughly than Emily Dickinson. The reassuringly familiar hymn meters of her verse are constantly challenged by the complexity of her syntax and by the unstable mixture of separation and conjunction represented in her use of dashes. Our first and deepest impressions of Dickinson's work often derive from the competition between a metrics of security and a grammar of insecurity that combine to make her poems a puzzling blend of the accessible and the inaccessible.

In the absence of some immediately recognizable tradition to which such an expressive mixture might be traced, Dickinson's work can seem almost perversely detached from referential meaning, as David Porter has recently argued, or utterly absorbed in private, psychic anxieties, as Vivian Pollak suggests.[1] Even a reader as sensitive to Dickinson's cultural context as Barton St. Armand can slip into this assumption of the poet's psychological or linguistic enclosure. In her struggle with what he describes as the "aloof cat-god" of Calvinism, Armand contends that "Dickinson constructed a closed imagistic world" in which she inverted the domestic pieties of Edward Taylor, envisioning God as a grim predator and identifying herself with his diminutive, nimble, but finally helpless victims.[2] Despite an equally perceptive grasp of Dickinson's place in New England's literary culture, Karl Keller still insists on her essential mystery, on the inability of the reader to enter completely into her imaginative world.[3]

There is a good deal of truth in this darkened picture of Dickinson – a writer of relentlessly private discourse who, as Sandra Gilbert and Susan Gubar have suggested, sought to turn her life into a Gothic novel the very complexity of which provides "signs of her own psychic fragmentation."[4] What is particularly clear from the unusual variety and richness of the scholarly dialogue on Dickinson, however, is that Dickinson challenges her readers in ways not at all unlike the challenge that Isabel Archer posed to the masculine circle at Gardencourt: subversive and respectful, hesitant and decisive, provocative and unapproachable.[5] This is a combination of qualities that seems to call for resolution, and readers have tended to want to solve Dickinson as an almost inevitable consequence of reading her, prompted in part by the tendency of many of her early poems to take the form of riddles:

> Some things that fly there be –
> Birds – Hours – the Bumblebee –
> Of these no Elegy.
>
> Some things that stay there be –
> Grief – Hills – Eternity –
> Nor this behooveth me.
>
> There are that resting, rise.
> Can I expound the skies?
> How still the Riddle lies!   [P-89][6]

Surely the "solution" to these lines is that it is the dead who, according to orthodox piety in Amherst, "resting, rise," but seeing into Dickinson in this way is tantamount to discovering that theological doctrine is not the issue here. This is an extraordinarily intimate meeting with death into which Dickinson has coyly, if a bit shyly, enticed us with six opening lines that sound notes of grief and elegy, but only in a dismissive way. Her reading of old poets would have taught her that prospects of Eternity, the flight of time, the innocent pleasures of the bumblebee could be the rhetorical prelude to an erotic invitation as well as to a mortal one. Dickinson worked openly in this seductive tradition in ways that subvert its conventionally gratifying, masculine purposes and imply that states of loneliness are not necessarily states of erotic deprivation:

> To make a prairie it takes a clover and one bee,
> One clover, and a bee,
> And revery.
> The revery alone will do,
> If bees are few.   [P-1755]

The subdued sexuality in "Some things that fly there be," masked by a childlike presentation, lures the reader into a final line for which the preceding ones (with their explicit disavowal of "elegy") have only partly prepared us. The riddle persists in its uncertain, perhaps deceitful still-ness, but more important than the riddle of death itself are the hints that Dickinson delivers, even in these brief examples of her work, of the extent of her involvement with the key elements of John Winthrop's vision and the unique intensity which she brings to its expression. A tentative, yet at the same time commanding and sensual Eve – the self-sufficient "clover" of "To make a prairie" – she sets before us life and death in a way that dramatically heightens our sense of the human inse-curities that Winthrop faced two hundred years earlier.

The unusually rich critical literature of recent years has made it clear that to a significant degree Dickinson's grasp of the artistic advantages of insecurity is due to her own experience of what Suzanne Juhasz terms the "double bind" of the woman poet.[7] That bind takes as a given a view of the world that is broadly defined by what Carl Degler calls the doctrine of two spheres, in which home is perceived as the woman's "natural" place, and nurturing as her primary skill, whereas the public arena of economic and political life is perceived as the responsibility of men.[8] In the face of such a division, a woman who claims an artistic vocation is already engaged in a particularly intense and unrelenting war between self-effacement and self-assertion, a predicament that Anne Bradstreet, for example, was able to convert into an unusually subtle poetic achieve-ment precisely because it coincided so perfectly with the Puritan view of the self. "Within Puritanism, womanhood *is* selfhood," as Karl Keller puts it, and Dickinson, in turn, built this joint sense of conflict and opportunity into the dramatic posture of her verse.[9] The predicaments of the poems that seem most private, or that lend themselves to the theme of the woman writer under psychic stress, are quite often reflections of Dickinson's conscious decision to rebuild the link between domestic life and epic meaning that Milton explored in *Paradise Lost,* a link that Dickinson establishes in many instances by appropriating as her speaker's voice the dramatic, typological identity of Eve.

As Jack Capps has most convincingly demonstrated, Dickinson's work is unusually rich in allusions, but her relationship to Milton is more nearly that of a successor and transformer than a reader.[10] Her use of the figures of Eve and Mary is a calculated act that signals not her sense of linguistic alienation from the male poetic tradition (as Margaret Homans has suggested) but her willingness to take up in detail Milton's subject, on Milton's terms, and reassert its vitality and pertinence.[11] Winthrop, then, is probably not the direct inspiration for Dickinson that he was for Bradstreet or Hawthorne, but Dickinson's reading of *Paradise Lost* settles on the same, central figure from Genesis that Winthrop chose to embody his communal ideals. For Dickinson, too, Eve articulates a range of

feeling that equals the extraordinary performance that Winthrop imagines for her in "A Modell of Christian Charity." In Dickinson's case this
performance includes a capacity for innocent rebellion that the stubbornness of Winthrop's Eve hints at only indirectly:

> Over the fence –
> Strawberries – grow –
> Over the fence –
> I could climb – if I tried, I know –
> Berries are nice!
>
> But – if I stained my Apron –
> God would certainly scold!
> Oh, dear, – I guess if He were a Boy –
> He'd – climb – if He could!   [P-251]

This is the sort of lyric that is easily dismissed as merely sentimental or as
evidence of Dickinson's mischievous irreverence for the scolding, patriarchal God of Calvinism.[12] But these childlike qualities belie the
poem's fundamental ambition: to retell not only the story of the Fall but
also the stories of Incarnation and Crucifixion in the smallest possible
space. There is no Adam in Dickinson's fable, only a girlish Eve in the
process of convincing herself to steal a bit of forbidden fruit. Her self-
temptation is apparently successful. The dashes in the last line (in this
instance almost a hybrid of drawing and punctuation) suggest that the
speaker may actually be climbing – or at any rate exulting in her prowess
at getting over fences – just as she is convincing herself that God would
do the same thing if he were in the same situation. The innocent diction
does not really conceal a number of points that were critical to Milton as
they are to Dickinson: that this wonderfully ingratiating speaker is in fact
self-tempted rather than deceived, that her actions will in all likelihood
first express themselves in an altered sexuality (the suggestively "stained"
apron), but that finally God will indeed become a "boy" whose own
"climbing" (of the cross? to Heaven?) will cancel the offense that is about
to be committed.

Part of Dickinson's artistic success in these lines depends upon our
recognition that this is clearly a great weight of meaning to place upon
such a slight poetic structure. But just that apparent mismatch between
vehicle and meaning was crucial to the divine injunction against eating
forbidden fruit in the first place. In Milton, the incongruity provokes
Satan to a certain degree of derisive amusement (4.505–22).[13] Dickinson
is only imitating God, much as she is glossing Milton, but her purposes
seem less to subvert than to condense. The ultimate significance of the
Genesis myth for Milton was not judgment but mercy, and the entire

journey from innocence through experience to forgiveness is in fact compressed into Dickinson's lines, captured in the voice of the child speaker, and reproduced in the reader, who progresses first from impressions of sentimental innocence, through an awareness of the biblical parallel, and back again to a wiser recognition that this speaker's crime truly is as harmless as she asserts it is, though harmless for different reasons and with consequences that are universal as well as private and familial.

In the essays on marriage that Henry James, Sr. published in the *Atlantic Monthly* this triumphant image of Eve also makes itself felt. There, in language very much in the spirit of Satan's temptation from *Paradise Lost,* James had envisioned woman as an emblem of regenerate humanity "divorced from any legal vassalage even to God" and feeling herself "freely and frankly at one with him." This exhilarating vision in turn led the elder James to his description of the great "creative Allegory" of marriage, which his son then subjected to fictional scrutiny in *The Portrait of a Lady.*[14] Dickinson's Eve seldom attains the full, Miltonic growth that Henry James, Sr. openly invokes, but part of Dickinson's purpose is to call attention to her rhetorical distance from Milton's exalted and authoritative style both in response to the requirements of the double bind of the woman poet and as a means of asserting a new sort of poetic authority in its place. More often Dickinson's approach to Eve's voice involves casting her speaker into the action of Milton's epic at some more or less precise moment and then reimagining the dramatic monologue upon which so much of the power of *Paradise Lost* itself depends. A simple example of this process is the use Dickinson makes of the passage in *Paradise Lost,* Book 10, when Eve attempts to console a despairing Adam during the night after Christ has pronounced his judgment on the fallen couple.

Seeing Adam in such anguish, Eve approaches and addresses "Soft words to his fierce passion," but Adam's reply to her solicitude is abrupt and harsh:

> Out of my sight, thou Serpent, that name best
> Befits thee with him leagu'd, thyself as false
> And hateful; nothing wants, but that thy shape,
> Like his, and color Serpentine may show
> Thy inward fraud, to warn all Creatures from thee
> Henceforth; lest that too heav'nly form, pretended
> To hellish falsehood snare them . . .   (10.867–73)

Stunned by this violence, Eve falls at Adam's feet, asking not explicitly for his forgiveness but for "His peace" (10.913). "Between us two let there be peace," Eve pleads, and she announces her intention to return to the place in Eden where Christ had judged them and ask God to let the judgment fall only on her.[15] These speeches are a critical moment in the poem, for they mark the beginning of a long exchange in which Eve finally despairs entirely of life and advises that the two of them commit suicide. The transition from despair to hope for both Adam and Eve brings this long night to a close, and at dawn they jointly return to the place of judgment and ask for mercy. Dickinson is able to capture all this range of emotion and significance in a strikingly compressed space:

> The Daisy follows soft the Sun –
> And when his golden walk is done –
> Sits shyly at his feet –
> He – waking – finds the flower there –
> Wherefore – Marauder – art thou here?
> Because, Sir, love is sweet!
>
> We are the Flower – Thou the Sun!
> Forgive us, if as days decline –
> We nearer steal to Thee!
> Enamored of the parting West –
> The peace – the flight – the Amethyst –
> Night's possibility!   [P-106]

The signs of Milton's direct presence here are few but unmistakable. The soft words that Eve first addresses to Adam in *Paradise Lost* are responsible for the gentle adverb of Dickinson's first line. Adam's violent reply to Eve's tenderness accounts for the otherwise puzzling nature of the Sun's harsh question: "Wherefore – Marauder – art thou here?" The time of day in Dickinson's poem corresponds to the time in Milton's – an issue to which we will return a bit later – and Adam's brutal equation between Eve and the serpent may explain the furtive, stealing movement to which the "Daisy" speaker alludes in the second stanza.

More important than any of these details of structure or language, however, is the use that Dickinson makes of her Daisy, her Eve. Rather than slip into a despair from which Adam's measured advice finally frees her, as she does in *Paradise Lost,* Dickinson's Eve is the one who explains the basis for hope, invoking the "peace" that Eve had pleaded for in *Paradise Lost* but also foretelling in the poem's last line the possibility for life that draws Milton's tenth book to a close at dawn and prepares for Michael's elaborate visions of the future. The range of "possibility" in Dickinson's lines is, in fact, vast, for it is at once local (and to some degree erotic) as well as timeless, metaphysical, and finally apocalyptic.[16]

But it remains only "possibility." Just as in Dickinson's whimsical treatment of the Fall as a raid on a strawberry patch, this poem loses a great deal of its suggestive power if it loses the Miltonic context. And Dickinson has not gone out of her way to make the context inescapable.

There are enough clues here – an unusually generous supply, by Dickinson's standards – to make her meaning clear, but it remains quite easy to mistake these lines for an episode in a private romance something like the courtship of Daisy and Phoebus that Barton St. Armand identifies as central to Dickinson's imagination, or the Gothic fiction that Sandra Gilbert and Susan Gubar discover. The "golden walk" of the second line could be either a beautiful synecdoche for all of prelapsarian life or simply what it seems to be, the passage of a single day. Dickinson appears to have sought out a kind of border ground between public and private discourse and positioned her poem quite carefully at precisely the point where it could either recede into a highly coded and personal confession or advance into public dialogue with a formidable poetic colleague on the largest subjects in redemptive history.

Dickinson explores border states of several kinds in her verse – the boundary between life and death, crossed at the instant of dying, for example, or the meeting place of land and sea – but her sense of the potential for blending public and private speech in the role of Eve suggests that Eve serves for Dickinson very much the purposes that she served for Winthrop, integrating the familiar moral setting of private life with the wider sphere of public enterprise. In Dickinson's case, this process involves fusing the images of the poet at home with the poet as national prophet who undertakes to justify the ways of God to men. In contrast to Milton, however, Dickinson found a formal equivalent for the fit audience, though few that Milton envisioned himself addressing. By reducing the epic machinery to its dramatic essence she has, in effect, placed the reader in the same position that Milton's God assigned Adam and Eve, free to "stand" and free to "fall," free to sense the full scope of her lines but equally free to mistake them for an eccentric (and erotically charged) variation of the domestic verse for which many of Dickinson's contemporary "lady singers" were celebrated.

Dickinson clearly meant a poem like "The Daisy follows soft the Sun" to evoke both the mystery of private passion and the Miltonic tradition to which she laid equal claim. Just as Winthrop appropriated Eve's familial passion as a resource of the state – as its "model" – Dickinson, in effect, claimed the epic status of Milton as a model for her private portfolio. Like Winthrop too Dickinson takes pleasure in reshaping Eve's role, giving her a greater authority over the events in which she plays such a major part, without ever completely sacrificing the privacy that gives Eve her special value for a poet like Dickinson, who understood her own life as a fusion of private and prophetic identities. This reshaping process can have the effect of turning Dickinson's verse into a penetrating commentary on the aspects of the Miltonic tradition that she has deliberately set out to follow.

In "They leave us with the Infinite," for example, Dickinson takes up one of Milton's most challenging lines and exposes a fresh dimension of meaning in it:

> They leave us with the Infinite.
> But He – is not a man –
> His fingers are the size of fists –
> His fists, the size of men –
>
> And whom he foundeth, with his Arm
> As Himmaleh, shall stand –
> Gibralter's Everlasting Shoe
> Poised lightly on his Hand,
>
> So trust him, Comrade –
> You for you, and I, for you and me
> Eternity is ample,
> And quick enough, if true.   [P-350]

As in most of Dickinson's treatments of Eve's voice, this one conflates different scenes in *Paradise Lost* in order to fit the greatest possible meaning into the shortest space. The third stanza alludes to the notorious description of Adam and Eve in Book 4, in which Milton appears to subordinate Eve to Adam's rule in no uncertain terms:

> Two of far nobler shape erect and tall,
> Godlike erect, with native Honor clad
> In naked Majesty seem'd Lords of all,
> And worthy seem'd, for in thir looks Divine
> The image of thir glorious Maker shone,
> Truth, Wisdom, Sanctitude severe and pure,
> Severe, but in true filial freedom plac't;
> Whence true autority in men; though both
> Not equal, as thir sex not equal seem'd;
> For contemplation hee and valor form'd,
> For softness shee and sweet attractive Grace,
> Hee for God only, shee for God in him . . .   (4.289–99)

Dickinson's cheerful "You for you, and I, for you and me" not only recasts Milton's hierarchical formula but conclusively identifies the speaker of Dickinson's poem. Once we recognize the speaker, it is fairly easy to see that the dramatic context of these lines is not Book 4 but some time later in Milton's poem, after the Fall, when trust in God has become an issue rather than a certainty and God Himself has become "the Infinite" rather than the paternal Creator of prelapsarian Paradise.

Dickinson's Eve, however, unlike Milton's, is the authoritative partner, the consoler, the advocate for life who recognizes that Eternity will come "quick enough" on its own and ought not to be embraced in suicidal despair. It is easy to imagine how fully Dickinson would have felt the implications of the double meaning in Milton's capitalized "Grace" in his description of Eve; her own fondness for emphatic capitals was a lifelong passion. Like the speaker in "The daisy follows soft the Sun," the speaker of "They leave us with the Infinite" too senses the possibilities for "grace" ahead and seeks to console her "Comrade." In Dickinson's formulation, it is Eve who makes others' conditions her own, maintaining what Winthrop called the unity of the spirit in the bond of peace, and addressing her husband with a word that symbolizes that comradely unity. Milton's troubling line "Hee for God only, shee for God in him" appears to place Eve in a derivative position but, as Dickinson affirms, it also expands her range of sympathetic power. Adam may be primary, in some sense, but he is also self-absorbed ("You for you"). Eve possesses the wider range of selflessness: "I, for you and me." In the assertive voice of "I'm ceded – I've stopped being Theirs" Dickinson apparently recalled the "Godlike erect" stature of Milton's First Parents in the passage from Book 4 and applied it once again to the voice of her speaker, "a half unconscious Queen" who celebrates the self-determination of her second baptism:

> But this time – Adequate – Erect,
> With Will to choose, or to reject,
> And I choose, just a Crown –   [P-508]

Dickinson's Eve is nearly always adequate, Godlike erect, though often her powers of choice are reduced to powers of endurance or, as in "They leave us with the Infinite," powers of trust. More accurately, perhaps, they are reduced to the ability to sustain the peculiar anguish of a transitional life – between what Dickinson punningly calls the moment of being "ceded" and the completion of birth.[17]

Particularly after the Fall, the figure of Milton's Eve concentrates for Dickinson the sense of momentously suspended existence – a condition that she expressed in a number of remarkable poems that seem to be forged out of an unusually intense encounter between personal circumstances and poetic influence:

> Behind Me – dips Eternity –
> Before Me – Immortality –
> Myself – the Term between –
> Death but the Drift of Eastern Gray,
> Dissolving into Dawn away,
> Before the West begin –

'Tis Kingdoms – afterward – they say –
In perfect – pauseless Monarchy –
Whose Prince – is Son of None –
Himself – His Dateless Dynasty –
Himself – Himself diversify –
In Duplicate divine –

'Tis Miracle before Me – then –
'Tis Miracle behind – between –
A Crescent in the Sea –
With Midnight to the North of Her –
And Midnight to the South of Her –
And Maelstrom – in the Sky –   [P-721]

There is little sign in these lines of much direct indebtedness to *Paradise Lost;* the association of death with dawn may allude to the fateful daybreak in Book 10 that Dickinson drew on for "The Daisy follows soft the Sun," or it may only refer to the dawning of an afterlife. Allusions to daybreak pervade Dickinson's poetry in ways that suggest a distinctly personal mythology at work. What is clear, however, is that this speaker too is female, adequate, and erect in the face of her suspension between two miracles that suggest creation and incarnation, the birth of a curiously unparented "Son" whose origins the closing prophecies of *Paradise Lost* explicitly trace to Eve, the bearer of the "Promised Seed" that "shall all restore" (11.621–3). Dickinson exploits the same typological network here that Anne Bradstreet employed in "The Author to Her Book," but she does so with a boldness that confronts the consequences of the Fall with absolute conviction in the adequacy of "Me," a speaker requiring no prospective "Prince" or absent father with fists the size of men upon whom to ground her confidence. The Tennysonian joke of the third stanza merely underscores Dickinson's adoption of a heroic voice that is aware of, and sublimely indifferent to, masculine precursors whose self-enclosed diversification the second stanza alludes to in language that comes surprisingly close to identifying the patriarchal trinity with a comically "versified" narcissism. The speaker of "Behind Me – dips Eternity" is both a witness to the maelstrom of judgment and, as the poem's last stanza suggests, a master of the design that enfolds chaos.

One of Dickinson's longest poems, "I cannot live with You," examines this complex posture in ways that intensify both the personal insecurity of the speaker and the self-confidence that derives from Dickinson's exultant appropriation of the Miltonic context. These lines touch on the same sources in *Paradise Lost* that Dickinson treated less ambitiously in "They leave us with the Infinite." The sense of grim trust in God is gone, however, and Dickinson builds this complex monologue out of a series of

confessions in which her speaker announces a degree of personal inadequacy that becomes an index to the strength and durability of her love:

> I cannot live with You –
> It would be Life –
> And Life is over there –
> Behind the Shelf
>
> The Sexton keeps the Key to –
> Putting up
> Our Life – His Porcelain –
> Like a Cup –
>
> Discarded of the Housewife –
> Quaint – or Broke –
> A newer Sevres pleases –
> Old Ones crack –   [P-640]

Milton's influence is part of the background of these first three stanzas,
but the origins of this "Housewife" who puts aside the cup of "Our Life"
become explicit three stanzas later in the third of the poem's confessions:

> Nor could I rise – with You –
> Because Your Face
> Would put out Jesus' –
> That New Grace
>
> Grow plain – and foreign
> On my homesick Eye –
> Except that You than He
> Shone closer by –
>
> They'd judge Us – How –
> For You – served Heaven – You know,
> Or sought to –
> I could not –
>
> Because You saturated Sight –
> And I had no more Eyes
> For sordid excellence
> As Paradise

In this more extended transformation of Milton's hierarchal formula,
"Hee for God only, shee for God in him," Dickinson's Eve sets the terms
of her existence in a way that emphasizes her powers of love and choice
rather than the condition of dependence and her need for mediation. Her
sight is limited only by its capacity for fullness, for saturation, and her
circumstantial understanding exceeds that of Adam, matches that of

Milton, and falls short only of God's, whose judgment is hidden in the uncertainty of "How." The poem denies the speaker's capacity to "rise," but in a perfect instance of what Robert Weisbuch has called Dickinson's powers of compound vision, it "rises" just the same.[18]

The closing lines briefly echo Satan's own famous confession from *Paradise Lost,* "myself am Hell," as a means of establishing simultaneously the speaker's predicament and her paradoxical adequacy to face the worst of sentences alone:

> And were You lost, I would be –
> Though My Name
> Rang loudest
> On the Heavenly fame –
>
> And were You – saved –
> And I – condemned to be
> Where You were not –
> That self – were Hell to Me –
>
> So We must meet apart –
> You there – I – here –
> With just the Door ajar
> That Oceans are – and Prayer –
> And that White Sustenance –
> Despair –

This despair, however, like the despair of Milton's tenth book, is full of possibility. These final stanzas restore the domestic intimacy that the first stanzas had appeared to put aside, but restore it provisionally, as God does for Adam and Eve in *Paradise Lost.* The poem closes with an expression of the "vitalized dread" that Robert Weisbuch identifies as Dickinson's one fixed value, but it is a value for which Dickinson herself finds a perfect dramatic equivalent in Milton's scenic expansion of Genesis.[19]

In these Edenic monologues, Dickinson has worked a double transformation upon the themes of *Paradise Lost.* She has given the greatest sense of private urgency to a remote, mythic structure and at the same time has asserted – not unlike Whitman – the mythic status of private life. This reciprocal imaginative influence was Winthrop's goal as well in "A Modell of Christian Charity": to claim for marriage the public importance of the state and to claim for the state the emotive bonds of marriage. In Dickinson's case as in Winthrop's, this metaphorical network implies a willingness to endure as much as to celebrate, to face the costs of failure as well as to rejoice in a triumphant vision of "Night's Possibility." Karl Keller traces this feature of Dickinson's imagination to her participation in the evangelical tradition of Jonathan Edwards. Edwards's "pit" in Keller's view is the setting from which Dickinson repeatedly chooses to begin her poetic recovery of hope.[20] But in light of the patterns of dramatic appropriation in her poems, it is more likely to be Milton's pit than Edwards's. When Dickinson envisions robbing her predecessors – as she does in one famous confessional instance – it is poets that she is thinking of despoiling, not ministers, and the crime is correspondingly less serious since its victims possess "a Fortune – / Exterior – to Time –" (P-448). In *Paradise Lost,* as much as in the psychology of Edwards's sermons, the route to mercy leads through death. Accordingly, Dickinson appropriated Eve's voice in a number of poems to express both the sense of irrevocable loss that is part of the providential design in Milton's poem and the sense of sacrifice and of peril that conditions Winthrop's vision too in his speech to the *Arbella* emigrants.

Dickinson returned repeatedly to the closing books of *Paradise Lost* in order to explore the mixture of hope and insecurity that characterize those moments, particularly when they are treated from Eve's point of view. The passages from Book 10 that she drew upon for "The Daisy follows soft the Sun" also provide the dramatic context for her reconsideration of Eve's desire to go alone to the place in Eden where Christ had passed his judgment and plead with God to exempt Adam from punishment "that all / The sentence from thy head remov'd may light / On me, sole cause to thee of all this woe, / Mee mee only just object of his ire" (10.935):

> Savior! I've no one else to tell –
> And so I trouble *thee.*
> I am the one forgot thee so –
> Dost thou remember me?
> Nor, for myself, I came so far –
> That were the little load –
> I brought thee the imperial Heart
> I had not strength to hold –
> The Heart I carried in my own –
> Till mine too heavy grew –
> Yet – strangest – *heavier* since it went –
> Is it too large for *you?*   [P-217]

The "imperial Heart" for which this speaker pleads is joined to her own heart with some of the intimacy with which a woman carries a child, but mysteriously it is the speaker's heart rather than the "Heart" she carries that grows too heavy, is apparently delivered of its imperial burden, and yet feels heavier still despite the fact that she names herself (derisively) "the little load." These marvelously entangled images are Dickinson's equivalent of the intimate bonds that join Adam and Eve, both as "one Flesh, one Heart, one Soul," according to Milton (8.499) and as a married couple. The scenes in *Paradise Lost* that recount the creation of Eve out of Adam's side describe that event as if it were a birth, and Dickinson's lines also suggest the image of one soul extracted from another, though the physical embodiment of that mysterious birth in Dickinson's case is a heart rather than a rib.

The connections between this poem and the Miltonic text it glosses are too complex to yield easily to her speaker's powers of explanation, but precisely the sense of being overwhelmed is Dickinson's subject. Her speaker, her Eve, seems to doubt the Savior's mercy, but forgiveness is really a given in this poem, as it is in *Paradise Lost*. The mystery that gives life to the lines is the nature of the mutually binding relationship between hearts: How is it formed? What does it entail? These, the poem suggests, are the "strangest" things the speaker confronts and before which she expresses her helplessness. In "The first Day's Night had come" Dickinson allows Eve to express a still more sweeping sense of helplessness that reaches beyond the boundaries of *Paradise Lost* to imagine Eve's description of the years after the expulsion from the Garden:

> The first Day's Night had come –
> And grateful that a thing –
> So terrible – had been endured –
> I told my Soul to sing –
>
> She said her Strings were snapt –
> Her Bow – to Atoms blown –
> And so to mend her – gave me work
> Until another Morn –
>
> And then – a Day as huge
> As Yesterdays in pairs,
> Unrolled its horror in my face –
> Until it blocked my eyes –
>
> My Brain – begun to laugh –
> I mumbled – like a fool –
> And tho' 'tis Years ago – that Day –
> My Brain keeps giggling – still.
>
> And Something's odd – within –
> That person that I was –
> And this One – do not feel the same –
> Could it be Madness – this?   [P-410]

The connection between these lines and *Paradise Lost* hinges on Dickinson's sensitivity to the passage of time in Milton's poem and on the relationship of that time sequence to Dickinson's own view of what Barton St. Armand has termed her "mystic Day."[21]

The concept of time applies only to one of the three settings of *Paradise Lost*. Heaven and hell, in Milton's view, are timeless places. Paradise, however, is under the influence of the movement of heavenly bodies, and it has a diurnal rhythm. The events in time that Milton relates, then, take place between sunset on the day of Satan's arrival in Paradise and sunset on the day that Michael expels Adam and Eve from the garden, when they turn back, facing west, toward the eastern gate of Paradise and witness a "sunset" composed of "that flaming Brand," the gate itself, and the "thronged and fiery Arms" of the angels sent to guard the Tree of Life (12.644). Between these two sunsets two complete days pass, one the day of the temptation and Fall and one the day on which Michael reveals to Adam the course of human history that will follow from his sin. The night between these two days marks the chronological midpoint in Book 10 in which Eve despairs of life and to which Dickinson has devoted such attention.

Sunset, in Milton's sequence, is the time both of expulsion and of consolation, of Christ's judgment and of the completion of the consoling visions of Michael, a dual significance that Dickinson responds to in her own poetic sunsets. Dawn is similarly critical in both poets' imaginative chronology, but the third important element of the Miltonic clock is noon. Noon is the time of day when Adam and Eve meet after she has eaten the fruit and the time that their newly awakened lust for one another expresses itself. Similarly, noon was the time of greatest sexual intensity in Dickinson's imagination. "Vespers – are sweeter than Matins – Signor," she observes seductively near the close of "I shall keep singing!": "Morning – only the seed of Noon." Morning was the seed of Noon in *Paradise Lost* as well, and if Dickinson did not take her symbolic language directly from Milton, she certainly would have noticed and enjoyed the poetic agreement between them.

In "The first Day's Night had come" Dickinson momentarily returns to the chronological center of *Paradise Lost* but situates her Eve there, this time, alone, mending her soul in preparation for "another Morn" that promises challenges as great as the day that has already been endured. The only sign of the broken marital partnership of Milton's poem is the appropriately broken pun on "Atoms" that suggests the extent of this Eve's isolation from her spouse. In *Paradise Lost,* on the second day, Michael takes Adam to a hilltop in Eden to witness a vision of the human future "thereby to learn / True patience, and to temper joy with fear / And pious sorrow, equally inur'd / By moderation either state to bear" (11.360). Eve is left sleeping below, her eyes "drencht . . . As once thou slep'st, while she to life was form'd." Dickinson follows Milton exactly enough to incorporate the image of Eve's "blocked" eyes, but the lesson that Dickinson's Eve learns on this "Day as huge / As Yesterdays in pairs" is not the lesson of true patience and moderation that Michael promises but a much more human and provisional awareness that "Something's odd – within."

In *Paradise Lost* Adam readily absorbs all that Michael teaches him, and Eve awakens from her sleep content to leave Paradise, grateful for the knowledge of their ultimate redemption. Dickinson, however, describes a response to this mythic pattern that is much more limited, much less sure of its role, far more insecure than that of the characters in Milton's poem. Insisting both on the structure of *Paradise Lost* and on the integrity of the private soul, Dickinson assembles a myth of her own in which the lesson that Eve discloses – in contrast to the compliant gratitude of Milton's First Parents – is uncertainty, a state of perpetual balance between madness and sanity, death and life, that reflects not so much Dickinson's private anxieties as it does her determination to reestablish the personal bearing of the Genesis myth, much as Milton sought to do in *Paradise Lost*.

If Milton's focus is on justifying God to men, however, Dickinson's is on justifying women and men to God, an advocate's role that she fulfills sometimes by simply retelling Milton's story in ways that significantly modify its outcome, insisting on the adequacy of its human participants. Dickinson's famous dream vision of a visit made to her room in winter first by a "Worm – / Pink, lank and warm" and then a "Trifle afterward" by a snake "ringed with power" has elicited a certain amount of attention from readers eager to document Dickinson's ambivalent attitudes toward sex. But it seems more likely that Dickinson is once again recasting Milton in a way that gives peculiar intensity to Eve's temptation and then celebrates her temporary escape by fusing elements of Book 9, in which the Fall takes place, with Book 5, in which Eve relates to Adam her prophetic and disturbing dream.

The formidably "ringed" snake "with mottles rare" that approaches Dickinson's speaker is suggestively similar to the magnificent creature that ultimately stalks Eve in the climactic book of *Paradise Lost:*

> not with indented wave,
> Prone on the ground, as since, but on his rear,
> Circular base of rising folds, that tow'r'd
> Fold above fold a surging Maze, his Head
> Crested aloft, and Carbuncle his Eyes;
> With burnisht Neck of verdant Gold, erect
> Amidst his circling Spires, that on the grass
> Floated redundant . . .   (11.496–504)

Wisely deciding not to compete directly with Milton's erotically charged, redundantly (and rhetorically) circular tempter, Dickinson imagines instead the moment when the "ringed" serpent responds to an energy "secreted in his form" – as Satan in fact is secreted in Milton's story – and tries to rape his victim:

> That time I flew
> Both eyes his way
> Lest he pursue
> Nor ever ceased to run
> Till in a distant Town
> Towns on from mine
> I set me down
> This was a dream.   [P-1670]

In the dream that Eve indeed relates to Adam at the beginning of Book 5 of *Paradise Lost*, she does not fly the angel tempter but yields, eats the forbidden fruit, and literally ascends to the clouds "wond'ring at my flight and change / To this high exaltation" (5.90). Dickinson's speaker is firmer in her resistance, calmer in the face of her disturbing vision, and wonderfully swift of foot, in every sense, as the unencumbered lines above deftly suggest. She does not need Adam – and we do not need psychoanalysis – to interpret her vision. The serpent's visit is in every respect a grimly Miltonic parody of the seasonal and sexual patterns of the poem just preceding it in the Johnson numbering. The manuscript evidence suggests that Dickinson may have thought of these poems as a sequence:[22]

> In snow thou comest –
> Thou shalt go with the resuming ground,
> The sweet derision of the crow,
> And Glee's advancing sound.
>
> In fear thou comest –
> Thou shalt go at such a gait of joy
> That man anew embark to live
> Upon the depth of thee.   [P-1669]

The visitor here is easily identifiable as the savior who comes in winter and who dies in spring, every year in Amherst. But the second stanza is another memory of Eden, a place where Christ comes clothed in "fear" to judge, but whose departing "gait" is a punning reference to the eastern gate of Paradise through which Milton's couple passes to begin a new life in a more vast, but equally reassuring landscape.

In the case of Dickinson's serpent guest, it is not the sexual nature of the assault itself that prompts her flight so much as it is the suitor in question. In "I started Early – took my Dog," Dickinson records a meeting with another transcendent lover in which her own role is much less tentative and her desire to escape much less urgent. The sexual intensity of her assignation with the "Tide" is every bit as great as in the encounter with the serpent, but this lover is much closer to the apocalyptic bridegroom of "In snow thou comest," a suitor whose values have nothing in common with the rituals of ordinary courtship and whose advances seem anything but unwelcome:

> But no Man moved Me – till the Tide
> Went past my simple Shoe –
> And past my Apron – and my Belt
> And past my Bodice – too –
>
> And made as He would eat me up –
> As wholly as a Dew
> Upon a Dandelion's Sleeve –
> And then – I started – too –
>
> And He – He followed – close behind –
> I felt His Silver Heel
> Upon my Ankle – Then my Shoes
> Would overflow with Pearl –   [P-520]

Like Milton's Eve (or like Anne Bradstreet), Dickinson's poetic persona welcomes "the Rites / Mysterious of connubial love" – even when that love is not, as it happens, connubial. This sexual candor establishes for Dickinson herself a second dramatic voice as Eve's typological heir, Mary, whose specifically sexual predicament interested Dickinson in a series of important poems that, like her adoption of Eve's voice, constitute a formal bridge between private and mythic experience.

The typological sequence, however, did not dictate imaginative priorities to Dickinson. The voice of Eve is an ongoing identity whose power of memory evokes and extends the events of Milton's drama into contemporary life. There is no explicit indication of the sex of Dickinson's speaker in "When I hoped, I recollect," any more than there is an open acknowledgment of dramatic context. But this poem represents an unusually bold variation upon the structure of *Paradise Lost,* drawing upon Milton's mystic chronology to reinforce Dickinson's own associations of time with psychological states. As in "The first Day's Night had come," Dickinson positions her speaker outside the boundaries of Milton's plot in an indeterminate present – the reader's time – and then reports a sequence of spiritual conditions that seems to mark a descent into blackness:

When I hoped, I recollect
Just the place I stood –
At a Window facing West –
Roughest Air – was good –
Not a sleet could bite me –
Not a frost could cool –
Hope it was that kept me warm –
Not Merino shawl –

When I feared – I recollect
Just the Day it was –
Worlds were lying out to Sun –
Yet how Nature froze –

Icicles upon my soul
Prickled Blue and Cool –
Bird went praising everywhere –
Only Me – was still –

And the Day that I despaired –
This – if I forget
Nature will – that it be Night
After Sun has set –
Darkness intersect her face –
And put out her eye –
Nature hesitate – before
Memory and I –   [P-768]

The sequence here from Hope to Fear to Despair seems a deathward progress, but Dickinson has carefully cast all three of these conditions of soul equally into the past. Despair is at least as remote as Hope, and once the identity of the speaker is clearly established, the movement of the poem will at least imply unsuspected possibilities for life.

These lines compress three scenes from *Paradise Lost* and establish the complete mastery of Dickinson's Eve over the significance of redemptive history and over private, psychological experience. Working backward through the poem makes the pattern of allusion clearest. The "Day" of Eve's despair in *Paradise Lost* occurs just at dawn of the day following the Fall – the "Day as huge / As Yesterdays in pairs" that Dickinson has already confronted in "The first Days Night had come." This sobering dawn follows a night of lamentation for Adam that Milton describes as peculiarly ominous, a "still Night":

> not now, as ere men fell,
> Wholesome and cool and mild, but with black Air
> Accompanied, with damps and dreadful gloom,

Which to his evil Conscience represented
All things with double terror . . .   (10.847–50)

This is the darkness that Dickinson has in mind (P-768) when she has her Eve invoke a night that "intersects" the face of Nature as a sign of her determination to remember the "vehement despair" that in Milton's own peculiar lexicon "dy'd her Cheeks with pale" (10.1009).

The day of fear in Dickinson's poem, on the other hand, corresponds to the beautiful morning in Book 5 when Adam awakens Eve from her prophetic dream. Milton establishes the mildness of unfallen Nature that contrasts with Eve's nightmare, a perpetual summer filled with "the shrill Matin song / Of Birds on every bough," which Dickinson has set in flight in "When I hoped, I recollect" with her graceful redaction, "Birds went praising everywhere." In the midst of these praises Milton's Eve describes the "damp horror" that "chill'd" her when the tempter in her dream tasted the forbidden fruit. Dickinson's version of Milton's setting is compressed and masterful, for she is able to capture both the seasonal appeal and the metaphysical scope of Paradise in a single line: "Worlds were lying out to Sun." Moreover, the frozen horror that Dickinson's Eve describes is inward, spiritually more self-aware than the sensation of Milton's Eve, and at the same time hauntingly appealing, as if these icicles "Blue and Cool" upon the soul contain promise as well as menace – a possibility that the recollected stillness of Dickinson's speaker also suggests, for she is waiting rather than trembling.

Hope, in the first stanza of Dickinson's poem, is identified only with a direction, west, but that is the geographical equivalent of sunset and nightfall, the time of day in *Paradise Lost* when Adam and Eve first appear, express their love for one another, and look forward to the fulfillment of God's promise to raise "from us two a Race / To fill the Earth, who shall with us extol / Thy Goodness infinite, both when we wake, / And when we seek, as now, thy gift of sleep" (4.732–5). As Dickinson dryly hints, Merino shawls would have been unnecessary encumbrances on the sublime nakedness of Paradise, and Milton's Eve too (like Dickinson's) had confessed that she forgot all times and all changes of season when conversing with Adam.

The pattern of allusion is, once again, hidden and yet sufficiently clear to break through and illuminate the poem's dramatic context. Dickinson is retelling the complete psychological experience of *Paradise Lost* from a perspective of some distance and some confidence. Despair is still very much a threat to Dickinson's speaker, or memory would not require such an extreme degree of resolve, but in Dickinson's Eve the resolution, the boldness, and even the humor that Milton hints at in Eve's character have triumphed over the circumstances that threaten them. More accurately perhaps, as Karl Keller has suggested, they have triumphed within the circumstances of the Puritan epic. That, in effect, is the significance of Dickinson's ideal of "adequacy." Her Eve, like Winthrop's, is free in all but the most implicit sense from any subservience to Adam, but she is free within the pattern of loyalty that both Winthrop and Milton celebrate. In these monologues from Eve, Dickinson performs an act of accommodation that recovers Milton for her own day as much as Milton undertook to recover Genesis or Winthrop undertook to recover for Massachusetts Bay both the example of Eve and the vision of Moses.

Indeed, like Winthrop, Dickinson did not confine herself to a single, all-consuming emblem for her poetic ambitions. In addition to the voice of Eve she also experimented with the voice of Adam, addressing Eve at the moment when she presents him with the forbidden fruit and explaining why he too is committed to join in her transgression:

> Me from Myself – to banish –
> Had I art –
> Impregnable my Fortress
> Unto All Heart –
>
> But since Myself – assault Me –
> How have I peace
> Except by subjugating
> Consciousness?
>
> And since We're mutual Monarch
> How this be
> Except by Abdication –
> Me – of Me?   [P-642]

Dickinson skillfully exploits the doctrine of one flesh, one heart, one soul to create a marriage poem of unusual power simply because of the insistence upon the inwardness of that bond.[23]

On at least one occasion, Dickinson tried out the voice of Christiana in the second part of John Bunyan's *The Pilgrim's Progress*. Bunyan was apparently one of the several enthusiasms that Dickinson shared with Benjamin Franklin, along with their joint love of picturing themselves in diminutive terms, their zestful independence of religious revivals, and their fondness for aphorism. In "I years had been from home" Dickinson describes pausing before a "Door / I dared not enter" and hesitating to knock for fear of a rejection that seems much more potent than simply a social slight. After some seconds that "like an Ocean rolled / And broke against my ear," the speaker just touches the latch of the "awful Door" with trembling Fingers, "Then moved my Fingers off / As cautiously as Glass / And held my ears, and like a Thief / Fled gasping from the

House" (P-609). The closing image of the speaker in flight pictures almost exactly the anxious escape of Christian from his own home in the
City of Destruction, when he plugs his ears and cries, "Life, Life, Eternal
Life." But the awful door itself is the one that Christiana fears to open at
the beginning of her own journey to the Celestial City: "What shall I do,
when I at such a door, / For pilgrims ask, and they shall rage the
more?"[24] Bunyan, of course, answers Christiana's fears and objections,
and she proceeds on her journey. Dickinson's pilgrim, though adequate
to the challenges of "Consternation," is also more sensitive to the implications of failure, less consoled by allegorical certainties, more acutely
aware of the predicament of being suspended between life and death.

Perhaps the most ambitious of Dickinson's monologues portrays her as
speaking for Moses:

>My Life had stood – a Loaded Gun –
>In Corners – till a Day
>The Owner passed – identified –
>And carried Me away –
>
>And now We roam in Sovereign Woods –
>And now We hunt the Doe –
>And every time I speak for Him –
>The Mountains straight reply –
>
>And do I smile, such cordial light
>Upon the Valley glow –
>It is as a Vesuvian face
>Had let its pleasure through –
>
>And when at Night – Our good Day done –
>I guard My Master's Head –
>'Tis better than the Eider-duck's
>Deep Pillow – to have shared –
>
>To foe of His – I'm deadly foe –
>None stir the second time –
>On whom I lay a Yellow Eye –
>Or an emphatic Thumb –
>
>Though I than He – may longer live
>He longer must – than I –
>For I have but the power to kill,
>Without – the power to die –   [P-754]

This celebrated poem has challenged the ingenuity of many students of
Dickinson's work, and we have no shortage of interpretations of it.[25] But
most readers take as their point of departure the assumption that this is

private discourse. The apparent perplexities of the last stanza, however, confirm again that Dickinson is applying the tradition of Puritan typology to her own habits of dramatic projection. Moses, according to a typological reading of the Bible, is a metaphorical precursor of Christ, whose later liberating powers will address the spirit rather than the body and whose message embraces all humanity and not just the people of Israel in bondage in Egypt. That liberating power will express itself, paradoxically, in a power of "dying" that conquers death, whereas the power of Moses is itself quite often "deadly," like the "Yellow Eye" cast by Dickinson's speaker in "My Life had stood – a Loaded Gun." Moses too, though a predecessor of Christ, was also (according to the Protestant exegesis of Dickinson's day) his servant or instrument who fulfilled his mission only when he was very old, though his "Master" lived a much shorter life. All these features of the typological structure of the Old and New Testaments come together in Dickinson's last stanza, in which her speaker explains a cryptic relationship to his "Master" that matches precisely the typological relationship of Moses to Christ.

Moses was indeed a sort of "Loaded Gun" in Egypt, a man of great strength and violent passion whose energies are channeled only after his "Owner" makes him a spokesman for God. The process of identification that Dickinson alludes to in her first stanza is sufficiently ambiguous to imply both the identification of the gun (as most readers have supposed) and the identification of the "Owner," who does in fact identify himself to Moses with an etymological riddle, "I am who I am," as a means of convincing the people of Israel that Moses' mission is genuine (Exodus 3:14). The choice of a loaded gun as an emblem for Moses is uniquely appropriate both to his powers of violence and to his limited capacity for speech, and the mountain wilderness and smiling valley of Dickinson's poetic landscape effectively compress the landscapes of Exodus and Deuteronomy as well as the setting and the import of genuinely prophetic speech. Moreover, the poem describes a succession of genders that corresponds to Dickinson's contemporary vision of biblical history, moving from a patriarchal Old Testament – "And now We hunt the Doe" – to the matriarchal virtues of receptivity, endurance, and "life" that dominate the New Testament.[26] Only the "Loaded Gun" in this poem seems associatively "male," and even it functions as a loving, if violent, spouse guarding its sleeping "master." The gun's owner is the androgynous Christ of Bunyan's vision at the Interpreter's House in The Pilgrim's Progress.

Just as Dickinson repeatedly sought to capture in a single lyric the complete experience of Paradise Lost, so she tries in these lines to evoke the full range of biblical mystery, violence, and mercy that was so central to the imaginative life of her culture. Dickinson's aspirations in this poem too are intimate and epic all at once, and it is this range of goals, more than any other single element, that unites her with Winthrop's purposes in "A Modell of Christian Charity." It is difficult to know for certain whether she expected these aspirations to be recognized, but it is at least clear that she did not really conceal them and that she found in her particular version of dramatic form a perfect fusion of the private and public identities that Winthrop evoked as a means of explaining the special conditions of life in America.

In search of that fusion Dickinson explored the possibilities of a final dramatic voice that enabled her to accomplish all of her strikingly ambitious artistic goals and that may have been responsible as well for the commencement of her most famous correspondence. She wrote to Thomas Wentworth Higginson for the first time after reading in the *Atlantic* his "Letter to a Young Contributor," in which part of Higginson's paternal purpose was to console the mute inglorious "Miltons," as he called them, who might not find an appreciative audience on earth but who could count on singing their "Paradise as Found" in Heaven.[27] A poet as sensitive to the example of Milton as was Emily Dickinson might have imagined (wrongly as it turned out) that Higginson would be able to read her ingeniously "Miltonic" texts with full appreciation. By 1862, when she began her correspondence with Higginson, she had already written the first of what proved to be an important body of "annunciation" poems – Dickinson's *Paradise Regained* – in which she composed her own extended version of the "Magnificat" from Luke:

> For this – accepted Breath –
> Through it – compete with Death –
> The fellow cannot touch this Crown –
> By it – my title take –
> Ah, what a royal sake
> To my necessity – stooped down!
>
> No Wilderness – can be
> Where this attendeth me –
> No Desert Noon –
> No fear of frost to come
> Haunt the perennial bloom –
> But Certain June!
>
> Get Gabriel – to tell – the royal syllable –
> Get Saints – with new – unsteady tongue –
> To say what trance below
> Most like their glory show –
> Fittest the Crown!   [P-195]

The biblical model upon which Dickinson draws in her first stanza is much more conventional in its humility than Dickinson's own lines. After receiving from Gabriel the news that she would bear a son by the Holy Spirit – and after this extraordinary message is confirmed by the greeting of Elizabeth, "Blessed are you among women, and blessed is the fruit of your womb!" – Mary expresses her own acceptance of this dramatic transformation: "My soul magnifies the Lord, and my spirit rejoices in God my savior, for he has regarded the low estate of his handmaiden" (Luke 1:47–8). Dickinson's "handmaiden," however, is overcome not so much with a sense of her low estate as with a grasp of her own "necessity" and her own distinction. Dickinson's pun on "necessity" is intended, for her speaker (like Anne Bradstreet in "The Author to Her Book") is filled with a sense of power, of indispensability, as well as a sense of need, that derives in part from her own imaginative exultation and in part from the celebratory atmosphere of *Paradise Regained,* Milton's treatment of Christ's temptation by Satan in the wilderness. It is from *Paradise Regained* that the wilderness and desert noon of Dickinson's second stanza derive, and also from *Paradise Regained* that Dickinson draws her vision of Mary as epitomizing the fusion of life and death that marks the human experience in so much of her poetry.[28]

Paradise Regained is a brief epic that seems ideally suited as a stimulus to Dickinson's work, for in it Milton makes explicit the mysterious conjunction of the private with the universal that Dickinson also explores. The purpose of this sequel to *Paradise Lost* is "to tell of deeds / Above Heroic, though in secret done / And unrecorded left through many an age" (1.15) – a combination of heroism and secrecy to which Dickinson herself frequently turned in her own poems, as well as in the management of her increasingly heroic body of "secret" work.[29] Moreover, the Mary of *Paradise Regained* is both the master of the "house private" to which Christ returns at the end of his temptations and the agent of recollection in the poem, who reveals to her son the circumstances of his birth and reflects on the years of his youth: "Private, unactive, calm, contemplative / Little suspicious to any King" (2.82). This is a portrait of Christ's private status that seems designed to have suggested to Dickinson an image of herself as well as a possible subject for poetry, and it is that blending of her personal artistic circumstances with the mythic ones of Mary and Christ that seems to be responsible for the exclamatory punctuation of "For this – accepted Breath –" as well as Dickinson's other annunciation poems.

Moreover, Milton's Mary sensed her own predicament to be what Dickinson herself would later describe as "acute":

> O what avails me now that honor high
> To have conceiv'd of God, or that salute

Hail highly favor'd, among women blest!
While I to sorrows am no less advanc't,
And fears as eminent, above the lot
Of other women, by the birth I bore   (2.67–72)

The fate foretold for her son gave her a special prominence in agony that
Milton called her "Exaltation to Afflictions high" and that Dickinson
would draw to a still sharper poetic edge in what is probably the finest of
her poems on Paradise found:

Title divine – is mine!
The Wife – without the Sign!
Acute Degree – conferred on me –
Empress of Calvary!
Royal – all but the Crown!
Betrothed – without the swoon
God sends us Women –
When you – hold – Garnet to Garnet –
Gold – to Gold –
Born – Bridalled – Shrouded –
In a Day –
Tri Victory
"My Husband" – women say –
Stroking the Melody –
Is *this* – the way?   [P-1072]

The exultantly accepted crown of "For this – accepted Breath" has assumed its full ambiguity in these lines, and Milton's "Exaltation to Afflictions high" has produced the superbly concrete and dramatic "Empress of Calvary." But these disturbing visions of the full burden of
marriage, with which the poem begins, gradually soften as the exclamation points yield to the less conclusive dash and finally to a provocative
question. The lines get shorter as the poem moves from the mythic
grandeur and resistance of the initial explosive outburst to the erotically
suggestive "this" of the final line, in which Dickinson seems willing to
imagine not only the doctrine but the physical fact of conception by God.
Milton's God in *Paradise Regained* briefly brags to Gabriel (with a kind of
Whitmanian fervor) that "I can produce a man / Of female seed" who
will decisively foil Satan's designs (1.50). Dickinson seizes on this sexual
hint and produces in "Title divine – is mine" a mythical epithalamion
that celebrates that "female seed," envisioning death and then, as in so
many of her deathbed monologues, conquering it not by the abstract
mechanisms of a covenant but sexually, in the bonds of a marriage the
terms of which her female speaker has completely mastered, just as

Winthrop's Eve was the master model of the marriage of American community. Like Anne Bradstreet's "As Weary Pilgrim," this Dickinson magnificat unites the experience of human weakness with a vision of human strength and historic purpose on a scale that absorbs the individual speaker into the selfless whole.

CONCLUSION

In these chapters I have tried to exploit as fully as possible the literary implications of John Winthrop's initial equation of community and domesticity in American experience. In the course of exploring these implications, Winthrop has sometimes yielded to more formidable influences – Shakespeare, Bunyan, Milton – and the ideas and images of his model have frequently given way to the particular ambitions of the artists who followed him. Emily Dickinson's dialogue with *Paradise Lost* or Thoreau's urgent call for "life" are not conscious responses to Winthrop's understanding of "charity," but together with the other writers we have considered they help establish the vitality of the domestic vision that Winthrop first expressed and that renews its appeal in the early work of one of the first of our modern writers, Robert Frost.

Richard Poirier has observed that Frost is, among other things, "a great poet of marriage, maybe the greatest since Milton."[1] Poirier means this comparison as a prelude to his extensive consideration of the role of the "home" in Frost and of Frost's own self-conscious appropriation of the English poetic tradition. But it is a useful comparison on quite specific grounds as well. Frost clearly set out to address the example of Milton, not only in the extraordinary dialogue poems from *North of Boston* that Poirier treats so effectively in *Robert Frost: The Work of Knowing,* but in the Miltonic aspirations of earlier, briefer poems – "The Trial By Existence," for example, in which Frost dramatically reimagines the heavenly setting of the third book of *Paradise Lost,* the apocalyptic regret of "Reluctance," or the careful echoes of Milton's "narrow" Eden that begin the fall of "Rose Pogonias":

> A saturated meadow,
>   Sun-shaped and jewel-small,
> A circle scarcely wider

Than the trees around were tall;
  Where winds were quite excluded,
    And the air was stifling sweet
With the breath of many flowers –
    A temple of the heat.

There we bowed us in the burning,
    As the sun's right worship is,
To pick where none could miss them
    A thousand orchises;
For though the grass was scattered,
    Yet every second spear
Seemed tipped with wings of color
    That tinged the atmosphere.

We raised a simple prayer
    Before we left the spot,
That in the general mowing
    That place might be forgot;
Or if not all so favored,
    Obtain such grace of hours
That none should mow the grass there
    While so confused with flowers.[2]

Very little in these lines insists on their essential ambition. The title, in fact, tries to put the reader off or encourages us to identify less epic models for Frost's idyll in the echoes of Marvell, for example, that Poirier so perceptively catches.[3] It quickly becomes apparent, however, that these three stanzas (like a number of Dickinson's most intense poems) compress the plot of *Paradise Lost,* giving us in the end an "Adam" and "Eve" who leave their "saturated meadow" with a wider vision and a richer grasp of life than they possessed in the stifling enclosure of their passion. Death ("the general mowing") asserts its power to eclipse the erotic life that the strikingly sexual allusiveness of the first stanza evokes. The "jewel-small circle" that contains the speaker's "burning" is as candidly physical (and female) an image as Anne Bradstreet's passionate anticipation of her husband's return:

But when thou northward to me shalt return,
I wish my Sun may never set, but burn
Within the Cancer of my glowing breast,
The welcome house of him my dearest guest.

But in Frost as in Bradstreet sexuality is not its own end. What opposes the general mowing is not physical passion but grace. To be sure it is only a "grace of hours" in Frost, and not of eternity, but though the range of hope seems more limited than in Bradstreet's openly religious vision, Frost's language suggests the possibility of more potent redemptive forces residing outside the speaker's simple prayer.

What counts most for our purposes is the degree to which a poem like "Rose Pogonias" demonstrates the continuing vigor of those images of gender, of marriage, and of the competition between death and life that formed the heart of Winthrop's communal idealism and Anne Bradstreet's verse. Clearly the same forces are at work in Frost's delicate lines, giving them a peculiar scope that their own apparent simplicity both disguises and evokes. Frost in fact is able to be so indirect – can afford his delicacy of suggestion – because he, like Dickinson, comes after Bradstreet, Milton, and the poetic tradition that they in part comprise. He has the advantages as well as the challenges of belatedness, a condition to which Frost gave his own mythological form in the longest and most ambitious poem from *A Boy's Will*, "The Trial by Existence."

William Pritchard looks with much justifiable suspicion upon what he calls the boy-scout "uplift" of the sentiments in "The Trial by Existence" and notes that Frost himself hinted at the presence of "lots of teasing" in some of his early poems.[4] But in comparison with Frost's later books of poetry, there is very little teasing in *A Boy's Will*, and if there is any in "The Trial by Existence" then it is teasing of a serious sort. In the course of presenting a fable of rebirth, "The Trial by Existence" illuminates Frost's own understanding of his relationship to an older poetic and spiritual vocabulary. The first six stanzas of the poem describe a chivalric vision of Heaven, where "valor" reigns as the chief virtue among an angelic host as enthusiastically military in its appetites as Milton's warlike Thrones, Dominations, Princedoms, and Powers from *Paradise Lost*. To Frost's community of "trooping" spirits, God addresses a challenge, much as Milton's God addresses a challenge to his assembled listeners in putative search of a spirit courageous enough to save the human race from death.

Frost's God too is looking for souls willing to take up the life that "opens earthward," as a means of forming rather than saving man, but as the last three stanzas make clear this is a peculiar trial offering none of the epic consolations that Frost's own lines both invoke and to some degree parody:

> But always God speaks at the end:
>   "One thought in agony of strife
> The bravest would have by for friend,
>   The memory that he chose the life;
> But the pure fate to which you go

Admits no memory of choice,
Or the woe were not earthly woe
    To which you give the assenting voice."

And so the choice must be again,
    But the last choice is still the same;
And the awe passes wonder then,
    And a hush falls for all acclaim.
And God has taken a flower of gold
    And broken it, and used therefrom
The mystic link to bind and hold
    Spirit to matter till death come.

'Tis of the essence of life here,
    Though we choose greatly, still to lack
The lasting memory at all clear,
    That life has for us on the wrack
Nothing but what we somehow chose;
    Thus are we wholly stripped of pride
In the pain that has but one close,
    Bearing it crushed and mystified.

In these final stanzas "The Trial by Existence" is saved from its own, dangerously cloying vision of its poetic predecessors by turning upon memory itself and establishing its limits as a condition of human life. The "pure fate" that Frost celebrates here, and that he embodies in many of his poems, entails a human figure "wholly stripped of pride" yet sanctified in a marriage ceremony designed to "bind and hold" the familiar antagonists, spirit and matter, death and life, in a mysteriously bearable union. That is precisely the union that Anne Bradstreet celebrates in her marriage vision at the conclusion of "As Weary Pilgrim," but in Frost's case the ecstatic anticipations of faith are absent and we get in their place a verse that "remembers" life even in the midst of what seems to be lifeless experience.

It is important to register Frost's characteristic hedging. The conditions of rebirth in "The Trial by Existence" do not entail the complete obliteration of memory but only of memory's absolute clarity and durability. Human life is haunted by the choice and the awe even in its darkest moments. The heavenly marriage remains to play some clouded role within the memory of the marriage that opens earthward. This capacity for memory in several senses is the source of the power of "Home Burial," for example, a poem in which the central issue dividing a husband and wife is their apparently opposed powers of remembrance and of mourning for their dead child. The circumstances of the poem are familiar to most readers, an argument on the stairs between a couple struggling to adjust to the pain of a loss that Frost himself understood all too well – the wife accusing her husband of callousness, the husband wondering in reply if his wife's sorrow has grown morbid:

> Give me my chance.
> I do think, though, you overdo it a little.
> What was it brought you up to think it the thing
> To take your mother-loss of a first child
> So inconsolably – in the face of love.
> You'd think his memory might be satisfied –

Memory is both the ground of contention within the parents in this poem and a kind of external presence – a spirit – to be propitiated, belonging not to the survivors but (as the husband suggests) to the dead. The climax of the wife's anguish occurs when she performs an act of perfect recollection, confronting her husband with the apparently unfeeling words he uttered on the day he dug his child's grave: "Three foggy mornings and one rainy day / Will rot the best birch fence a man can build." Insensitive as these words may seem, however, they too "remember" the occasion on which they are spoken; they reflect the sense of vacancy that marks all conversation in a house that is stricken with loss, and they constitute almost on their own an extraordinarily concise, and moving, expression of the husband's awkward fusion of sorrow and clumsiness.

Memory is also a property of setting in "Home Burial." The stairs upon which Frost places his speakers recall the vertical universe of popular piety, in which ascent and descent are images of spiritual progress as well as movements in space. The opening lines of the poem exploit this potential for meaning in the wife's rhythmic attempts to descend and to "raise herself" and in her husband's half-menacing, half-redemptive "mounting." Moreover, the bickering between the parents, the images they use, awaken recollection at the same time that they signify the "burial" of the home. Their dialogue suggests both the animation of their lost child and the lingering capacities for childishness (or child making perhaps) that reside still within themselves:

> "There you go sneering now!"
>
> "I'm not, I'm not!
> You make me angry. I'll come down to you.
> God, what a woman! And it's come to this,
> A man can't speak of his own child that's dead."
>
> "You can't because you don't know how to speak.
> If you had any feelings, you that dug

With your own hand – how could you? – his little grave;
I saw you from that very window there,
Making the gravel leap and leap in air,
Leap up, like that, like that, and land so lightly
And roll back down the mound beside the hole.
I thought, Who is that man? I didn't know you.
And I crept down the stairs and up the stairs
To look again, and still your spade kept lifting.
Then you came in.

In this poem not only people but language itself makes "the best of [its] way back to life," but it does so, as Frost suggests in "The Trial by Existence," indirectly and with no "lasting memory at all clear" of the choice it is actually making.

Frost's best readers have often suggested that the most formative influence upon him was exercised by William James, a teacher whom Frost never actually encountered at Harvard but whose work he knew well. Lawrence Thompson detects signs of James's presence in "The Trial by Existence"; Richard Poirier draws a compelling reading of "Design" out of a long passage from the third lecture in *Pragmatism* that addresses the problem of design in nature.[5] In that same lecture James confronts yet another metaphysical problem his treatment of which identifies him quite closely not only with the life-affirming sensibility of Robert Frost but with the older rhetorical traditions of John Winthrop. The issue in this case is not the possibility of design in nature but the competition between theism and materialism for the loyalties of the twentieth century mind. Materialism, James suggests, offers us a universe doomed to entropic decay, a fate he characterizes by quoting at length from Arthur James Balfour's *The Foundations of Belief*:

> I cannot state it better than in Mr. Balfour's words: "The energies of our system will decay, the glory of the sun will be dimmed, and the earth, tideless and inert, will no longer tolerate the race which has for a moment disturbed its solitude. Man will go down into the pit, and all his thoughts will perish. The uneasy consciousness which in this obscure corner has for a brief space broken the contented silence of the universe, will be at rest. Matter will know itself no longer, 'Imperishable monuments' and 'immortal deeds,' death itself, and love stronger than death, will be as though they had never been. Nor will anything that is, be better or be worse for all that the labour, genius, devotion, and suffering of man have striven through countless generations to effect."

For James, Balfour's vision sums up the spiritual consequences in his time and, largely, in ours of the "faith" of science: "This utter final wreck and tragedy is of the essence of scientific materialism as at present understood."[6]

Against this vision of death the pragmatic theist is able to bring to bear the possibility – not the certainty – of purpose. Such theism, in James's view, will always fall short of the clarity and factual power of science, but it has "at least this practical superiority" in its favor:

> that it guarantees an ideal order that shall be permanently preserved. A world with a God in it to say the last word, may indeed burn up or freeze, but we then think of him as still mindful of the old ideals and sure to bring them elsewhere to fruition; so that, where he is, tragedy is only provisional and partial, and shipwreck and dissolution not the absolutely final things.

This possibility of hope amid shipwreck is at the basis of Frost's myth in "The Trial by Existence" and sustains the complex powers of memory in "Home Burial." But these are also the metaphors of John Winthrop's discourse to the *Arbella* emigrants, whose own fears of shipwreck were spiritual as well as material, and whose confrontation with death and life anticipates the apocalyptic scope of James's modern predicament. In many ways *Pragmatism* offers at the outset of the social and artistic enterprises of a new century precisely the framework of understanding that John Winthrop offered at the outset of the enterprises of Massachusetts Bay. In giving poetic expression to that framework, Robert Frost identified himself more decisively than by any other act with the literary and spiritual heritage of the Puritans.

In the next-to-last lecture of *Pragmatism* James restates the conditions of radical isolation and radical dependence that form both the poetic circumstances of "Home Burial" and the communal circumstances of seventeenth-century New England. In both cases domesticity and emptiness are the extremes between which human existence is poised: "All 'homes' are in finite experience," James affirms, "finite experience as such is homeless. Nothing outside of the flux secures the issue of it. It can hope salvation only from its own intrinsic promises and potencies."[7] That recognition and that hope are the grounds of Winthrop's urgency in "A Modell of Christian Charity" as well, and they are the impetus behind much of the most ambitious literary work produced in America through the beginning of the twentieth century.

NOTES

INTRODUCTION

1 See Leonard Barkan, *Nature's Work of Art: The Human Body as Image of the World* (New Haven, Conn.: Yale University Press, 1975) for the tradition upon which Winthrop draws. Barkan identifies Renaissance England as "the heyday of the anthropomorphic image of the commonwealth" (p. 75).

2 Edmund Morgan, *The Puritan Family* (1944, rpt. New York: Harper & Row, 1966).

3 Ibid., p. 133.

4 See especially Philip J. Greven, *The Protestant Temperament: Patterns of Child-rearing, Religious Experience, and the Self in Early America* (New York: Knopf, 1977), pp. 28–43, 87–109. The account of child rearing in Plymouth Colony by John Demos seems to me much more sensitive to the limitations of the historian's knowledge and to the Puritan predicament. See Demos, *A Little Commonwealth: Family Life in Plymouth Colony* (New York: Oxford University Press, 1970).

5 On the operation of the Puritan household see David Leverenz's informative overview of Puritan family manuals in *The Language of Puritan Feeling* (New Brunswick, N.J.: Rutgers University Press, 1980), pp. 70–104. In summary Leverenz writes that "Puritan tracts encourage a distinctive intensity of loving in parents, especially in mothers, and a loving gravity of restraint in fathers" (p. 92). For an account of how such a distinctive intensity operated in practice, see David Levin's description of Cotton Mather's experience both as child and parent in *Cotton Mather: The Young Life of the Lord's Remembrancer* (Cambridge, Mass.: Harvard University Press, 1978), especially Chapter 9, "Suffering and Doing: The Mystery of Particular Faiths and Deaths," pp. 269–310.

6 Lawrence Stone, *The Family, Sex, and Marriage in England 1500–1800*, abridged ed. (New York: Harper & Row, 1979), pp. 173–90, 274. In many key areas of domestic relations, Stone affirms, "middle-class dissenters seem to

have been in advance of the rest of society" (274). Philippe Aries identifies a similar pattern to the one that Stone describes, finding the seventeenth and eighteenth centuries to be critical for the emergence of a new iconography of the family out of traditional, medieval iconographies. See Aries, *Centuries of Childhood,* trans. Robert Baldick (New York: Vintage, 1962), pp. 339–64. Linda Pollock's important critique of what she calls "the Aries thesis" is contained in the opening chapters of *Forgotten Children: Parent–Child Relations from 1500 to 1900* (Cambridge University Press, 1983), pp. 1–67.

7 Michael Gilmore, *The Middle Way: Puritanism and Ideology in American Romantic Fiction* (New Brunswick, N.J.: Rutgers University Press, 1977), pp. 107–14.

8 For Sacvan Bercovitch's formulation of the predicament of choice, see *The American Jeremiad* (Madison: University of Wisconsin Press, 1978), pp. 20–5. David Minter takes the jeremiad as the conceptual origin of his own study of American prose, but he identifies the genre almost exclusively with what he calls the "caretaker" (rather than "founder") generations in New England and associates it with a strategy of substituting the act of telling a story for the act of pursuing a goal. See Minter's chapter on the jeremiad in *The Interpreted Design as a Structural Principle in American Prose* (New Haven, Conn.: Yale University Press, 1969), pp. 50–66.

9 See Perry Miller, *The New England Mind: The Seventeenth Century* (Cambridge, Mass.: Harvard University Press, 1939), pp. 419–22.

10 Loren Baritz, *City on a Hill: A History of Ideas and Myths in America* (New York: Wiley, 1964), pp. 3–45, and Wilson C. McWilliams, *The Idea of Fraternity in America* (Berkeley and Los Angeles: University of California Press, 1973), pp. 133–49.

11 Philip Gura, *A Glimpse of Sion's Glory* (Middletown, Conn.: Wesleyan University Press, 1984), p. 30.

12 Amy Lang, *Prophetic Woman: Anne Hutchinson and the Problem of Dissent in the Literature of New England* (Berkeley and Los Angeles: University of California Press, 1987), pp. 28–50.

13 Ann Douglas, *The Feminization of American Culture* (New York: Knopf, 1977), p. 13.

14 Douglas's assessment of this feminizing evolution needs to be qualified by the work of Edmund Morgan and David Leverenz, who note the preponderance of female imagery in the rhetoric of the earliest Puritan ministers. See Morgan, *The Puritan Family,* pp. 161–8, and Leverenz, *The Language of Puritan Feeling,* pp. 138–61. David Stannard notes that the first signs of the sentimentalizing of death in New England appear during the Great Awakening. See *The Puritan Way of Death* (New York: Oxford University Press, 1977), pp. 148–57. See also David S. Reynolds's argument for a mixture of masculinization and feminization in nineteenth-century American religion, "The Feminization Controversy: Sexual Stereotypes and the Paradoxes of Piety in Nineteenth-Century America," *New England Quarterly* 53 (March 1980), 96–106.

15 See George Forgie, *Patricide in the House Divided: A Psychological Interpretation of Lincoln and His Age* (New York: Norton, 1979). Forgie tends to see this

domesticating and sentimentalizing process as largely a nineteenth-century response to the predicament of living in a post-heroic age. William Spengemann's argument in *The Adventurous Muse: The Poetics of American Fiction, 1789–1900* (New Haven, Conn.: Yale University Press, 1977) is that America's most distinctive imaginative tradition is that of "adventure" and derives from travel writing in the New World. "Domesticity" of the sort that Lincoln exploited is, according to Spengemann's account, an imported literary value that is ultimately overwhelmed by history and nature. Spengemann's terms seem to me a logical extension of Winthrop's, with the important exception that Spengemann finds the "adventurous self" to be the more native American construct. I would argue that Winthrop's enterprise establishes both the power and the priority of the domestic self.

16 Barton Levi St. Armand has provided a recent example of the value of reestablishing the link between major figures in the "literary" canon and the frequently sentimental expressions of popular culture. See St. Armand, *Emily Dickinson and Her Culture* (Cambridge University Press, 1984).

17 Mary Kelley, *Private Woman, Public Stage* (New York: Oxford University Press, 1984).

18 Joyce Warren, *The American Narcissus: Individualism and Women in Nineteenth-Century American Fiction* (New Brunswick, N.J.: Rutgers University Press, 1984) and Spengemann, *The Adventurous Muse.*

19 Kelley, *Private Woman, Public Stage,* Cathy Davidson, *Revolution and the Word: The Rise of the Novel in America* (New York: Oxford University Press, 1986), Nina Baym, *Woman's Fiction: A Guide to Novels by and about Women in America, 1820–1870* (Ithaca, N.Y.: Cornell University Press, 1978), Jane Tompkins, *Sensational Designs: The Cultural Work of American Fiction, 1790–1860* (New York: Oxford University Press, 1985).

20 Tompkins, *Sensational Designs,* pp. 11–16.

21 See David Reynolds, *Beneath the American Renaissance: The Subversive Imagination in the Age of Emerson and Melville* (New York: Knopf, 1988). On the concept of biformities, see Michael Kammen, *People of Paradox: An Inquiry Concerning the Origins of American Civilization* (New York: Knopf, 1972).

22 Nancy Cott, *The Bonds of Womanhood: Woman's Sphere in New England, 1780–1835* (New Haven, Conn.: Yale University Press, 1977).

23 Cotton Mather, *Magnalia Christi Americana: Books 1 and 2,* ed. Kenneth W. Murdock (Cambridge, Mass.: Harvard University Press, 1977), p. 228.

1. "THIS GREAT HOUSEHOLD UPON THE EARTH"

Because of differing editorial practices, the orthography of quotations in this chapter varies from the carefully modernized spelling and punctuation of Morison's edition of William Bradford's *Of Plymouth Plantation* to the faithfully transcribed irregularities of the manuscript of Winthrop's prose in Edmund Morgan's text of "A Modell of Christian Charity." The reader must not therefore assume that Winthrop was less literate than Bradford, or that Ann Bradstreet was more polished than Edward Taylor.

1 For an examination of this network of sources in connection with Shakespeare's play see Barbara Lewalski, "Biblical Allusion and Allegory in *The Merchant of Venice*," *Shakespeare Quarterly* 13 (1962), 327–43, and Douglas Anderson, "The Old Testament Presence in *The Merchant of Venice*," *ELH* 52 (Spring 1985), 119–32.

2 John Winthrop, "A Modell of Christian Charity," in *The Founding of Massachusetts: Historians and the Sources*, ed. Edmund S. Morgan (Indianapolis, Ind.: Bobbs-Merrill, 1964), p. 204. All page numbers in parentheses referring to Winthrop's work are citations to this edition.

3 It is, at any rate, quite clear from the text that Winthrop takes considerably less satisfaction in the image of a city on a hill than subsequent readers have done. He had good reason to wish to avoid too close a scrutiny of New England, particularly during the first ten years of the colony's existence. See, for example, Edmund Morgan, *The Puritan Dilemma* (Boston: Little, Brown, 1958), p. 75.

4 Perry Miller, *Errand into the Wilderness* (Cambridge, Mass.: Harvard University Press, 1956), p. 5. Miller asserts as well that "A Modell of Christian Charity" represents Winthrop's intentions to frame a government the first duty of which was to be "deliberately, vigorously, and consistently intolerant." If that was, in fact, Winthrop's intention, then we must suppose him almost totally impervious to irony. Stephen Foster has more recently endorsed Miller's skepticism about Winthrop's intentions by concluding from an unusually strict reading of the text of "A Modell of Christian Charity" that Winthrop meant its ideal of communal love to apply only to those who, literally, communed in church congregations. See Foster, *Their Solitary Way: The Puritan Social Ethic in the First Century of Settlement in New England* (New Haven, Conn.: Yale University Press, 1971), pp. 40–4.

5 On the tradition of Puritan antagonism to selfishness see Sacvan Bercovitch, *The Puritan Origins of the American Self* (New Haven, Conn.: Yale University Press, 1975), pp. 1–34. Andrew Delbanco's discussion of Winthrop's text also emphasizes its communitarian idealism. See Delbanco, *The Puritan Ordeal* (Cambridge, Mass.: Harvard University Press, 1989), pp. 72–80.

6 Amy Lang takes the view that Winthrop's sense of the necessity of accommodating the ideal of the church "body" to the urgent need for wider ideals of citizenship is behind much of the language in "A Modell of Christian Charity." See Amy Lang, *Prophetic Woman: Anne Hutchinson and the Problem of Dissent in the Literature of New England* (Berkeley and Los Angeles: University of California Press, 1987), p. 31.

7 Invocations of the family as a metaphor of considerable metaphysical importance were familiar in Puritan thought and theology. The most thorough and informative treatment of this tradition is Edmund Morgan's *The Puritan Family* (1944, rpt. New York: Harper & Row, 1966), especially pp. 29–64 and 133–60. See also Larzer Ziff, *Puritanism in America* (New York: Viking, 1973), and David Leverenz, *The Language of Puritan Feeling* (New Brunswick, N.J.: Rutgers University Press, 1980).

8 See Lang, *Prophetic Woman*, pp. 28–31.

9 The egalitarian attitudes implied here need to be qualified by – but not necessarily contradicted by – the part Winthrop played in the trial and exile of Anne
Hutchinson. See John Winthrop, *The History of New England from 1630 to
1649*, 2 vols., Vol. 1, ed. James Savage (Boston: Little, Brown, 1853), pp.
239–328. These pages give a full account of the antinomian controversy,
including Winthrop's gruesome satisfaction in recording the details of the
miscarriages of Hutchinson and one of her followers, Mary Dyer, as judgments of Divine Providence on their conduct. David Hall has collected all the
pertinent documents on the Hutchinson case, including Winthrop's anonymous pamphlet, "A Short Story of the Rise, Reign, and Ruin of the Antinomians," published in England, and the extraordinary records of Hutchinson's
appearances before the General Court. See *The Antinomian Controversy 1636–
1638: A Documentary History,* ed. David D. Hall (Middletown, Conn.:
Wesleyan University Press, 1968), pp. 199–348. See also Emery Battis, *Saints
and Sectaries* (Chapel Hill: University of North Carolina Press, 1962). Though
Winthrop clearly felt that Hutchinson's sex was an aggravation of her theological heresies, it is critical to note that he and a number of his colleagues on
the General Court treated her with great seriousness and with a wary respect
for her intelligence. Hutchinson was by no means simply "foolish" in
Winthrop's eyes; she was a force to be rescued for the good of the state if
possible. Failing such a rescue, she required firm but balanced treatment. His
remarkable use of Eve in "A Modell of Christian Charity" is fundamentally
consistent with his conduct in Hutchinson's case. Winthrop's commitment to
living by truths that others merely profess is central and deeply felt. Perry
Miller affirmed that to understand America one has to understand that commitment. See *The New England Mind: From Colony to Province* (Cambridge,
Mass.: Harvard University Press, 1954), p. 8.

10 See the discussion of Eve and the garden in Joseph A. Galdon, S. J., *Typology
and Seventeenth-Century Literature* (The Hague: Mouton, 1975), pp. 95–112.
For a more specialized treatment of the pervasiveness of typological thought
in American writing, see Mason I. Lowance, Jr., *The Language of Canaan:
Metaphor and Symbol in New England from the Puritans to the Transcendentalists*
(Cambridge, Mass.: Harvard University Press, 1980).

11 For a fine characterization of Winthrop's relationship with Margaret Tyndal,
his third wife, see Morgan, *The Puritan Dilemma*, pp. 13–14, 48–53. See also
Morgan, *The Puritan Family,* pp. 47–60.

12 William Bradford, *Of Plymouth Plantation* (New York: Random House, 1981),
pp. 13, 25. Edmund Morgan notes that by the end of the seventeenth century
accepted tradition held that the Puritan founders had come to New England
for the sake of their children. See Morgan, *The Puritan Family,* p. 168.

13 Bradford, *Of Plymouth Plantation,* p. 86.

14 In Perry Miller's book, for example, Winthrop's model serves as the touch-
stone by which he measures and criticizes the Mathers. Cotton Mather's
Bonifacius becomes for Miller "a calculated plot" rather than an extension of
Winthrop's tradition. See Miller, *The New England Mind,* pp. 414–16.

15 Bradstreet, however, might have sensed from the outset more familial friction

than Winthrop would have liked. It is likely that, even during the voyage on the *Arbella,* Bradstreet's father, Thomas Dudley, would already have come into some degree of personal conflict with Winthrop. On the Winthrop–Dudley antagonism, see Morgan, *The Puritan Dilemma.*

16 Ann Stanford (and others) insist perhaps too strongly on the antagonistic climate of the seventeenth century toward women writers. It is clear that many men prized Bradstreet's work on its own merits and not simply because she was, in addition to being a poet, an accomplished housewife. One might more justifiably chide the prominent (and prominently male) modern critics who have patronized Bradstreet's work. See, for example, Roy Harvey Pearce, *The Continuity of American Poetry* (Princeton, N.J.: Princeton University Press, 1961), pp. 21–4 ("Mrs. Bradstreet is above all gentle, genteel"), and Hyatt Waggoner, *American Poets From the Puritans to the Present* (1968, rev., Baton Rouge: Louisiana State University Press, 1984), pp. 8–16. Bradstreet certainly felt a significant and disturbing degree of male antagonism, but she also enjoyed significant male support. See Ann Stanford, "Anne Bradstreet, Dogmatist and Rebel," *New England Quarterly* 39 (September 1966), 373–89.

17 *The Works of Anne Bradstreet,* ed. Jeanine Hensley (Cambridge, Mass.: Harvard University Press, 1967), p. 4. Page numbers in parentheses citing Bradstreet's work refer to this edition. Joseph McElrath and Allan P. Robb make an argument for reading Bradstreet in seventeenth-century orthography in their more recent edition, *The Complete Works of Anne Bradstreet,* eds. Joseph McElrath and Allan P. Robb (Boston: Twayne, 1981).

18 Bradstreet's clear exploitation of the status of the home suggests that Mary Kelley is in error when she says that linking "the private world of the home to the public world of politics" was "unprecedented" before the Revolution. See Kelley, *Private Woman, Public Stage* (New York: Oxford University Press), p. 61.

19 For Daly's complete and sensitive discussion of Bradstreet's poetry see Robert Daly, *God's Altar: The World and the Flesh in Puritan Poetry* (Berkeley and Los Angeles: University of California Press, 1978), pp. 82–127. The phrase "willed resignation" itself occurs on p. 112.

20 Quoted in Samuel Eliot Morison, *Builders of the Bay Colony* (Boston: Houghton Mifflin, 1930), p. 72.

21 Eileen Margerum has discussed Bradstreet's uses of humility in her "public" verse. The private verse seems equally interesting for the uses to which it puts the conventions of self-effacement. See "Anne Bradstreet's Public Poetry and the Tradition of Humility," *Early American Literature* 17 (Fall 1982), 152–160. David Leverenz has perceptively remarked that the Puritan "plain style reflects Puritan disgust at self-centeredness." See Leverenz, *The Language of Puritan Feeling,* p. 9. Elizabeth Wade White discusses "In Reference to Her Children" in some detail, though primarily from a bibliographic standpoint in *Anne Bradstreet: "The Tenth Muse"* (New York: Oxford University Press, 1971).

22 Ann Stanford would argue for a greater sense of antagonism between

Bradstreet and conventional gestures of piety, like the humility represented in these laments for example. Karl Keller's view of Bradstreet's grasp of the value of such traditional elements of her inherited cultural context, both as aids to life and as aids to art, seems to me a more promising approach, and I have tried to follow Keller's lead here. See Keller, *The Only Kangaroo Among the Beauty* (Baltimore: Johns Hopkins University Press, 1979), pp. 8–37. For Robert Daly's emphasis on the familial relations between Bradstreet and God, see Daly, *God's Altar,* p. 91.

23 Josephine Piercy finds in the marriage poems "unashamed passion" and largely satisfactory amorous relations. The poems themselves clearly record a more mixed, and more interesting, relationship. See Josephine Piercy, *Anne Bradstreet* (New York: Twayne, 1965), pp. 87–8. See also Robert Daly's comparison of the lines from "A Letter to My Husband Absent Upon Public Employment" to a biblical source in Matthew 22:2–14. See Daly, *God's Altar,* pp. 106–7.

24 John Cotton makes the traditional connection between marriage and covenant quite clear in his commentary on Canticles: "And looke what affection is between Husband and Wife, hath there been the like affection in your soules towards the Lord Jesus Christ?" Quoted in Leverenz, *The Language of Puritan Feeling,* p. 22. See also Daly, *God's Altar,* pp. 104–5.

25 Both Norman Grabo and Alan Howard have noted Taylor's dependence upon a number of sources for this profusion of metaphor – primarily the Bible and contemporary emblem books. Howard is particularly severe with Taylor, concluding finally that Taylor preferred a world view derived largely from books to the world in which he lived as a source for his poetry. See Alan Howard, "The World as Emblem: Language and Vision in the Poetry of Edward Taylor," *American Literature* 44 (1972), 359–84, and Norman Grabo, *Edward Taylor* (New York: Twayne, 1961), pp. 156–8.

26 See Karl Keller, *The Example of Edward Taylor* (Amherst: University of Massachusetts Press, 1975), Chap. 3. This essay is also printed as "The Example of Edward Taylor" in *The American Puritan Imagination,* ed. Sacvan Bercovitch (Cambridge University Press, 1974), pp. 123–38.

27 *The Poems of Edward Taylor,* ed. Donald E. Stanford (New Haven, Conn.: Yale University Press, 1960), Ser. 2, No. 82. Citations to the meditations by series and number in parentheses refer to the text printed in this edition. Citations to "God's Determinations Touching His Elect" by page number in parentheses also refer to this edition.

28 Norman Grabo observes as well that much of what appears to be Taylor's poetic extravagance is, in fact, indebted to the conventions of religious expression at the time and to Taylor's sources. See Grabo, *Edward Taylor,* p. 153.

29 That, in fact, is how Robert Daly presents Bradstreet and Taylor, the first as a puritan "naturalist," trusting in her earthly images as sources of consolation, the second as a more consistently unworldly skeptic, suspicious of his own metaphorical profusion.

30 See in particular Daly's treatment in *God's Altar,* pp. 162–99.

31 William J. Scheick, *The Will and the Word: The Poetry of Edward Taylor* (Athens: University of Georgia Press, 1974), p. 123.
32 Norman Grabo, by contrast, sees Taylor as theologically committed to the view of the inadequate human speaker. That commitment, though, was clearly not so great as to forbid speaking directly to God in a quite familiar, informal manner. See Grabo, *Edward Taylor*, p. 109.
33 Karl Keller notes that Taylor's language "simulates" salvation. See Keller, *The Example of Edward Taylor*, p. 109.
34 Karen Rowe, *Saint and Singer: Edward Taylor's Typology and the Poetics of Meditation* (Cambridge University Press, 1986), p. 105.
35 Edmund Morgan, *The Gentle Puritan* (1962, rpt. New York: Norton, 1983), p. 141.
36 On Milton's sense of this contentedly domesticated God see Joan Malory Webber, "The Politics of Poetry: Feminism in *Paradise Lost*," *Milton Studies* 14 (1980), 3–20.

2. *"TO BE GREAT AND DOMESTIC"*

1 *The Autobiography of Benjamin Franklin*, eds. Leonard W. Labaree, Ralph L. Ketcham, Helen C. Boatfield, and Helene H. Fineman (New Haven, Conn.: Yale University Press, 1964), p. 139.
2 Ibid., p. 49.
3 Daniel Shea has noted a general critical concern over Franklin's status as "the last Puritan" or the first American. It is important to keep in mind that Franklin was the first to see himself in this transitional capacity. See Shea, *Spiritual Autobiography in Early America* (Princeton, N.J.: Princeton University Press, 1968), p. 234. Esmond Wright describes the relationship between the form of the *Autobiography* and Franklin's Puritan background. See Wright, *Franklin of Philadelphia* (Cambridge, Mass.: Harvard University Press, 1986), pp. 6–9. The most familiar manifestation of this transitional property of Franklin's example is his indebtedness to, and acquaintance with, Cotton Mather. See David Levin, *In Defense of Historical Literature* (New York: Hill & Wang, 1967), pp. 58–76, and M. R. Breitwieser, *Cotton Mather and Benjamin Franklin: The Price of Representative Personality* (Cambridge University Press, 1985).
4 Thomas Philbrick, by contrast, finds the modest title of the *Notes* "accurate." See Philbrick, "Thomas Jefferson" in *American Literature, 1764–1789: The Revolutionary Years*, ed. Everett Emerson (Madison: University of Wisconsin Press, 1977), pp. 161–6.
5 Thomas Jefferson, *Notes on the State of Virginia* in *Writings* (New York: Library of America, 1984), p. 127. All page numbers in parentheses referring to passages from the *Notes* are citations to this edition.
6 Thomas Philbrick gives a good summary of the circumstances under which Jefferson wrote the *Notes*. See Philbrick, *American Literature, 1764–1789*, pp. 160–1.
7 This vision of a revolution in peril is not inconsistent with – though it sug-

gests a different picture of the *Notes* from – Leo Marx's characterization of the book as the quintessential statement of the case for the American pastoral ideal. That ideal also incorporates a sense of menace. See Marx, *The Machine in the Garden* (New York: Oxford University Press, 1964), p. 118.

8 J. Hector St. John de Crevecoeur, *Letters from an American Farmer,* ed. Albert E. Stone (New York: Penguin, 1981), p. 201. All page numbers in parentheses refer to this edition.

9 Behind this issue of textual selection and exclusion is a critical debate concerning the degree of Crevecoeur's involvement in the final form that the *Letters* took. A. W. Plumstead reviews the relevant facts in "Hector St. John de Crevecoeur," *American Literature, 1754–1789,* pp. 218–21.

10 James's status as a character has impressed other readers more favorably. Thomas Philbrick regards him as "a concretely realized individual." See Philbrick, *St. John de Crevecoeur* (New York: Twayne, 1970), p. 75. More recently David Robinson has argued for a unity in the book founded on James's developing consciousness. See Robinson, "Crevecoeur's James: The Education of an American Farmer," *Journal of English and Germanic Philology* 80 (1981), 552–70. A fair conclusion might be that Crevecoeur is just as committed to the idea of character in James as Swift is committed to the idea of character in Lemuel Gulliver. This position skirts the issue to some degree, but it emphasizes the possibility that what is involved in the nature of "James" is the difference between twentieth-century notions of fictional responsibility and eighteenth-century visions of fictional opportunity.

11 An interesting critical disagreement exists over the extent of James's own commitment to this agrarian myth. Philip Beidler contends that James, unlike Benjamin Franklin, represents a mind "hopelessly trapped" by its ideals. See Beidler, "Franklin's and Crevecoeur's 'Literary' Americans," *Early American Literature* 13 (Spring 1978), 50–63. James C. Mohr, in contrast, regards the *Letters* as a whole as Crevecoeur's definition of the American capacity knowingly to embrace unachievable ideals. See Mohr, "Calculated Disillusionment: Crevecoeur's *Letters* Reconsidered," *South Atlantic Quarterly* 69 (1970), 354–63.

12 It is important to recognize that this vision of America's potential failure in Crevecoeur – and for that matter in much of Jefferson – differs from the social anxieties that Emory Elliott finds to have motivated the postrevolutionary generation: Dwight, Freneau, Barlow, and Brackenridge. Crevecoeur does not immediately concern himself with the effects of a triumphant American materialism upon revolutionary virtue. It is not backsliding that worries him, so much as a direct contest between the forces of life and death inherent in revolutionary America from the beginning. See Emory Elliott, *Revolutionary Writers: Literature and Authority in the New Republic 1725–1810* (New York: Oxford University Press, 1982). William Hedges covers much of the same ground briefly but suggestively in Hedges, "The Old World Yet: Writers and Writing in Post-Revolutionary America," *Early American Literature* 16 (Spring 1981), 3–17.

13 Crevecoeur's focus upon the contradiction of slavery is part of a tradition of American self-criticism that was well established even in the eighteenth century. See Bernard Bailyn, *The Ideological Origins of the American Revolution* (Cambridge, Mass.: Harvard University Press, 1967), pp. 232–46.

14 Jay Fliegelman describes the pervasive nature of familial metaphors (including those of New World infancy) in eighteenth-century political debate. See Fliegelman, *Prodigals and Pilgrims: The American Revolution Against Patriarchal Authority, 1750–1800* (Cambridge University Press, 1982). Annette Kolodny discusses Crevecoeur's use of the metaphor of the land as a woman, promoting rebirth particularly among new immigrants, in a curiously error-filled section of *The Lay of the Land* (Chapel Hill: University of North Carolina Press, 1975), pp. 52–66.

15 I have been unable to find any confirmation of Crevecoeur's claims of widespread opium addiction among women of Nantucket in the eighteenth century. This detail is, it would seem, intended to appear credible to those who also believe that hornets make good house pets. It is one of Crevecoeur's meaningful hoaxes.

16 Crevecoeur had the opportunity to correct these wildly inaccurate directions and distances in later editions of his book. That he let them stand suggests that they have a purpose in his fable as parts of a pattern of doubt cast over the ideal significance of Nantucket.

17 Marius Bewley's sacramental reading of the slave's predicament – though brief and aimed at rebuking Charles Feidelson rather than at illuminating Crevecoeur – is consistent with the slave's broadly representative status. See Bewley, *The Eccentric Design* (New York: Columbia University Press, 1959), pp. 101–2.

18 Philbrick, *St. John de Crevecoeur,* p. 94.

19 Thomas Philbrick was the first to read this section of the book carefully, but the "sinister significance" that he finds in the snakes that James describes has little to do with slavery and more to do with what Philbrick views as James's increasing fascination with violence. See ibid., pp. 95–106.

20 James's "covenant" metaphor in the *Letters* (p. 50) in fact seems to underscore the pertinence of Sacvan Bercovitch's witty definition of a jeremiad as a "state of the covenant address." See Bercovitch, *The American Jeremiad* (Madison: University of Wisconsin Press, 1978), p. 4.

21 George Forgie, *Patricide in the House Divided: A Psychological Interpretation of Lincoln and His Age* (New York: Norton, 1979), pp. 3–53.

22 *The Autobiography of Benjamin Franklin,* eds. Labaree et al. (New Haven, Conn.: Yale University Press, 1964), p. 137. All page numbers in parentheses refer to this edition.

23 Franklin, in fact, near the end of his life seems willfully to have participated in the process of text dispersal and fragmentation that modern editors have been able only partly to reverse. In his own autobiography, Thomas Jefferson records a visit he made to Franklin a month before the older man's death in which Franklin stubbornly, and rather mysteriously, insisted that Jefferson take and keep a portion of what was clearly Franklin's memoir describing

some of his negotiations with the British government just before the beginning of the Revolution. Jefferson too scrupulously returned the manuscript fragment to Temple Franklin after Franklin's death and it appears now to be lost. See Jefferson, *Autobiography* in *Thomas Jefferson, Writings* (New York: The Library of America, 1984), pp. 99–100.

24 That attribution is characteristic of many of Franklin's readers, who – with a few notable exceptions – appear to agree that the *Autobiography* as a whole is formless, largely as a result of its haphazard composition. See, for example, an essay by Hugh J. Dawson, "Fathers and Sons: Franklin's 'Memoirs' as Myth and Metaphor," *Early American Literature* 14 (Winter 1979–80), 269.

25 Robert Sayre, *The Examined Self* (Princeton, N.J.: Princeton University Press, 1964), p. 16. Franklin's diffuseness becomes a kind of problem for Sayre, in spite of his attempt to set it in the context of Henry Adams's early modernism.

26 Locke noted apologetically in his "Epistle to the Reader" that the *Essay* might well have been shorter were it not for the fact that it was "written by incoherent parcels; and, after long intervals of neglect, resumed again, as my humor or occasions permitted." He claimed to be "too lazy, or too busy" to improve it. See John Locke, *An Essay Concerning Human Understanding* (Chicago: Henry Regnery, 1956), pp. 3–4.

27 David Levin emphasizes the qualities of informality and candor that characterize the *Autobiography*. A key expression of such candor and ease is Franklin's determination to expose the structure of composition rather than conceal it. See Levin, *In Defense of Historical Literature*, pp. 58–76.

28 On Franklin's relations with women, particularly during his residence in France, see Claude-Anne Lopez, *Mon Cher Papa: Franklin and the Ladies of Paris* (New Haven, Conn.: Yale University Press, 1966). A fuller account of Franklin in a domestic context is Claude-Anne Lopez and Eugenia W. Herbert, *The Private Franklin: The Man and His Family* (New York: Norton, 1975).

29 Charles L. Sanford, "An American Pilgrim's Progress," *American Quarterly* 6 (Winter 1954), 297–310.

30 See John Bunyan, *The Pilgrim's Progress*, ed. Roger Sharrock (Harmondsworth: Penguin, 1965), p. 60.

31 Josiah in fact is only the first of many people in the *Autobiography* who appear to have given thoughtful consideration to John Locke's astute and humane views on the rearing of children in *Some Thoughts on Education*, which had already gone through several English editions by the time Franklin was a boy. Carl Van Doren noted Franklin's own acquaintance with Locke's educational writings and his application of those writings to the conduct of the Junto in *Benjamin Franklin* (New York: Viking, 1938), pp. 190–2. Jay Fliegelman eloquently summarizes Locke and describes the importance of Locke's educational paradigm to the revolution in concepts of authority taking place throughout the eighteenth century in Anglo-American culture. Fliegelman points out briefly how Franklin's critique of his brother's management of Franklin's own apprenticeship draws upon Locke's precepts about educating the young to independence rather than to obedience. See Fliegelman, *Prodigals and Pilgrims*, pp. 12–15, 108. In important respects, Locke's parenting advice

reinforced qualities already present in the family traditions of New England in the mid-seventeenth century. See, for example, David Levin's account of the parental principles of Cotton Mather in *Cotton Mather: The Young Life of the Lord's Remembrancer* (Cambridge, Mass.: Harvard University Press, 1978), pp. 298–309.

32 For far less positive accounts of Franklin's relations with his father see Hugh J. Dawson, "Fathers and Sons: Franklin's 'Memoirs' as Myth and Metaphor," *Early American Literature* 14 (Winter 1979–80), 269–92, and Jay Fliegelman, *Prodigals and Pilgrims*, p. 111.

33 For David Levin, this charity toward Keith in particular is part of Franklin's ongoing interest in human nature – a subject he pursued completely "without rancor." I tend to agree with Levin's assessment, though I find more gentleness and less disinterested curiosity in Franklin's examination of these events. See Levin, *In Defense of Historical Literature*, p. 67.

34 Franklin explicitly uses the metaphors of parent and child in a political context in his letters and other writings. See passages quoted in Bernard Bailyn, *The Ideological Origins of the American Revolution*, p. 89, and David Freeman Hawke, *Franklin* (New York: Harper & Row, 1976), p. 94, for some examples. On the child–parent metaphor in England's colonial relations, see Fliegelman, *Prodigals and Pilgrims*, p. 93.

35 See Nancy Cott, *The Bonds of Womanhood: Woman's Sphere in New England, 1780–1835* (New Haven, Conn.: Yale University Press, 1977), in particular Chapters 3, 4, and 5.

36 The draft of the Declaration of Independence is the most well known of Jefferson's efforts to expose the legislative and political process. But he also printed in his *Autobiography* what are virtually minutes of the proceedings of the Continental Congress. The contrast to Franklin's book could not be more marked. In the recent Library of America edition Jefferson's *Autobiography* runs to one hundred pages, nearly all of which is political reporting, beginning with the Stamp Act Crisis. Jefferson devotes six paragraphs to his early life, before 1765.

37 This is not the same thing as saying, with William Spengemann, that Franklin suppressed his personal accomplishments in order to make his life more imitable. Franklin suppressed few accomplishments that he lived to discuss in the *Autobiography*. He gave his vanity free play, as he cheerfully notes. He merely insisted that his achievements were won by domestic virtues rather than by publicly (or conventionally) heroic ones. William C. Spengemann, *The Forms of Autobiography* (New Haven, Conn.: Yale University Press, 1980), pp. 51–61.

38 John Bunyan, *Grace Abounding to the Chief of Sinners and The Pilgrim's Progress,* ed. Roger Sharrock (London: Oxford University Press, 1966), p. 10.

39 Ibid., p. 104.

40 Ibid., p. 69.

41 Robert Bell has argued that Franklin's autobiography reduces the spiritual dimension of Bunyan's example to little more than a social gesture, losing all sense of "transcendent Augustinian unity." Like Robert Sayre, however, Bell tends to see what Franklin has abandoned of the earlier heritage rather than what he has preserved. See Bell, "Metamorphoses of Spiritual Autobiography," *ELH* 44 (1977), 108–26.

42 John Lynen suggests that the mottoes reflect Franklin's taste for "satiric" exaggeration and overstatement. This view clearly has things backward. The mottoes are measured and thoughtful. Only the aspiration reflected by the list of virtues itself could be thought of as brash or overstated. See Lynen, "Benjamin Franklin and the Choice of a Single Point of View," *The American Puritan Imagination: Essays in Revaluation,* ed. Sacvan Bercovitch (Cambridge University Press, 1974), p. 182.

43 I do not mean that Franklin was never exasperated with the Quakers. Once when fuming over their pacifist stubbornness, Franklin called them, rather colorfully, the "stiff rumps." See David Freeman Hawke, *Franklin,* p. 148.

44 Daniel Shea noted in connection with Franklin's description of the eccentricities of Samuel Keimer a quality that is generally present in the *Autobiography* as a whole: "What Franklin enjoys is the vanquished dogmatist." See Shea, *Spiritual Autobiography in Early America,* p. 247.

45 Adams's observation is quoted in Van Doren, *Benjamin Franklin,* p. 530.

3. AZADS IN CONCORD

1 See Marilyn Butler, "Against Tradition: The Case for a Particularized Historical Method" in *Historical Studies and Literary Criticism,* ed. Jerome J. McGann (Madison: University of Wisconsin Press, 1985), pp. 25–47, and Philip F. Gura, "The Study of Colonial American Literature, 1966–1987: A Vade Mecum" in *The William and Mary Quarterly,* 45 (April 1988), 305–41.

2 Henry D. Thoreau, *Walden,* ed. J. Lyndon Shanley (Princeton, N.J.: Princeton University Press, 1971), p. 79. All page numbers in parentheses identifying passages from *Walden* refer to this edition.

3 Indeed, Charles Anderson has suggested that social reform is not "the real goal" even of Thoreau's first two chapters, the most openly (or apparently) reformist chapters in the book. See Anderson, *The Magic Circle of Walden* (New York: Holt, Rinehart, & Winston, 1968), p. 37.

4 The idea of an extended household at Walden has close affinities with Frederick Garber's emphasis on the role of the clearing, the redeemed space, as Thoreau's central image for the healthy soul. See Garber, *Thoreau's Redemptive Imagination* (New York: New York University Press, 1977). I should note here my debt throughout this discussion to Joel Porte's sympathetic view of Thoreau and the figurative value of "life" in *Emerson and Thoreau: Transcendentalists in Conflict* (Middletown, Conn.: Wesleyan University Press, 1965).

5 William Howarth emphasizes the contradiction between Thoreau's ideal of organic form and the way in which he actually wrote *Walden.* See Howarth, *The Book of Concord* (New York: Viking Press, 1982). Joseph Wood Krutch makes this point about Thoreau's method most graphically. See Krutch, *Henry David Thoreau* (New York: William Sloane, 1948), p. 120. Lawrence Buell has commented on the tendency of antebellum literature to remain strongly "research based" – a reflection, as Buell sees it, of the artists' view of themselves as to some degree civic figures with a public responsibility to instruct their readership. See Buell, *New England Literary Culture* (Cambridge University Press, 1986), p. 40.

6 The similarities and differences between Franklin and Thoreau have intrigued

scholars for years. David Levin suggests the stylistic affinities between them in "The Autobiography of Benjamin Franklin: The Puritan Experimenter in Life and Art," *Yale Review* 53 (Winter 1964), 273. John Lynen notes the way that Franklin seems to anticipate Thoreau, yet he finally contends that Thoreau satirizes Franklin's "prudential philosophy," a conclusion with which Sherman Paul largely agrees. See Lynen, "Benjamin Franklin and the Choice of a Single Point of View," *The American Puritan Imagination: Essays in Revaluation,* ed. Sacvan Bercovitch (Cambridge University Press, 1974), p. 193, and Paul, *The Shores of America* (1958, rpt. New York: Russell & Russell, 1971), p. 308. Thoreau himself invites the comparison with Franklin in his wry allusions to Poor Richard's aphorisms and in his fascination with the modest economic means necessary for sustaining a healthy life. It does not seem to me that Thoreau's Franklinian lists of accounts in "Economy" are quite so prophetically ominous as Stanley Cavell finds them in *The Senses of Walden* (1972, rpt. San Francisco: North Point, 1981).

7 Michael Gilmore has argued that Thoreau did indeed aspire to social potency when he began *Walden* but that he gradually abandoned his hopes and withdrew from "history" into the isolated self. He describes these as the "privatizing and antihistorical" tendencies of *Walden*. Gilmore quotes in support of his view precisely the sentence that Stanley Cavell has identified as partial evidence of Thoreau's continued embrace of the public role of prophet. See Gilmore, *American Romanticism and the Marketplace* (Chicago: University of Chicago Press, 1985), p. 49. Cavell finds that Thoreau's expressed despair over his inability to influence his times echoes the words of Jeremiah. See Cavell, *The Senses of Walden,* p. 22.

8 See Frederick Garber on Thoreau's "totemism" in "Higher Laws," *Thoreau's Redemptive Imagination,* p. 38. Sherman Paul paradoxically contends that "Brute Neighbors" is committed to the higher, spiritual meanings of nature, a view that seems stubbornly opposed to Thoreau's charming beginning of that chapter, whereas Charles Anderson insists that the structural pattern of "Higher Laws" is indeed an "ascent" to Heaven. See Paul, *The Shores of America,* p. 340, and Anderson, *The Magic Circle of Walden,* p. 151. Both Anderson and Paul impose a degree of consistency and architectonic skill on these portions of *Walden* that Thoreau does not really seem to welcome. On the important, formal assumptions of the book see especially Lawrence Buell, *Literary Transcendentalism: Style and Vision in the American Renaissance* (Ithaca, N.Y.: Cornell University Press, 1973), pp. 188–208.

9 I am thinking mainly of Thoreau's role as a spectator within, rather than as a member of, families around Concord, including the Emersons. He did have a wide social network and a complex "family" life of his own to draw on, but not as a parent or a spouse, and by the time he was writing *Walden* his two favorite siblings, John and Helen, were dead. Thoreau's life as a social being, nevertheless, is a rewarding study. See Mary Elkins Moller, *Thoreau in the Human Community* (Amherst: University of Massachusetts Press, 1980).

10 On this oscillation between intimacy and distance – one of many – in Thoreau, see Frederick Garber on the interplay between seclusion and contact, *Thoreau's Redemptive Imagination,* p. 26.

11 For Thoreau's exploitation of the myths of Isis and Osiris in Plutarch's *Moralia* see Meg McGavran Murray, "Thoreau's Moon Mythology: Lunar Clues to the Hieroglyphics of *Walden*," *American Literature* 58 (March 1986), 15–32. H. Bruce Franklin discusses Melville's use of the same mythic model in *Moby-Dick*. See Franklin, *The Wake of the Gods* (Stanford, Calif.: Stanford University Press, 1963), pp. 53–98.

12 See Michael West, "Scatology and Eschatology: The Heroic Dimensions of Thoreau's Wordplay," *PMLA* 89 (October 1974), 1043–64.

13 The images of birth in these passages have struck virtually every careful reader of *Walden*, particularly since Perry Miller and Sherman Paul called attention to them. In Paul, however, they constitute primarily a vivid analogy to the organic ideal of creativity that the transcendentalists embraced. See Paul, *The Shores of America*, pp. 348–350. Miller found in them a "derisive, tortured" irony, for the "afterbirth of mud and clay is filthy" and finally sterile. See Miller, *Consciousness in Concord* (Boston: Houghton Mifflin, 1958), pp. 126–7. Miller's view in particular substitutes his own concerns for those of Thoreau, whose presence at this birth has as many implications for Thoreau's own status as it does for the conventionally maternal image of nature.

14 It has become traditional to view Thoreau's portraits of these Irish working families as far harsher in tone than they really are. See, for example, Charles Anderson's comments in *The Magic Circle of Walden*, pp. 46, 143, or Sherman Paul in *The Shores of America*, p. 325. Recently John Hildebidle has joined in these earlier, negative judgments in *Thoreau: A Naturalist's Liberty* (Cambridge, Mass.: Harvard University Press, 1983), pp. 119–20. All three critics are much harder on Thoreau than Thoreau is on either Collins or Field.

15 Some of the most persuasive paragraphs of Philip Gura's chapter on Thoreau's philological interests have to do with Thoreau's success in avoiding the sort of despair about human promise that could afflict Melville, for example, in the face of the grimmer levels of life. For Thoreau, the Fields were as much a part of nature as field mice or Walden Pond – Thoreau would have found this identity well expressed in their name – and as such they participated in, rather than defaced, the Walden landscape. See Gura, *The Wisdom of Words: Language, Theology, and Literature in the New England Renaissance* (Middletown, Conn.: Wesleyan University Press, 1981), pp. 141–4.

16 Charles Anderson notes that Therien's name, like that of the Fields, is a pun, echoing *therion* the Greek for "animal." Unfortunately Anderson concludes that this pun underscores Therien's "low rank" in *Walden's* scale of being. It seems clear to me, in view of the reflexive nature of Thoreau's verbal portrait, that Therien's rank is very high indeed. See Anderson, *The Magic Circle of Walden*, pp. 146–7.

17 Indeed, Thoreau's hostility to Concord life is another of those durable critical axioms about *Walden* that seems singularly overemphasized. See Hildebidle's recent expression of it in *Thoreau: A Naturalist's Liberty*, p. 112.

18 In Philip Gura's view, Thoreau's philology confirmed for him this sense of the unity of life. See Gura, *The Wisdom of Words*, pp. 109–44. For the most eloquent account of Thoreau's sense of "fellowship" with all life, see Joseph Krutch, "The Style and the Man" in *Henry David Thoreau*, pp. 249–87.

19 Sherman Paul quotes Thoreau's long celebration of commercial activity as if it

were merely figurative rather than, in some measure at least, sincere in its appreciation. And Michael Gilmore argues that Thoreau drifts a bit furtively toward the values of the marketplace, as if he were ashamed of them but incapable of escape. In this sense, Gilmore refers to *Walden* as a "defeated text." Neither view seems willing to allow Thoreau's transactions with his community to be as open and aboveboard as they are, particularly in his enthusiastic response to commerce as a metaphor and as an expression of life. See Paul, *The Shores of America*, p. 323, and Gilmore, *American Romanticism and the Marketplace*, pp. 41–4.

20 Stanley Cavell has persuasively linked these hoeing passages to the metaphors of the Old Testament prophets, but if Thoreau does resemble Ezekiel and Jeremiah, then that resemblance by no means explains the richer charities of Thoreau's tone. See Cavell, *The Senses of Walden*, pp. 18–40.

21 Indeed, the railroad is the most conspicuous evidence for Thoreau of what Stanley Cavell calls the potential for "apocalyptic concord" in *Walden*, the sense that a new city of man may yet be possible in America. See Cavell, *The Senses of Walden*, p. 17.

22 See Stephen Whicher's fine opening chapter in *Freedom and Fate* (Philadelphia: University of Pennsylvania Press, 1953).

23 See Emerson's affirmation of this vocation in "The Poet," *Ralph Waldo Emerson: Essays and Lectures*, ed. Joel Porte (New York: Library of America, 1983), pp. 455–56. All page numbers in parentheses identifying passages from Emerson's work refer to this edition.

24 "Life" becomes, as well, a key term in what we might call Emerson's theory of literature. In the "Divinity School Address" Emerson stressed the importance of the speaker's "life" as a formal ingredient in sermons or in oratory. He extended that importance to secular prose in his comments on Montaigne (*Essays and Lectures*, p. 700) and in his admiration for the vitality of Carlyle's writing. See Jonathan Bishop, *Emerson on the Soul* (Cambridge, Mass.: Harvard University Press, 1964), pp. 128–9. Emerson is not a theorist, and the looseness with which he applies "life" to literature is a reflection of the tendency that Lawrence Buell has noted of Emerson's arguments to become metaphors. See Buell, *Literary Transcendentalism*, pp. 147–53. Robert Richardson gives a useful treatment of the extent to which Emerson read history as evidence of the unity of life. See Richardson, "Emerson on History," *Emerson: Prospect and Retrospect*, ed. Joel Porte (Cambridge, Mass.: Harvard University Press, 1982), pp. 49–64. B. L. Packer describes the formative role that "life" and "death" both as concepts and as experiences had on the composition of *Nature* in particular. Emerson's brother Charles died on May 9, 1836, as Emerson was completing the text of his first book. See Packer, *Emerson's Fall* (New York: Continuum, 1982), pp. 48–57.

25 Emerson's difficulties with Thoreau, for example, are well known. Equally poignant are friendships he both prized and failed to reciprocate with women, especially with Margaret Fuller. See particularly Gay Wilson Allen, *Waldo Emerson* (New York: Viking, 1981), pp. 350–6.

26 *Emerson in His Journals*, ed. Joel Porte (Cambridge, Mass.: Harvard University Press, 1982), p. 288.

27 The parallel between *Nature* and "A Modell of Christian Charity" rests almost

entirely on internal evidence, but Joel Porte has noted that Emerson was reading Winthrop's journal in 1835 as he was preparing to write a history of Concord and was on the point of beginning *Nature*. Porte describes the similarities of spirit between Anne Hutchinson's antinomianism and Emerson's own rebellion against the religious establishment, a resemblance that would make the affinities between *Nature* and John Winthrop's work yet another of Emerson's invigorating paradoxes. See Porte, *Representative Man* (New York: Oxford University Press, 1979), pp. 98–100.

28 Ibid., p. 75.

29 This metaphor of the fragmented body is Emerson's favorite means for describing what Carolyn Porter has called his sense of the "reification" of contemporary life. It was, in fact, the basis of Emerson's objection to the socialism of Fourier that it reassembled this fragmented man only mechanically: "Fourier has skipped no fact but one, namely Life." See Porter, *Seeing and Being* (Middletown, Conn.: Wesleyan University Press, 1981), p. 92.

30 *The Founding of Massachusetts: Historians and the Sources,* ed. Edmund S. Morgan (Indianapolis, Ind.: Bobbs Merrill, 1964), p. 203.

31 Erik Thurin, *Emerson as Priest of Pan* (Lawrence: Regents Press of Kansas, 1981), p. 162. Joel Porte has pointed out the sources of this marital imagery in Wordsworth, in whom Emerson would also have encountered it. See Porte, *Representative Man,* pp. 72–3. Eric Cheyfitz as well treats the subject of gender in Emerson, though less informatively than Thurin, in *The Transparent: Sexual Politics in the Language of Emerson* (Baltimore: Johns Hopkins University Press, 1981). Karl Keller's recent article, "The Puritan Perverse," is a stimulating, brief treatment of how the sexual suggestiveness of Emerson's work "licensed" the erotic intensity of Whitman: "American literary history is a history of the production of licensed monsters: Anne Hutchinson and Roger Williams out of the belly of John Cotton . . . Whitman out of the belly of Emerson." See *Texas Studies in Literature and Language* 25 (Spring 1983), 139–64.

32 Daniel Shea quotes this passage from "Compensation" as an instance of the pervasive images of metamorphosis in Emerson's language, but it lends itself as readily to the portrait of a socially concerned Emerson that Phyllis Cole describes. See Shea, "Emerson and the American Metamorphosis," in *Emerson: Prophecy, Metamorphosis, and Influence,* ed. David Levin (New York: Columbia University Press, 1975), pp. 29–56, and Cole's essay in the same collection, "Emerson, England, and Fate," pp. 83–105. Emerson's propensity to rewrite, again and again, fables of the "Fall," as he does here in this passage from "Compensation," is the central thesis of Barbara Packer's stimulating discussion of Emerson's major essays. Packer's emphasis, though, is not on Emerson's obsession with the marriage in Genesis but on his own "falls" of what she calls contraction, dislocation, ossification, and reflexion. See *Emerson's Fall,* pp. 1–84, for the application of Packer's reading to *Nature*. Emerson himself makes the connection between household life and political life much more bluntly in the lecture "Home" that he delivered as part of a series on "Human Life" in 1838: "A household is the school of power." See *The Early Lectures of Ralph Waldo Emerson,* Vol. 3, eds. Robert E. Spiller and Wallace E. Williams (Cambridge, Mass.: Harvard University Press, 1972), p. 24.

33 This conviction, in fact, is the core of what Lawrence Buell describes as

Emerson's sense of "microcosmic form" in *Literary Transcendentalism,* pp. 145–65.

34 See *The Founding of Massachusetts: Historians and the Sources,* p. 198.

35 This, in effect, is the argument of Quentin Anderson in *The Imperial Self* (New York: Knopf, 1971): that Emerson transvalues the terms of social life and makes them serve "the uses of the inward empire" (p. 47). It should be clear that I am describing a different view of Emerson's accomplishment.

36 See particularly Stephen Whicher's *Selections from Ralph Waldo Emerson* (Boston: Houghton Mifflin, 1957), pp. 4–6.

4. HAWTHORNE'S MARRIAGES

1 See *The Collections of the Massachusetts Historical Society,* Third Series, Vol. 7 (Boston: Little Brown, 1838), pp. 31–48, for this early text of Winthrop's speech.

2 Winthrop is a direct and indirect presence in two very early sketches, "Mrs. Hutchinson" and "Endicott and the Red Cross."

3 The sense of the primacy of marriage in Hawthorne is familiar to students of his work. It has provided some of the richest criticism we have seen of his fiction, most notably Frederick Crews's study, *The Sins of the Fathers: Psychological Themes and Hawthorne's Fiction* (London: Oxford University Press, 1966), but more recently Gloria Erlich's fascinating and sympathetic account of Hawthorne's family life, *Family Themes and Hawthorne's Fiction* (New Brunswick, N.J.: Rutgers University Press, 1984). The poles between which criticism of Hawthorne is suspended are the private, psychologizing readings such as these on the one hand and the equally rich, historicist approaches exemplified by the work of Michael Colacurcio. It seems to me that this division of study itself is oddly harmonious with Winthrop's intertwining of public and private spheres in his communal vision.

4 See, for example, Gloria Erlich's ingenious treatment of "The Wives of the Dead" in *Family Themes and Hawthorne's Fiction,* pp. 107–8.

5 *The Centenary Edition of the Works of Nathaniel Hawthorne,* Vol. 8, ed. Claude M. Simpson (Columbus: Ohio State University Press, 1972), pp. 423–30.

6 See Erlich's *Family Themes and Hawthorne's Fiction* and Nina Baym, "Nathaniel Hawthorne and His Mother: A Biographical Speculation," *American Literature* 54 (March 1982), 1–27.

7 *Nathaniel Hawthorne: Tales and Sketches,* ed. Roy Harvey Pearce (New York: Library of America, 1982), p. 370. All page numbers in parentheses identifying passages from Hawthorne's short fiction refer to this edition.

8 In addition to the work of Crews and Erlich already noted, the most important treatments of sexuality in Hawthorne begin with Leslie Fiedler, *Love and Death in the American Novel* (1960, rpt. New York: Stein & Day, 1966), particularly pp. 222–41 and 432–50, and include recent books by Allan Gardner Lloyd-Smith, *Eve Tempted: Writing and Sexuality in Hawthorne's Fiction* (London: Croom Helm, 1984) and Philip Young, *Hawthorne's Secret: An Untold Tale* (Boston: Godine, 1984).

9 Frederick Crews has argued that this "escapist" pattern of male protagonists is

widespread in Hawthorne's fiction. See Crews, *The Sins of the Fathers*, p. 134 and throughout.

10 Sharon Cameron treats "Ethan Brand" in this context with a somewhat different emphasis from mine in *The Corporeal Self: Allegories of the Body in Melville and Hawthorne* (Baltimore: Johns Hopkins University Press, 1981), pp. 90–100.

11 The persistence of the incest motif in Hawthorne is discussed by Leslie Fiedler in *Love and Death*, pp. 229, 241, 418–19, and at some length by Philip Young in *Hawthorne's Secret*. In effect, incest is Young's "untold tale", though Fiedler at least had already told it so far as the fiction itself is concerned. Neither Young nor Fiedler discusses "Ethan Brand" in this context. See also James B. Twitchell's discussion of the theme of incest in romantic literature, including Hawthorne, *Forbidden Partners: The Incest Taboo in Modern Culture* (New York: Columbia University Press, 1987). Twitchell's discussion of *Manfred* contains quotations from Byron's poem that resemble quite closely the passages in "Ethan Brand" in which Hawthorne describes Brand's sins against the soul of Esther. See *Manfred*, 2.3.120–1, quoted in Twitchell, *Forbidden Partners*, p. 89.

12 The first clue to this humor is the name of Endicott's "Ancient," which Hawthorne borrowed from John Gorham Palfrey, a booster of American literary materials in the *North American Review* who in 1821 had suggested a long list of figures from American history suitable for use in fiction, including Winthrop and Endicott. See Neal F. Doubleday, *Hawthorne's Early Tales* (Durham, N.C.: Duke University Press, 1972), pp. 23–24.

13 Michael Colacurcio, *The Province of Piety: Moral History in Hawthorne's Early Tales* (Cambridge, Mass.: Harvard University Press, 1984), pp. 255–8.

14 Michael Davitt Bell first suggested the idea of a competition in Hawthorne's imagination between conflicting evaluations of the past in *Hawthorne and the Historical Romance of New England* (Princeton, N.J.: Princeton University Press, 1971). In Bell's discussion Winthrop emerges as the paradigm of the Puritan as "noble patriarch" (pp. 20–1). More recently Frederick Newberry has explored some of the same ground in "Tradition and Disinheritance in *The Scarlet Letter*," *ESQ* 23 (1977), 1–26. Newberry's argument (presented most fully in the book of which this article is a chapter) is that Hawthorne is exploring the cultural transition from Old to New World in search of mediating figures who can fuse the best of both cultures – yet another of Hawthorne's marriages. Surveyor Pue, for example, the preserver of the story of Hester Prynne and Hawthorne's imaginative savior from the stagnation of the customhouse, becomes what Newberry calls an "upper-storey ancestor" whom Hawthorne substitutes both for his actual Puritan forebears and for the political "fathers" of the customhouse. See Newberry, *Hawthorne's Divided Loyalties: England and America in His Works* (London: Associated University Presses, 1987).

15 Philip Young, in particular, has noted the "spermatic" associations of Aylmer's laboratory in *Hawthorne's Secret*, p. 68.

16 See Edgar Dryden, *Nathaniel Hawthorne: The Poetics of Enchantment* (Ithaca, N.Y.: Cornell University Press, 1977), pp. 60–7.

17 Crews's comment comes during his discussion of "The Birth-mark" in *The Sins of the Fathers,* p. 112.

18 See Joel Porte, *The Romance in America* (Middletown, Conn.: Wesleyan University Press, 1969).

19 The wedding of extremes has, in fact, a second generic significance that Richard Brodhead emphasizes when he describes the fusion of the "ghostly logic" of romance with the full exposure of the novel in *The Scarlet Letter.* In *Hawthorne, Melville, and the Novel* (Chicago: University of Chicago Press, 1976) Brodhead argues that the artistic success of *The Scarlet Letter* is a result of Hawthorne's ability to make the novel and the romance function simultaneously in his text as ways of seeing character and events. The power of the book's last scene, Brodhead contends, does not derive from its ambiguity – is there or is there not a letter on Dimmesdale's chest? – but from its ability to join novel vision and romance into a single perception of the "deep life-matter" that the book itself retells. Brodhead does not do so, but it seems clear to me that this generic fusion might be compared to a marriage – as Hawthorne himself suggests in "The Custom-House."

20 The critical treatment of "Roger Malvin's Burial" illustrates pointedly the oscillation between psychological and historical poles that I noted earlier. See Crews's famous discussion in *The Sins of the Fathers* balanced against Michael Colacurcio's in *The Province of Piety* as enriched (anachronistically) by David Levin, "Modern Misjudgments of Racial Imperialism in Hawthorne and Parkman," *The Yearbook of English Studies* 13 (1983), 145–58. William Spengemann argues that "Roger Malvin's Burial" illustrates the tension between domesticity and romantic adventure by dramatizing a "sequence of increasingly desperate attempts to restore domestic peace" that only succeed in widening the domestic "fissures" that Reuben initially generated by failing to confess fully to Dorcas and failing to return and bury her father. Spengemann's reading is one of the most persuasive responses to this challenging tale. See Spengemann, *The Adventurous Muse: The Poetics of American Fiction, 1789–1900* (New Haven, Conn.: Yale University Press, 1977), pp. 153–60.

21 Gloria Erlich discusses the entire plot of "Roger Malvin's Burial" in the context of Reuben's desire to revenge himself against the main patriarch, Malvin, for enticing him to betray his self-sacrificial ideals in the beginning of the story. The result is an intensification of what Erlich calls Hawthorne's "intolerable ironies" to the point where they become much too difficult to accept either as plausible motives for Reuben or as artistic purposes for Hawthorne. See Erlich, "Guilt and Expiation in 'Roger Malvin's Burial,'" *Nineteenth-Century Fiction* 26 (March 1972), 377–89.

22 Nathaniel Hawthorne, *The Scarlet Letter,* ed. Larzer Ziff (Indianapolis, Ind.: Bobbs Merrill, 1963), p. 75. All page numbers in parentheses are citations to this edition, a printing of the centenary text.

23 Michael Colacurcio sees this moment as an allusion to the fable of Zeus and Europa, but the context of allusions to the Minotaur suggests that Hawthorne is thinking of the Cretan bull riders whom Theseus and his Athenian youths joined when they came as sacrifices to the Minotaur. See Colacurio, *The Province of Piety,* p. 269.

24 I have quoted Winthrop here in the version that Hawthorne knew, a text rather different from, and less revolutionary than, the manuscript, in part because the editors of the Massachusetts Historical Society *Collections* silently corrected Winthrop's supplanting of Adam by Eve. See *The Collections of the Massachusetts Historical Society,* Third Series, Vol. 7 (Boston: Little, Brown, 1838), pp. 31–48. An important treatment of *The Scarlet Letter* in connection with the Puritan past, specifically the antinomian crisis, is that of Michael Colacurcio, "Footsteps of Ann Hutchinson: The Context of *The Scarlet Letter,*" *ELH* 39 (1972), 459–94.

25 Leslie Fiedler notes this mixture of childlike and adult qualities in Dimmesdale at the end of the story, but he sees these traits as indicative of the failure of love in the New World – as part of the inadequacies of what Fiedler calls the convention of the "pale lover" in Hawthorne's fiction. See Fiedler, *Love and Death,* p. 238.

26 The account here of Hester's impact is consistent with Charles Feidelson's influential view of her role as the overcomer of the book's pattern of alienation. See Feidelson, "The Scarlet Letter" in *Hawthorne Centenary Essays,* ed. Roy Harvey Pearce (Columbus: Ohio State University Press, 1954), pp. 31–77. I tend to disagree, on the other hand, with Nina Baym, who finds *The Scarlet Letter* markedly different from Hawthorne's earlier work and his earlier value for integration in community. See Baym, *The Shape of Hawthorne's Career* (Ithaca, N.Y.: Cornell University Press, 1976), p. 142.

5. MELVILLE, WHITMAN, AND THE PREDICAMENT OF INTIMACY

1 Sacvan Bercovitch has emphasized this imaginative continuity in the concluding chapter of his book on the jeremiad tradition. See Bercovitch, "Epilogue: The Symbol of America" in *The American Jeremiad* (Madison: University of Wisconsin Press, 1978), pp. 176–210.

2 Michael Gilmore, *The Middle Way: Puritanism and Ideology in American Romantic Fiction* (New Brunswick, N.J.: Rutgers University Press, 1977), pp. 131–6.

3 Along with Gilmore, both Carolyn Karcher and John P. McWilliams have discussed this political dimension in Melville's art. See Karcher, *Shadow Over the Promised Land: Slavery, Race, and Violence in Melville's America* (Baton Rouge: Louisiana State University Press, 1980) and McWilliams, *Hawthorne, Melville and the American Character* (Cambridge University Press, 1984). Michael Paul Rogin has documented the extent to which *Moby-Dick* is saturated with the metaphors of the antislavery struggle in the midst of which it was written. See Rogin, *Subversive Genealogy: The Politics and Art of Herman Melville* (1983, rpt. Berkeley and Los Angeles: University of California Press, 1985), pp. 102–51.

4 The thesis of Edgar Dryden's book, *Melville's Thematics of Form: The Great Art of Telling the Truth* (Baltimore: Johns Hopkins University Press, 1968) is that Melville's narrators are a fictional accommodation to the dangers to "sanity and life" represented by truth telling (p. 26). The phrases of Melville's in this paragraph are from "Hawthorne and His Mosses" in Herman Melville, *Pierre,*

Israel Potter, The Piazza Tales, The Confidence-Man, Uncollected Prose, Billy Budd (New York: Library of America, 1984), pp. 1154–71.

5 Ibid., p. 1158.

6 T. Walter Herbert, Jr., *Moby-Dick and Calvinism: A World Dismantled* (New Brunswick, N.J.: Rutgers University Press, 1977), pp. 73–5.

7 Edward Rosenberry suggests this propensity in Melville toward fusion rather than logical resolution in his view of what Rosenberry calls the "marriage" of comic and tragic vision in Melville's work. See Rosenberry, *Melville and the Comic Spirit* (Cambridge, Mass.: Harvard University Press, 1955), p. 145. Warner Berthoff notes, too, the characteristic ability Melville displays in his fiction "to hold apparently contradictory discoveries in mind at once, in free solution." The emphasis falls, I think, not on contradiction but on the comparative ease with which it is sustained. See Berthoff, *The Example of Melville* (Princeton, N.J.: Princeton University Press, 1962), p. 38.

8 Herman Melville, *Moby-Dick, or The Whale* (Berkeley and Los Angeles: University of California Press, 1979), p. 237. Page citations in parentheses to *Moby-Dick* refer to this edition.

9 Sacvan Bercovitch points out that Melville's favorite biblical source in *Moby-Dick*, the Book of Job, was a staple of jeremiad literature in New England, used by preachers and politicians both as a means of dramatizing the sufferings of New England and of foretelling the happy resolution of those sufferings. See Bercovitch, *The American Jeremiad*, p. 59. Nathalia Wright suggests in a note on Melville's Leviathan that the prominence of Job among Melville's sources suggests his willingness to accept the absence of a moral order in creation in favor of a Job-like submission to the "marvellous" in the physical universe, a conclusion that seems to me consistent with Melville's appetite for experience if not with the Book of Job itself. See Wright, "Moby Dick: Jonah's or Job's Whale?" *American Literature* 37 (March 1965), 190–5.

10 Sacvan Bercovitch notes the affirmative role of what he calls "the Pequod Community" in *The American Jeremiad*, p. 192, but the best short account of Melville's celebration of shipboard life is Warner Berthoff's discussion of the world of the ship in *The Example of Melville*, pp. 80–4.

11 Herman Melville, *Typee, Omoo, Mardi* (New York: Library of America, 1982), pp. 401–7.

12 Ibid., p. 672. John P. McWilliams gives a good account of Melville's egalitarian enthusiasm in his chapter, "Distrust in Confidence," from *Hawthorne, Melville, and the American Character*, pp. 133–54.

13 R. W. B. Lewis, *The American Adam* (Chicago: University of Chicago Press, 1955), p. 146.

14 Newton Arvin finds Melville still playfully punning on the idea of a "counterpain" during his recuperative trip to the Holy Land in 1857. An Italian promontory near Naples, Posilipo, visited by Melville on that trip, has a Greek name that means "abating pain." As his journey progressed Melville used "Posilipo" in his journal as a synecdoche for the sort of healing encounter that Ishmael experienced with Queequeg: "Floating about philosophizing with Antonio the Merry [a gondolier in Venice]. Ah, it was Posilipo." See Newton Arvin, *Herman Melville* (New York: William Sloane, 1950), p. 214.

15 F. O. Matthiessen was the first to discuss this feature of Melville's imagination in the context of Emerson's admiration for the English metaphysical poets in the remarkable short essay "Ishmael's Loom of Time" from *American Renaissance* (New York: Oxford University Press, 1941), pp. 119–32. See Lawrance Thompson for some specific echoes of Milton in Ahab's language, *Melville's Quarrel with God* (Princeton, N.J.: Princeton University Press, 1952), pp. 178, 188–9. Henry F. Pommer has traced Melville's indebtedness to Milton most thoroughly. See Pommer, *Milton and Melville* (Pittsburgh, Pa.: University of Pittsburgh Press, 1950).

16 Paul Brodtkorb, among others, has noted the perplexities of this passage and comments that it gives us a description of Ahab "fragmented almost into incoherence," but it is, I think, an incoherence that makes its elements clear. We can discern what has been broken. See Brodtkorb, *Ishmael's White World: A Phenomenological Reading of Moby-Dick* (New Haven, Conn.: Yale University Press, 1965), pp. 63–4. See Edgar Dryden's treatment of the passage as well in *Melville's Thematics of Form*, p. 103.

17 Edgar Dryden explores the formal implications of the leg injury as a representation of Tommo's bondage to time in *Melville's Thematics of Form*, pp. 42–6. William Spengemann discusses *Typee* as representative of the sequential advances and retreats in Melville's fiction. Tatooing is the most irrevocable of the "advances" in *Typee*, from which Tommo turns back, as Ishmael does from the irrevocable advances of Ahab. See Spengemann, *The Adventurous Muse: The Poetics of American Fiction, 1789–1900* (New Haven, Conn.: Yale University Press, 1977), pp. 178–88.

18 Samuel Kimball, "Uncanny Narration in *Moby-Dick*," *American Literature* 59 (December 1987), 528–47.

19 T. W. Herbert, *Moby-Dick and Calvinism*, p. 100.

20 See the text of *Israel Potter* published in Melville, *Pierre, Israel Potter, The Piazza Tales, The Confidence-Man, Uncollected Prose, Billy Budd*, pp. 477–80.

21 In his study of the confidence man, Gary Lindberg includes both Franklin and Melville without directly linking them. His view of Franklin's example is, interestingly, less favorable than Melville's. See *The Confidence Man in American Literature* (New York: Oxford University Press, 1982). Michael Davitt Bell makes a representative case for the bleakness of Melville's vision in *The Confidence-Man* in the final chapter of *The Development of American Romance* (Chicago: University of Chicago Press, 1980).

22 See the text of *The Confidence-Man* in Melville, *Pierre, Israel Potter, The Piazza Tales, The Confidence-Man, Uncollected Prose, Billy Budd*, p. 862. Citations in parentheses to *The Confidence-Man* hereafter are references to this edition.

23 As one dimension of this "communal self," see H. Bruce Franklin's discussion of the mythological implications of the confidence man's "shape-shifting" in *The Wake of the Gods* (Stanford, Calif.: Stanford University Press, 1963), pp. 184–7.

24 Many other readers take Ishmael's nameless horror quite seriously here. See for example, Newton Arvin, *Herman Melville*, p. 28, and Paul Brodtkorb, *Ishmael's White World*, pp. 106–10.

25 As many readers have noted, a sense of Ahab's sexual impairment is clearly conveyed by the crippling groin injury he sustained on the streets of New

Bedford, but even sympathetic critics are reluctant to follow Ishmael in his most explicit descriptions of Ahab's suffering. Paul Brodtkorb and Richard Brodhead, for example, agree that Ishmael's descent into the Roman baths defies analysis and signals Ahab's unknowableness. See Richard Brodhead, *Hawthorne, Melville, and the Novel* (Chicago: University of Chicago Press, 1976), pp. 123–6, and idem, *Ishmael's White World*, p. 49. H. Bruce Franklin identifies Ahab with the dismemberment myths of Osiris but also stops short of Ishmael's confirmation. See Franklin, *The Wake of of the Gods*, pp. 71–4.

26 Melville's narrators have been the stimulus for much of the best criticism of his work. See in particular Warner Berthoff's chapter in *The Example of Melville*, pp. 115–32, and the narrator-based studies of Edgar Dryden and Paul Brodtkorb, cited above. Dryden is especially helpful on the significance of "The Town-Ho's Story" as evidence of the transformation of Ishmael into a teller. See Dryden, *Melville's Thematics of Form*, pp. 109–11.

27 Edward Rosenberry astutely notes the parallels between characters in *The Confidence-Man* and those in *Moby-Dick*, especially Stubb and Ahab. See Rosenberry, *Melville and the Comic Spirit*, p. 143.

28 Carolyn Karcher's lawyer-like examination of the first half of *The Confidence-Man* is an impressive – if exhausting – cross examination of dialogue in search of signs of the racist complicity of each of the confidence man's victims in the institution of slavery. It is, as criticism, a stunningly "uncharitable" performance, though Karcher significantly stops short of probing the influence of the Cosmopolitan, the most elaborate and extensive of the confidence man's avatars in the book. One of the achievements of Melville's novel is that it tends to turn its best and most sensitive readers into characters, as it has turned Karcher into a version of the cynical Canada thistle. Edward Rosenberry, fortified though he is by his association of the beginning and ending of *The Confidence-Man* with *Tristram Shandy*, still finds Melville's book demonic. See Karcher, *Shadow Over the Promised Land*, pp. 186–257, and Rosenberry, *Melville and the Comic Spirit*, pp. 146–154.

29 See "Benito Cereno" in Melville, *Pierre, Israel Potter, The Piazza Tales, The Confidence–Man, Uncollected Prose, Billy Budd*, pp. 708–9. Citations in parentheses to "Benito Cereno" hereafter refer to this text.

30 John P. McWilliams is representative of the great weight of opinion that holds Delano accountable for a "thoughtless optimism," particularly in the story's closing moments. See McWilliams, *Hawthorne, Melville and the American Character*, pp. 181–3. It seems to me much truer to the story to emphasize its resistance to such blanket judgments either on the part of critics or characters. Paul Brodtkorb describes this feature of Melville's fictional procedure quite beautifully in the context of *Moby-Dick* and the problem of Ahab's moral status. See Brodtkorb, *Ishmael's White World*, p. 81. Eric Sundquist has recently compared Delano's consolation of Cereno to Daniel Webster's complacent celebration of the Compromise of 1850, part of which entailed the notorious Fugitive Slave Act. Webster's words, however, ("The heavens, the skies, smile upon us") are clearly more shallow, less rich in implication than De-

lano's. If Melville was in fact using Webster as a source, he modified the source considerably in ways that Sundquist overlooks. See "Benito Cereno and New World Slavery" in *Reconstructing American Literary History*, ed. Sacvan Bercovitch (Cambridge, Mass.: Harvard University Press, 1986), pp. 93–122.

31 Arvin, *Herman Melville*, p. 174.

32 See Bercovitch for this convincing formulation in *The American Jeremiad*, pp. 176–210.

33 "Adamic" loneliness is the quality that R. W. B. Lewis identifies as the most characteristic mark of Whitman's imagination in *The American Adam*, pp. 49–50. Stephen Whicher describes the competition between death and life in Whitman's poetic vision as a means of identifying stages in the artist's spiritual progress. See Whicher, "Whitman's Awakening to Death" in *The Presence of Walt Whitman*, ed. R. W. B. Lewis (New York: Columbia University Press, 1962), pp. 1–27.

34 Jerome Loving, *Emerson, Whitman and The American Muse* (Chapel Hill: University of North Carolina Press, 1982), p. 136.

35 See, by contrast, Jerome Loving's discussion of how the autoerotic element in Whitman is finally transcended, becoming a marriage of body and soul within the self, in *Emerson, Whitman and The American Muse*, pp. 145–52.

36 Walt Whitman, *Poetry and Prose*, ed. Justin Kaplan (New York: Library of America, 1982), p. 27. All page numbers in parentheses hereafter refer to the reprinting of the 1855 edition in this volume.

37 Robert S. Frederickson has made the case for Whitman's impenetrable isolation most emphatically in "Public Onanism: Whitman's Song of Himself," *Modern Language Quarterly* 46 (June 1985), 143–60.

38 Kerry Larson, *Whitman's Drama of Consensus* (Chicago: University of Chicago Press, 1988), p. 53.

39 For Larson's Whitmanian oxymorons, see ibid., pp. 98–9.

40 James E. Miller, Jr., *The American Quest for a Supreme Fiction* (Chicago: University of Chicago Press, 1979), pp. 31–49.

41 Quoted in Lewis Hyde, *The Gift: Imagination and the Erotic Life of Property* (New York: Random House, 1983), p. 164.

42 Ibid., p. 163. The catalogues are not, of course, entirely new forms. Sandra Gilbert has called attention to the resemblance of Whitman's catalogues to the common nineteenth-century journalistic practice of the impressionistic column as represented by Fanny Fern in "Hour-Glass Thoughts." See Gilbert, "The American Sexual Poetics of Walt Whitman and Emily Dickinson" in *Reconstructing American Literary History*, pp. 123–54. Jerome Loving notes that Whitman too was a practiced hand at the journalist's catalogue. See Loving, *Emerson, Whitman and The American Muse*, p. 19.

43 Whitman's assumption of the identity of God in particular is familiar to many readers. See for example R. W. B. Lewis, *The American Adam*, pp. 43–51.

44 Kerry Larson notes in other contexts the implicit desperation of the catalogues. See Larson, *Whitman's Drama of Consensus*, pp. 130–1.

45 Whitman in fact responds in such passages to the extraordinarily visionary

science of his day, particularly as represented by Robert Chambers in *Vestiges of the Natural History of Creation* (1844). See Robert J. Scholnick, "The Password Primeval: Whitman's Use of Science in Song of Myself," *Studies in the American Renaissance 1986,* ed. Joel Myerson (Charlottesville: University of Virginia Press, 1986), pp. 385–425.

46 Larson, *Whitman's Drama of Consensus,* p. 117.

6. *LITERARY ARCHAEOLOGY AND* THE PORTRAIT OF A LADY

1 See Quentin Anderson, *The Imperial Self* (New York: Knopf, 1971), p. 3, where the author affirms his thesis that, with Emerson, Whitman and James, the American imagination signals a "flight from culture, from the institutions and emotional dispositions of associated life." The phrases from the following sentence come from Anderson's comparison of James and Whitman, p. 171.

2 Daniel Mark Fogel, *Henry James and the Structure of the Romantic Imagination* (Baton Rouge: Louisiana State University Press, 1981), pp. 49–84.

3 Richard Brodhead, *The School of Hawthorne* (New York: Oxford University Press, 1986), pp. 104–39.

4 Henry James, *The Portrait of a Lady* (New York: Viking-Penguin, 1986), p. 79. All page numbers in parentheses refer to this Penguin Classics printing of the New York edition text.

5 See for background Barbara Tedford, "The Attitudes of Henry James and Ivan Turgenev toward the Russo–Turkish War," *Henry James Review* 1 (Spring 1980), 257–61. Richard Poirier notes too the role these "Germanic" references have in establishing Isabel's relationship to Emerson. See Poirier, *The Comic Sense of Henry James: A Study of the Early Novels* (London: Chatto & Windus, 1960), pp. 219–20.

6 See Laurence B. Holland, *The Expense of Vision: Essays on the Craft of Henry James* (Princeton, N.J.: Princeton University Press, 1964), pp. 3–54. The association between *The Scarlet Letter* and *The Portrait of a Lady,* like the larger question of the relationship of Hawthorne and James, dates back to James's own lifetime, but Holland is the first to explore systematically the extent of the parallel in these two books. See Richard Brodhead's *The School of Hawthorne,* pp. 104–20, for a recapitulation of the James–Hawthorne connection in criticism. See also John Carlos Rowe, *The Theoretical Dimension of Henry James* (Madison: University of Wisconsin Press, 1984), pp. 32–4.

7 Holland, *The Expense of Vision,* p. 25.

8 Ibid., p. 52.

9 Ibid., p. 53.

10 John Winthrop, "A Modell of Christian Charity" in *The Founding of Massachusetts: Historians and the Sources,* ed. Edmund S. Morgan (Indianapolis: Bobbs-Merrill, 1964), pp. 191–204.

11 James does, however, display a sensitivity to the themes of Genesis that unites him directly to Winthrop. Dorothy Van Ghent first drew the parallel between Isabel's thirst for "life" in *The Portrait* and the alternating patterns of "life" and "knowledge" in the second chapter of Genesis. See Van Ghent, *The English Novel: Form and Function* (1953, rpt. New York: Harper & Row, 1961), p. 214.

David Hirsch has recently expanded on the biblical archaeology of *The Portrait* by adding to its sources key passages from the Song of Solomon. See *Hirsch,* "Henry James and the Seal of Love," *Modern Language Studies* 13 (Fall 1983), 39–60.

12 See Annette Niemtzow's comments on this fantasy vision in "Marriage and the New Woman in *The Portrait of a Lady,*" *American Literature* 47 (1975–6), 377–95.

13 Identifying and describing James's relation to his predecessors has been an established approach to his work for some years. For a focused treatment of this dimension to James criticism, see Robert Emmet Long, *The Great Succession: Henry James and the Legacy of Hawthorne* (Pittsburgh, P.A.: University of Pittsburgh Press, 1979), particularly pp. 98–116, in which Long connects *The Portrait of a Lady* most closely with *Daniel Deronda,* "Rappaccini's Daughter," and *The Marble Faun.*

14 See John Carlos Rowe, "What the Thunder Said: James's *Hawthorne* and the American Anxiety of Influence," *Henry James Review* 4 (Winter 1983), 83. This essay appears in somewhat shorter form in *The Theoretical Dimensions of Henry James.*

15 It is not precisely a "child's teacup," of course, but it is brightly colored and unusually large, as if Daniel Touchett himself were a child holding a toy cup.

16 Brodhead, *The School of Hawthorne,* pp. 129–30.

17 Bloom's terminology is most useful if we are careful to avoid displacing a critic's anxiety upon a writer. Critics are notoriously sensitive about influential and stifling predecessors – as these notes testify. Artists tend to take a less anxious, and certainly less systematic attitude.

18 Paul John Eakin, *The New England Girl: Cultural Ideals in Hawthorne, Stowe, Howells, and James* (Athens: University of Georgia Press, 1976), p. 188.

19 Isabel's eagerness to witness a revolution may also reinforce the parallels with Margaret Fuller Ossoli. Ossoli was returning to America with the manuscript of a book that described her first-hand experience of the Roman revolution of 1848 when she drowned. The manuscript was lost in the shipwreck.

20 Annette Niemtzow sees the conclusion as a bursting of the Victorian framework to "make room" for the modern novel, but the direction of the book's movement still seems to me more backward than forward. See Niemtzow, "Marriage and the New Woman in *The Portrait of a Lady,*" 394.

21 Nina Baym, "Revision and Thematic Change in *The Portrait of a Lady,*" *Modern Fiction Studies* 22 (Summer 1976), 183–200. For a second account of the import of the revisions see Anthony J. Mazzella, "The New Isabel," in *The Portrait of a Lady,* ed. Robert D. Bamberg (New York: Norton, 1975), pp. 597–619.

22 See Mary Jane King, "The Touch of the Earth: A Word and a Theme in *The Portrait of a Lady,*" *Nineteenth-Century Fiction* 29 (December 1974), 345–7.

23 David Hirsch takes the love between Ralph and Isabel to be the central relationship of the book and, accordingly, finds the theme of *The Portrait* to be the failure of love to triumph over death. Such a view seems unacceptably schematic but suggestive nonetheless. See Hirsch, "Henry James and the Seal of Love," pp. 41–6. Richard Poirier's account of the import of the relationship between Ralph and Isabel seems more persuasive in that it fixes responsibility

not upon "love" but upon Isabel for failing to recognize the "significance of comedy" in Ralph's temperament – how comedy and love are intertwined. See Poirier, *The Comic Sense of Henry James,* p. 200.

24 I am indebted to Annette Niemtzow's article for calling my attention to these essays by Henry James, Sr. The most important of the essays, "The Woman Thou Gavest With Me," appears in *Atlantic Monthly* 25 (January 1870), 66–72.

25 Ibid., p. 67.

26 Ibid. For a contrasting view of this marital idealism, see Alfred Habegger's view of these *Atlantic* essays in Habegger, "Henry James's *Bostonians* and the Fiction of Democratic Vulgarity," *American Literary Landscapes: The Fiction and the Fact,* eds. Ian F. A. Bell and D. K. Adams (New York: St. Martins, 1989), pp. 102–21.

27 Ibid., p. 72.

28 See Lauren T. Cowdery, "Henry James and the 'Transcendent Adventure': The Search for the Self in the Introduction to *The Tempest,*" *Henry James Review* 3 (Winter 1982), 145–53.

29 Quoted by Lauren Cowdery in her essay cited in ibid., 146.

7. EMILY DICKINSON'S ADEQUATE EVE

1 In David Porter's judgment, "Dickinson had no subject, least of all reality." Her poems replace the "mimetic function" of literature with what Porter describes as "language pyrotechnics." See Porter, *Dickinson: The Modern Idiom* (Cambridge, Mass.: Harvard University Press, 1981), pp. 112, 192. Vivian Pollak's central argument is that Dickinson sought through language to free herself from the "dread" of her own sexuality. See Pollak, *Dickinson: The Anxiety of Gender* (Ithaca, N.Y.: Cornell University Press, 1984), p. 26.

2 Barton Levi St. Armand, *Emily Dickinson and Her Culture* (Cambridge University Press, 1984), p. 166.

3 Karl Keller, *The Only Kangaroo Among the Beauty: Emily Dickinson and America* (Baltimore, M.D.: Johns Hopkins University Press, 1979), pp. 1–2.

4 Sandra Gilbert and Susan Gubar, *The Madwoman in the Attic: The Woman Writer and the Nineteenth-Century Literary Imagination* (New Haven, Conn.: Yale University Press, 1979), pp. 594, 622–6.

5 Albert Gelpi first suggested the comparison between Dickinson and Isabel Archer. See Gelpi, *Emily Dickinson: The Mind of the Poet* (1964, rpt. New York: Norton, 1971), p. 173.

6 The numbers identifying Dickinson's poems are those of Thomas Johnson in *The Poems of Emily Dickinson,* 3 vols. (Cambridge, Mass.: Harvard University Press, 1951–5).

7 Juhasz's formulation appears in *Naked and Fiery Forms* (New York: Harper & Row, 1976), pp. 1–6, and serves as a useful concept for Gilbert and Gubar in *The Madwoman in the Attic.* Other important voices in the feminist dialogue on Dickinson that I have made use of here are Barbara Mossberg, *Emily Dickinson: When a Writer is a Daughter* (Bloomington: Indiana University Press, 1982), Margaret Homans, *Women Writers and Poetic Identity* (Princeton, N.J.: Princeton University Press, 1980), Suzanne Juhasz again in *The Un-*

discovered Continent: Emily Dickinson and the Space of the Mind (Bloomington: Indiana University Press, 1983), and Jean McClure Mudge, *Emily Dickinson and the Image of Home* (Amherst: University of Massachusetts Press, 1975).

8 Carl Degler, *At Odds: Women and the Family in America from the Revolution to the Present* (New York: Oxford University Press, 1980), pp. 8–50. Degler's examination of American conditions serves as a detailed and lucid extension of Michel Foucault's brief and fragmentary assessment of the uses of women's sexuality in the nineteenth century. See Foucault, *The History of Sexuality*, Vol. 1, trans. Robert Hurley (1976, New York: Random House, 1980), pp. 103–14. Nancy Cott gives the most thorough account of the evolution of the doctrine of spheres in *The Bonds of Womanhood: Woman's Sphere in New England, 1780–1835* (New Haven, Conn.: Yale University Press, 1977). Cott's discussion is especially useful for understanding Dickinson since she draws so extensively on women's journals in the years just before and after Dickinson's birth.

9 Karl Keller, *The Only Kangaroo Among the Beauty*, p. 13.

10 Jack L. Capps, *Emily Dickinson's Reading* (Cambridge, Mass.: Harvard University Press, 1966). Capps is thorough and informative, particularly on Dickinson's indebtedness to nineteenth-century writers. But he concludes that there is no method to her biblical allusions and that she "found no place in her own writing" for the complex example of Milton (pp. 58, 72). The only other detailed comment on Dickinson's relation to Milton involves an allusion to *Paradise Lost* in a single poem. See Wolfgang Rudat, "Dickinson and Immortality: Virgilian and Miltonic Allusions in 'Of Death I try to think like this,' " *American Notes and Queries* 16 (February 1978), 85–7. William Sherwood, in the course of describing Dickinson's spiritual growth, suggests the similarity of that process to Milton's poetic goals, arguing that, "in her own quiet way, Dickinson too tried to justify God's ways." Sherwood does not pursue the comparison. See Sherwood, *Circumference and Circumstance: Stages in the Mind and Art of Emily Dickinson* (New York: Columbia University Press, 1968), p. 161. In general, despite the suggestive labors of Jack Capps, readers have tended to agree with Charles Anderson's early contention that literary sources are among the "least fruitful approaches" to Dickinson's work. See Anderson, *Emily Dickinson's Poetry: Stairway of Surprise* (New York: Holt, Rinehart, & Winston, 1960), pp. 33, 69. The most important exceptions to this trend are Ruth Miller's examination of Dickinson's reaction to her reading and her response to the influence of Francis Quarles's *Emblems Divine and Moral* in *The Poetry of Emily Dickinson* (Middletown, Conn.: Wesleyan University Press, 1968), and St. Armand, *Emily Dickinson and Her Culture*. See also Richard Sewall's fine chapter "Books and Reading" in *The Life of Emily Dickinson*, 2 vols. (New York: Farrar, Straus, & Giroux, 1974), pp. 668–705.

11 See Margaret Homans, *Women Writers and Poetic Identity*, pp. 200–11, in which Homans argues that the lesson of Eve for Dickinson is "the potential detachment of words from their referents." Dickinson is more often compared directly to Eve herself, as Barbara Mossberg does when she calls Dickinson a "shameless, self-confident Eve in writing her poetry." But Mossberg means

this phrase as her own metaphor rather than as a means of describing a systematic tool of Dickinson's. See Mossberg, *Emily Dickinson: When a Writer is a Daughter*, p. 156.

12 See, for example, Barbara Mossberg, who recognizes the poem as an "allegory of Christian disobedience" but who finally concludes that it is a "classic feminist argument against the injunctions against a women's success." See ibid., pp. 117–18.

13 Citations to *Paradise Lost* are to the edition prepared by Merritt Y. Hughes, *John Milton: Complete Poems and Major Prose* (Indianapolis, Ind.: Bobbs-Merrill 1957).

14 Henry James, Sr., "The Woman Thou Gavest With Me," *Atlantic Monthly* 25 (January 1870), 66–72.

15 Margaret Olofson Thickstun notes the influence that this passage from *Paradise Lost*, Book 10, had on Hawthorne's treatment of the scene between Dimmesdale and Hester in the forest in *The Scarlet Letter*, though for Thickstun this instance of literary influence is part of a pattern of Puritan "devaluation of womanhood" that results in making Dimmesdale the "heroine" of the book. Dickinson's response to Milton's text is, I think, more complex than either Hawthorne's or Thickstun's. See Thickstun, *Fictions of the Feminine: Puritan Doctrine and the Representation of Women* (Ithaca, N.Y.: Cornell University Press, 1988), pp. 132–56.

16 This poem is a good example of what Robert Weisbuch has called the tendency of Dickinson's lines to raise their bets. Weisbuch thinks of this process as completely "sceneless" and analogical, but I do not find his persuasive treatment of Dickinson's poetics at all inconsistent with the dramatic structure derived from Milton. See Weisbuch, *Emily Dickinson's Poetry* (Chicago: University of Chicago Press, 1975), pp. 1–17.

17 The predominance of such a transitional, or suspended, mode of existence in Dickinson has struck many readers, often as a special form of willfully embraced ambiguity that Robert Weisbuch has most usefully characterized as her compound vision. What I would argue is that the religious imagery in such a poem as "I'm ceded – I've stopped being Theirs" is not finally pressed into the service of a secular aesthetic (as Joanne Feit Diehl, for example, contends) but that the dramatically realized piety of her culture in a significant degree produced the "compound vision" of the poetry. See Diehl, *Dickinson and the Romantic Imagination* (Princeton, N.J.: Princeton University Press, 1981), pp. 110–11.

18 See Robert Weisbuch, *Emily Dickinson's Poetry*, pp. 98–9, in which he notes the "compound of pain and power" in the best of Dickinson's poems of "veto."

19 Ibid., p. 10.

20 Karl Keller, *The Only Kangaroo Among the Beauty*, pp. 80–9.

21 St. Armand, *Emily Dickinson and Her Culture*, p. 317. See especially Armand's treatment of sunset in Dickinson's mystic day, in conjunction with the natural piety of John Ruskin and Thomas Wentworth Higginson, pp. 269–79.

22 The only manuscript for both poems is in the hand of Susan Gilbert Dickinson. They may have been received together, copied together, and kept to-

gether by Susan, though of Dickinson's large output of poems, sixty-one exist only in transcripts in Susan Gilbert's hand, so these two may well be only arbitrarily associated. See *The Poems of Emily Dickinson,* ed. Johnson, Vol. 3, pp. 1137–8.

23 This poem is a good example of the ease with which even perceptive readers can find evidence of psychic anguish where Dickinson herself is expressing great strength. See Suzanne Juhasz's discussion, for example, in *The Undiscovered Continent,* pp. 17–18.

24 John Bunyan, *The Pilgrim's Progress,* ed. Roger Sharrock (Harmondsworth: Penguin Books, 1965), p. 213. Dickinson is imitating the whole introductory dialogue between the voice of Christiana and the voice of the poet.

25 Robert Weisbuch calls this poem the single most difficult one in Dickinson's canon (*Emily Dickinson's Poetry,* p. 25) and then goes on to read it as "a pattern of joy eroded by self-betrayal" and "a condemnation of subservience." Charles Anderson connected it to "the special climate of frontier America" (*Emily Dickinson's Poetry: Stairway of Surprise,* p. 174), a suggestion pursued with more detail and ingenuity by Albert Gelpi in "Emily Dickinson and the Deerslayer: The Dilemma of the Woman Poet in America," *Shakespeare's Sisters: Feminist Essays on Woman Poets,* eds. Sandra Gilbert and Susan Gubar (Bloomington: Indiana University Press, 1979), pp. 122–34. Gelpi argues that the poem is built around the myth of the pioneering male vanquishing Mother Nature and reads the last stanza as a riddle of the poet who "dies into her art." The most common reading of the poem is to see it as an examination of artistic vocation, a view in some ways consistent with its "prophetic" meaning.

26 On the triumph of what he calls "the matriarchal amplitude of the New Testament" in nineteenth-century popular culture, see St. Armand, *Emily Dickinson and Her Culture,* p. 94.

27 Higginson's advice is quoted in Sewall, *The Life of Emily Dickinson,* p. 551.

28 A cult of Mariolatry was widespread in nineteenth-century popular culture in America, as St. Armand shows in *Emily Dickinson and Her Culture,* pp. 89–97. The disparity between popular, sentimental piety and Calvinist rigor took the form of what Armand calls "the conflict between the Deacon and the Madonna." Dickinson's clear response to this conflict is an important qualification of Nina Baym's argument that there are no archetypes of maternity in Dickinson's poetry. In fact the voices of Eve and Mary are both potent, maternal forces in her work. See Baym, "God, Father, and Lover in Dickinson's Poetry," *Puritan Influences in American Literature,* ed. Emory Elliott (Urbana: University of Illinois Press, 1979), pp. 193–209.

29 Quotations from *Paradise Regained* are from the edition prepared by Merritt Hughes cited above, Note 13.

CONCLUSION

1 Richard Poirier, *Robert Frost: The Work of Knowing* (New York: Oxford University Press, 1977), p. 22.

2 *The Poetry of Robert Frost,* ed. Edward Connery Lathem (New York: Holt, Rinehart, & Winston, 1969), p. 13. Quotations from Frost's poems are all taken from this edition.

3 Poirier, *Robert Frost: The Work of Knowing,* pp. 206–10. Poirier notes the Miltonic background of several of Frost's lyrics, "The Most of It," "The Subverted Flower," "Never Again Would Birds' Song Be the Same," pp. 158–72.

4 William H. Pritchard, *Frost: A Literary Life Reconsidered* (New York: Oxford University Press, 1984), pp. 55–6.

5 For some discussion of the influence of James's *Pragmatism* on Frost see Lawrance Thompson, *Robert Frost: The Early Years 1874–1915* (New York: Holt, Rinehart, & Winston, 1966), pp. 383–6, Pritchard, *Frost: A Literary Life Reconsidered,* pp. 49–50, Poirier, *Robert Frost: The Work of Knowing,* pp. 250–4, Frank Lentricchia, *Robert Frost: Modern Poetics and the Landscapes of the Self* (Durham, N.C.: Duke University Press, 1975), pp. 3–19.

6 William James, *Pragmatism and The Meaning of Truth* (Cambridge, Mass.: Harvard University Press, 1978), pp. 54–5.

7 Ibid., p. 125.

INDEX

Cambridge Studies in American Literature and Culture

Editor
Albert Gelpi, Stanford University